Bilingualism in Action

Bilingual language behaviour is driven by numerous factors that are usually studied in isolation, even though individual factors never operate alone. Bringing together key insights from psycholinguistics and sociolinguistics, Luna Filipović presents a new model of bilingual language processing that captures bilingualism within and across minds. The model enables readers to explain traditional puzzles in the field, and accounts for some apparently contradictory reports in different studies. It shows how theory can be applied in practice and how practice feeds back into theory, with mutual benefits. Bilinguals are studied in action, when they interact with other bilinguals or monolinguals, when they recall witnessed events in real life and in the lab and when they translate and interpret for the benefit of monolinguals. This interdisciplinary take on bilingualism in action will lead to new research on bilingualism itself, and will lend itself to applications in forensic linguistics and translation studies.

LUNA FILIPOVIĆ is Professor of Language and Cognition at the University of East Anglia. Her research focuses on connections and relationships between different approaches to studying language. She has authored or edited six books in the areas of language typology, language and cognition, and bilingualism, including *Talking about Motion: A Crosslinguistic Investigation of Lexicalization Patterns* (2007) and *Criterial Features in L2 English: Specifying the Reference Levels of the Common European Framework* (2012, with John Hawkins).

Bilingualism in Action

Theory and Practice

Luna Filipović

University of East Anglia

CAMBRIDGE
UNIVERSITY PRESS

CAMBRIDGE
UNIVERSITY PRESS

University Printing House, Cambridge CB2 8BS, United Kingdom

One Liberty Plaza, 20th Floor, New York, NY 10006, USA

477 Williamstown Road, Port Melbourne, VIC 3207, Australia

314–321, 3rd Floor, Plot 3, Splendor Forum, Jasola District Centre,
New Delhi – 110025, India

79 Anson Road, #06–04/06, Singapore 079906

Cambridge University Press is part of the University of Cambridge.

It furthers the University's mission by disseminating knowledge in the pursuit of
education, learning, and research at the highest international levels of excellence.

www.cambridge.org
Information on this title: www.cambridge.org/9781108470353
DOI: 10.1017/9781108602235

First published 2019

Printed in the United Kingdom by TJ International Ltd, Padstow Cornwall

A catalogue record for this publication is available from the British Library.

Library of Congress Cataloging-in-Publication Data
Names: Filipovic, Luna, author.
Title: Bilingualism in action : theory and practice / Luna Filipovic.
Description: New York, NY : Cambridge University Press, [2019] | Includes index.
Identifiers: LCCN 2019019727 | ISBN 9781108470353
Subjects: LCSH: Bilingualism.
Classification: LCC P115 .F45 2019 | DDC 404/.2–dc23
LC record available at https://lccn.loc.gov/2019019727

ISBN 978-1-108-47035-3 Hardback
ISBN 978-1-108-45590-9 Paperback

To the loves of my life, Luzzi, Aria, Jack and mama Marina, who made it possible, and at times almost impossible, to write this book.

Contents

Figures

Tables

Preface

Bilingualism in action is about how and why bilinguals use their languages in the many ways they do. This book is not 'everything you need to know about bilingualism', but it offers something you will want to know and that you will find fascinating if you are a bilingual, or if you study bilinguals or work or live around them. It offers a holistic view of *bilingualism within minds and across minds* and provides a uniform account of psycholinguistic and sociolinguistic factors that shape bilingual behaviours in individuals and societies. Its primary intended audience is academic; more precisely, professional researchers of bilingualism and university teachers of language-related disciplines, such as theoretical and applied linguistics, psycholinguistics, sociolinguistics, forensic linguistics, cognitive science and translation studies. The book also offers novel insights of relevance to language professionals more generally, such as teachers of foreign languages, interpreters, translators and communication consultants.

Human communication itself is complex and bilingual human communication has an additional layer of complexity, whereby multiple factors interact but the product of their interaction is not always the same. We often get disparate research results in the literature precisely because there are many factors involved and some play a more prominent role than others in different circumstances. Mapping the patterns of this interaction and being in a position to predict outcomes based on the interplay of different factors in different circumstances will enable us to provide a more unified account of bilingual language use. We will take a novel and interdisciplinary approach here to some traditional puzzles and point out some new challenges as well as provide suggestions about how to approach and overcome them in the future.

It is well known that bilinguals differ with respect to how proficient they are in each of the two languages. They are also known to adjust their linguistic behaviour and behave differently depending on who they are talking to. For instance, I am a very proficient L2 English speaker whose first language is Serbian. I keep my Serbian in check very well when I am just speaking English to other English speakers. But if I know that my interlocutor is another Serbian–English bilingual I may switch to Serbian occasionally, which is not something

I would do with interlocutors who are monolingual in English. My linguistic behaviour is therefore different in these two situations. Yet another different situation is when I am at my dinner table at home, surrounded by my friends or family, who range from monolingual speakers (e.g. of either English or Serbian) to multilingual speakers (of two or more languages). Then I will speak to my mother in Serbian, to my husband in English and to my elder daughter in Serbian or English (and occasionally also Italian, when we want to keep something super-private). When I do this, I find myself less able to monitor my use of each language successfully than when I speak just one in a single conversation. This is precisely when I would tend to use more of the words or structures that English and Serbian share. I would try to bring my English and my Serbian as close together as possible without making mistakes and creating misunderstandings in either (at least that is what I hope for!). For example, I have noticed that, when using both languages in a single communicative situation, I use many more so-called 'overt subjects' in my Serbian sentences even though Serbian is what is known as a 'pro-drop language' and it allows subjects not to be expressed (because other parts of the sentence make it clear who or what the subject is). In contrast, I do habitually 'drop my subjects' when I am speaking only Serbian. I have also noticed that even when I am using just one language, English, I tend to insist on disambiguating the past simple tense. When my husband says 'the baby ate the food you left for her', I always ask 'Did she it eat all up?' This difference is all-important if you are trying to feed a reluctant baby! Saying just 'ate the food' could have either a perfective-complete interpretation (i.e. the baby ate the whole thing) or an imperfective-incomplete one (i.e. the baby ate some but not all of it). The English past simple tense does not strictly specify each meaning, but Serbian does: you must always decide if the whole thing was consumed or not because different verb forms signal one or the other meaning (this is called 'aspect' in language). My Serbian (and, on this occasion, my motherly care) urges me to seek a resolution for even the slightest possible ambiguity between perfective and imperfective that the English past simple tense does not give me. I do not insist on this distinction in English all of the time, but I am much more aware of it and use it whenever it matters to me. And I am sure that every bilingual speaker on the planet has similar stories to tell. In this book I want to capture what lies behind such stories, and what all bilinguals share as well as what makes them different from each other. Different languages, different personal linguistic narratives and different circumstances under which they use their languages all have a role to play, and here we analyse these roles separately and also, more importantly, together.

These multilingual dinner-table struggles of mine actually inspired me to write this book. They gave me the basic insight that *bilingualism in action* is characterised by malleability, conditioned by who the interlocutors are and what the purpose of the communication is (e.g. multilingual dinner-table chat vs. monolingual international boardroom meeting).

In spite of the increased interest in bilingualism as a phenomenon and the growth of bilingual research, there has not yet been **a holistic account** of both the psychology of bilingualism, i.e. the knowledge and representation of more than one language within minds, and the social and communicative use of that knowledge across minds in different contexts of use. Moreover, the field of bilingualism research seems to be addressing a myriad of different issues under different conditions and coming up with an overwhelming variety of outcomes. The aim of this book is to provide a unifying framework that can enable us to make predictions about, and find explanations for, the different outcomes when different types of languages are used by different kinds of bilingual speakers in different contexts. It is about all bilinguals, and it is for all bilinguals.

Acknowledgements

I owe a debt of gratitude to many people who I have been lucky to have in my personal and professional life. First on the thanks list is my family, mum Marina, dad Filjka, grandma Zana, grandpa Sava, aunt Vesna and uncle Zoran, who had an essential formative influence on me in my early life and encouraged my eagerness to learn and know more. My extended Italian family, Leti Pozzuto and Giovanni Venturini in particular, put an indelible stamp on this book, for which I am immensely grateful, by inspiring examples that I cite in my writing from our long conversations in Italian. Additionally, I thank Giovanni Venturini for granting me permission to use one of his many beautiful paintings for the book cover.

I am profoundly grateful to my kids, Lucrezia and Aria, for teaching me a lot about bilingualism first-hand and for filling our dinner-table conversations with insights about bilingual minds, in addition to revelations about their wonderful, happy worlds. And a big thank you to Jack, for loving me the right way.

I was also incredibly fortunate to have had an excellent education, both in my motherland, Serbia, and in my adopted homeland, England. My first steps in linguistics were made under the supervision of Ranko Bugarski, at the University of Belgrade, who introduced me to his novel ideas in linguistics, which would later turn into important subfields (such as cognitive linguistics) and in which Ranko was a pioneer as early as the 1960s. It was an honour to be his student and it is to him that I owe my preparedness for PhD research at the University of Cambridge. I got lucky again in having Peter Matthews as my PhD supervisor; Peter taught me how to think critically, to scratch below the surface of nicely phrased claims and see what, if anything, lay underneath before I got too excited about them. My interest in typology in general and motion events in particular was inspired by Dan Slobin, and led to my specialisation in psycholinguistics. I feel privileged to have been able to think and talk about motion, and all things language, with Dan, and to call him my friend. And this segues nicely into thanking all my friends. This book would not have been here without them because they helped me arrive at a place where I was able to write it; so thank you Macki, Vlada, Mara, Ivan Mica, Gaga, Aca, Vesna, Ljuba, Cica, Duško, Mina, Ana, Nigel, Debs, Tom, Sharon, Mario, Matt, Tomoko, Lena and Diane.

My gratitude goes also to numerous agencies that have funded my work, on which I reported in parts of this book: the Economic and Social Research Council (ESRC), the Leverhulme Trust, the Newton Trust and the Spanish Ministry of Economy and Competitiveness. I would also like to extend warm thanks to the legal interpreters in the United States and the United Kingdom, as well as representatives from numerous legal jurisdictions in both countries, who granted me access to authentic and sensitive data for my forensic linguistic work and who will have to remain anonymous. I have also benefited from co-authoring, collaborating or discussing my work with colleagues over many years. Thank you (alphabetically) to Suzanne Abad Vergara, Teresa Cadierno, Paola Cifuentes-Feréz, Ginny Gathercole, Sharon Geva, Liz Hales, John Hawkins, Alberto Hijazo-Gascón, Jan Hulstijn, Iraide Ibarretxe-Antuñano, Kasia Jaszczolt, Andreas Musolff, Carlos de Pablos-Ortega, Aneta Pavlenko, Gabrina Pounds, Martin Putz, Ana Rojo, Vera da Silva Sinha, Chris Sinha, Larry Solan, Peter Trudgill, Ivana Vidaković and Gabriella Vigliocco.

I wrote the first draft of this book during a period of study leave, for which I am most grateful to the University of East Anglia. Many thanks also to Andrew Winnard of Cambridge University Press. The reviewing, editing and production of this book were seamless and joyful experiences for me, and I hope also for the publisher. The anonymous reviews secured at different stages of the writing were extremely beneficial in terms of clarifying a number of my points as well as to the formulation and presentation of my scholarly arguments. Additional and fundamental contributions to the reviewing and revision process were made by John Hawkins, whom I can never thank enough. Any errors that may remain are solely and exclusively my own.

Finally, *Bilingualism in Action* started as an intriguing idea about bilingual linguistic behaviour that came to me during one of those exuberant conversations at my multilingual family dinner table, and it was not long before I realised that I had actually figured out a way to capture the multifaceted nature of bilingual language representation and use. I hope this work inspires further research into bilingual and multilingual communication at dinner tables across the world, as well as in other situations and with many different language combinations.

1   Introduction

The Research Domain of Applied Bilingual Studies

1.1   Defining Bilingual

Question: Who is bilingual?
Answer: Somebody who speaks two languages.

Very simple. Or not? In one respect, knowing two languages, not necessarily to the same degree, can be a criterion for saying that somebody is bilingual. However, a more precise definition is required, since we cannot really claim that an adult English speaker, for instance, who has just embarked on a beginner's course in French is bilingual in the same way as somebody who has been speaking both French and English from birth. We normally think of bilinguals as people with a substantial degree of knowledge and competence in two languages. Finding a proper definition of what 'substantial' means in the context of bilingualism is no small task. A very high level of competence in any two languages, with similar frequency of use in both, is a possible criterion that we can use to qualify a speaker as bilingual. On the other hand, all second-language learners are bilingual to different degrees, so the term 'bilingual' could apply to them as well, probably to more advanced learners rather than those who are just starting to learn a second language (an L2).

In addition, there are different classification systems for bilingualism based on how and when the two languages were acquired: early vs. late, simultaneously vs. consecutively, selectively (e.g. specialised competence related to a professional field) or generally, with or without formal class-room instruction, and so on. In this book the aim is to provide a framework for bilingualism that takes into account all the different types of bilingual speakers that have so far received varying degrees of academic attention. I will consider bilingualism to be a *cline*, comprising a spectrum of linguistic histories of different speakers and their abilities, which are not fixed and constant but rather flexible and malleable both in the short term (e.g. conditioned by different communicative situations) and long term, over the lifespan.

The real challenge for an inclusive approach such as this is to find a way to compare, and contrast, research findings about bilingualism that include very different methodologies, and that report on different language types, speaker types and communicative situation types. For a start, categorising bilinguals into dichotomous groups is somewhat artificial. Speakers may have very different capabilities in the two languages even when they are put in the same category: they may differ substantially with respect to how often and in what contexts they use each of their two languages (e.g. daily vs. a few times a year, at home vs. at work, etc.). Bilingualism changes over the lifespan, and proficiency in a language that was learnt early can diminish or be lost, whilst language proficiency in the weaker language can be enhanced through continuous use. Psycholinguistics has only relatively recently come to appreciate that individual differences must take centre stage in bilingualism research (see Hulstijn, 2018 for a recent inspiring overview).

In some respects, early and late bilinguals exhibit the same linguistic behaviour, but in others, their outputs differ significantly (see Chapter 2 for details). It has been reported that certain cognitive benefits are available to both early and late bilinguals who are very fluent in both languages, but not to those who do not have equal command in their two languages (Luk, De Sa & Bialystok, 2011). It may be the case that in some respects, all bilinguals are similar whereas in others they are quite different. The field of bilingualism research needs to address bilingualism in a more finely grained manner than it has hitherto, and at the same time, offer a more holistic perspective that takes into consideration all the relevant factors that may impact outcomes in bilingual communication. I make an attempt to do this here.

In this book I focus on the more *explanatory side of things* (the why), rather than the descriptive (the what). I draw on the invaluable descriptions in the previous literature and in my own research of what different bilinguals do on different occasions when they use their language(s), and I show how a variety of (sometimes conflicting) insights (Chapter 2) can be incorporated into a unified model of bilingual language processing (Chapter 3) that can help us account for why bilinguals do the different things that they do (Chapter 4). At the same time, we will see the effects of *bilingualism in action*; that is, in normal everyday conversations with other bilinguals or with monolinguals, as well as in more specific types of situations, for example when witnessing events, passing a judgement or employing their linguistic skills as language professionals (Chapters 5 and 6). *Bilingualism in Action* is an *interdisciplinary study of what happens within and across bilingual minds* when they are engaged in different activities that are performed using their languages explicitly or implicitly.

Fortunately for the work presented in this book, bilingualism has been gaining in popularity as a research area within the various disciplines and subdisciplines of the language sciences. For instance, research in the area of *applied language typology* (Filipović, 2017a, 2017b) has focused on certain parameters of typological contrast between languages that have *significant real-life consequences*, and on the ways in which different types of bilinguals resolve these contrasts in concrete communicative situations and in different contexts of use (e.g. in translation of suspect narratives or witness memory elicitation; see Filipović, 2019a; Filipović & Hijazo-Gascón, 2018; Hijazo-Gascón, 2019). Psycholinguistic research has always been interested in the ways in which bilinguals remember things *about* their languages; for example, how they process their two languages, and store and retrieve form–meaning mappings in each language. More recently a different type of research on bilingual memory has been gaining pace and prominence, involving the effects of bilingualism on how events are remembered, with empirical studies in autobiographical bilingual memory (see Pavlenko, 2014 for a detailed overview) and bilingual witness memory (Filipović, 2011, 2018, 2019b). These kinds of studies offer us invaluable insights into the role of the particular language in which the memory was created and the role of the language used to access it in later recall. Translation studies have also seen the development of an applied perspective building on their earlier theoretical and more philosophical origins. This applied turn has been driven by empirical research on how interpreting and translating may be affected by the differences between the two languages of a bilingual language professional; by an improved understanding of the different professional and practical circumstances that may affect the process and the product of translation; and by increasing awareness of how translation can impact real-life outcomes, for example in legal and medical contexts (e.g. see Filipović, 2007a, 2019a; Trbojević, 2012).

In other words, *Bilingualism in Action* unifies a number of *cross-cutting theoretical and empirical issues that arise in the study of bilingual communication*. I provide examples from the fields of forensic linguistics, translation and second-language learning and teaching in order to highlight the effects that language contrasts can have on bilingual information exchange. Certain contrasts can have very real practical consequences both for the everyday lives of bilinguals and for the numerous professional contexts in which bilingual interactions feature prominently. The findings presented and discussed here are by no means limited to the areas that are highlighted. In fact, this book is an attempt to bring together theory and empirical findings from many different areas of bilingualism research in order to create a framework that can be used much more broadly in *applied bilingualism research*; thus, it is a study of bilingualism and its concrete effects in different personal and professional environments.

I deliberately do not enter into the debates here on certain important aspects of language processing, such as the differences between language production and comprehension and the implications of any differences between these two mechanisms for bilingualism, though I do include discussion of examples from both types of study. This is not because I think such analysis is not warranted or relevant – these types of debates have been amongst the fundamental battle-grounds in psycholinguistics for many years – but rather I feel that these discussions do not quite fall within the interdisciplinary remit of this book. When bringing multiple fields together we cannot encompass everything that constitutes each discipline. This is neither necessary, nor indeed possible. We should rather try to combine and integrate those aspects and established findings from each field that help us answer our specific interdisciplinary research questions. In the present case, we want to discover *how any two languages interact in different bilingual minds when bilinguals actively use one or both their languages, and what the real and potential consequences of these interactions may be in different social or communicative contexts.*

1.2   What Unites and What Divides Different Bilinguals

When we look at how different types of bilingual speakers are categorised and defined in various studies, we see very little unanimous agreement. For example, what some researchers classify as early bilingualism others consider to be late bilingualism (see Myers-Scotton, 2006). To make matters more complex, more than one parameter may be considered as significant in this context; for example, age of onset for each language, or age of arrival into the speech community (Bylund, 2011). And then there are so many other factors that affect bilingual development, bilingual linguistic behaviour and the potential cognitive consequences of bilingualism. For example, the level of proficiency in each language is clearly a very significant factor (Abutalebi, Cappa & Perani, 2009) as is language dominance (Silva-Corvalán & Treffers-Daller, 2015).

Finally, with even a fleeting browse through the literature on bilingualism, one is overwhelmed by the number of different and often opposing claims that pervade the field. In some studies, it is the language used for speaking in the experiment that guides bilingual linguistic responses and affects aspects of non-linguistic behaviour, such as the grouping together of events based on perceived similarities among them (e.g. Athanasopoulos et al., 2015). In other studies, it is the overall dominant language of the environment where the bilingual speakers live and work that drives their decision-making, not the language used in the experiment (e.g. Dussias, 2001; Dussias & Sagarra, 2007). There are also studies that show how neither the language spoken in the task nor the language of the living environment guide bilingual linguistic and non-linguistic behaviour; rather, it is some common language pattern shared by both languages that is used by some bilinguals (early and balanced) in the task, regardless of which one is being spoken (e.g. Filipović, 2011; Kersten et al.,

2010; Lai, Rodriguez & Narasimhan, 2014). Numerous different experimental approaches and methods (e.g. self-paced reading, eye-tracking, recognition and recall memory elicitation tasks, similarity judgment triads, etc.) as well different aspects of the lexicon and grammar (colour, gender, tense, aspect, motion constructions, etc.) have been discussed and studied, but no unifying approach has been proposed that can encompass all the different results and outcomes, and contextualise them within a systematic overview of bilingualism and its different manifestations. Crucially, there has been no comprehensive account of what the different studies can tell us about the similarities and differences between different bilinguals. There is also a lack of information about the different linguistic behaviours of one and the same bilingual under different communicative conditions.

Some notable attempts have been made towards accounting for different outputs of different bilinguals. For instance, Pavlenko (2005) provides a clear account of the kinds of cross-linguistic influences that are found in various studies and offers a systematisation of the different outcomes (e.g. with L1 influencing L2, or vice versa, etc.). However, we still need an account that enables us *to predict and explain when and why certain outcomes are more or less likely* based on the different factors that play a role in bilingual acquisition and use.

To this end, I introduce in this book an integrated **multifactor model CASP for Bilingualism** (as proposed in Filipović & Hawkins, 2018) and illustrate how it captures all bilingual linguistic behaviour and enables us to predict, and account for, linguistic behaviours by different bilingual speaker types and in different communicative situations. I show (in Chapter 3) that the underlying bilingual processing mechanisms modelled here are fundamentally the same for all bilinguals, regardless of their respective linguistic backgrounds, histories and abilities. Specifically, levels of proficiency, interlocutor type or communicative situation type may all differ, but the underlying mechanisms of language processing and language use are shared by all speakers and driven by their goal of getting their intended meanings across. The ways in which this is done, and the outputs produced on each occasion, will differ, but this is not because different general mechanisms are at play: rather it is because *the same mechanisms interact differently with one another under different circumstances and contexts of use.* Just as with monolingual exchanges, the ultimate goal of bilingual communication is to understand and be understood.

The different circumstances that affect bilingual linguistic behaviour are created by both internal and external factors. The **internal (variability) factors** are those of *bilingualism within minds.* They condition variability among bilinguals, and involve age of acquisition, proficiency and dominance, which characterise the linguistic profiles of bilingual individuals or groups. The **external (adjustability) factors**, which *calibrate bilingualism across minds,* are the different conditions under which bilinguals use their languages, to which each bilingual adjusts (monolingual vs. bilingual interactions, formal vs. informal communication, etc.). Internal factors are also termed 'variability factors' within the CASP model of bilingualism (Chapter 3) in order to reflect the nature of these factors: they vary across bilingual groups and consequently classification of those groups varies in accordance with these factors. Some of them (proficiency) can also vary over time for a single speaker. External factors are termed 'adjustability factors' in Filipović and Hawkins (2018) because bilinguals adjust their behaviour to different communicative environments and circumstances. The variability and adjustability factors are interconnected: the ability of bilinguals to adjust their linguistic behaviour to the demands of each communicative situation ultimately depends on their linguistic profiles as characterised by the variability factors.

All of these factors have been discussed extensively in the literature on bilingualism, though variability factors have been studied significantly more than adjustability factors. I provide a succinct overview of the key ideas and empirical findings for both factor types (Chapter 2). The central novelty and advantage of the present approach is its integration of findings from many different studies, which have usually investigated one factor at a time, and their synthesis into a multifactor model that explains how, when and why the different factors interact and what the outcome is likely to be in a particular interaction involving a particular bilingual. The processing mechanisms that bilinguals use can be seen a *complex adaptive system*, ever evolving and constantly in flux (see Chapter 3 for details). This means that a single factor does not govern bilingual behaviour; rather it is *the interplay of multiple factors that sometimes compete and sometimes collaborate* that produces the linguistic outputs that we observe (see Filipović & Hawkins, 2013, 2018).

1.3   Bilinguals in Action: Remembering, Judging, Translating

The reason for this book's focus on bilingual memory, judgments and professional language services as the principal contexts for examining bilinguals in action is not solely because the author's expertise covers these areas. The inherent connection between forensic linguistics, translation and psycholinguistics has only partially been made explicit and described in the literature, and more systematic attention is needed. Psycholinguistic aspects of translation have been researched most notably by de Groot (1997, 2011). Forensic linguistics and translation have been linked together in the discussion of non-native speakers and the law (e.g. Berk-Seligson, 2002 [1990], 2009, 2011; Filipović, 2007a, 2008, 2009, 2010a, 2013a, 2019a; Gibbons, 2003). But forensic linguistics and psycholinguistics have not yet been connected as much as they should be, and there is much potential for innovative research at the intersection of these two areas. The current lack of interdisciplinary interaction between them may be at least in part because forensic linguistics has mainly focused on themes and methodologies adopted from discourse analysis and sociolinguistics, whilst psycholinguistics favours experimental approaches to the study of language and the mind more generally, methodologies which have not been widely adopted in forensic linguistic research. The author of this book (Filipović, 2010a, 2010b, 2011, 2013b, 2016, 2018, 2019a, 2019b) has been one of the pioneers in bringing forensic linguistics and psycholinguistics closer together, and she has also added translation and language typology to the mix, with the goal of investigating empirically the real-life consequences of language contrasts and translation on witness memory and jury judgment.

Nowadays, we live in bilingual and multilingual societies throughout the world. Indeed, more people are bilingual than monolingual and the behaviour of bilinguals is fundamental to any interdisciplinary research in the language sciences. For example, in contexts relevant for forensic linguistic research, we can note that the chances of having a bilingual witness, victim or a suspect are now greater than ever. The same is true when it comes to the composition of juries in court. Therefore, addressing the practical consequences of bilingualism in authentic interactive situations is of considerable social importance, in addition to enabling us to understand bilingualism better by providing insights into what happens when bilinguals are in action. The current book is a contribution to the knowledge base of both the theory and practice of bilingualism.

1.4   Bilingualism Within and Across Minds: What Is This All About?

Many phenomena discussed in different areas of psycholinguistics and sociolinguistics are actually the product of language contact within minds and across minds, types of contact which need to be brought together under one model of bilingual processing, as proposed and exemplified in this book (Chapter 3). We will see how both psycholinguistic and sociolinguistic factors jointly affect the linguistic outputs of bilinguals and lead them to behave very differently in different contexts. There needs to be a closer co-operation between the vast fields within which bilingualism is studied. As Benmamoun, Montrul and Polinsky (2013a: 11) emphasise:

It seems to us that psycholinguists studying bilingualism and sociolinguists studying language acquisition and change in ethnic minority communities often look at different populations. The two research communities need to come together to understand the reasons behind their divergent findings.

Psycholinguistics has traditionally been interested in bilingual lexical storage and retrieval (e.g. is the meaning and conceptual content of a certain word shared by the two languages and to what extent: always, sometimes or never?) and in bilingual syntactic processing (e.g. are syntactic representations shared or separate: always, sometimes or never?). More recently, bilingualism has begun to be seen as a vital source of information about language and cognition more generally, for example in the study of cognitive functions such as categorisation and memory (see Bassetti & Cook, 2011; Altarriba & Isurin, 2013; Pavlenko, 2014). Bilingualism has also been explored from numerous sociolinguistic perspectives in studies that have had different foci, for example language change (Heine & Kuteva, 2005; Trudgill, 2010, 2011), code-switching (Silva-Corvalán, 1994, 2014) or code-mixing (Muysken, 2000). It is the findings from these and other similar studies that have been most valuable for the current enterprise, in part because they have made clear what still remains to be done in order to get a fuller picture of bilingualism.

We will also look in some detail at the sociolinguistic factors that modulate the interactions amongst psycholinguistic principles of language processing, and consider how they affect bilingual linguistic outputs. For instance, the processing principle of **efficiency** in bilingual production encourages the use of the same structures in both languages, but how this takes place exactly depends on sociolinguistic factors, such as what the majority language is in a social group and what the social relationships are among the group members (Trudgill, 2010, 2011). We shall see that bilinguals can sometimes 'gain' and sometimes 'lose' grammatical and semantic features in one of their languages, depending on a number of factors (typological features of the two languages involved, linguistic profiles of bilingual individuals and characteristics of the social situations in which bilinguals communicate). Ultimately, these factors will affect the directions in which languages can change as a result of language contact through bilingualism. I shall also discuss examples of how bilingualism leads to language change through time and explain how psycholinguistic and sociolinguistic factors come together within and across bilingual minds to create both short-term and long-term change in one or both of bilinguals' languages (Chapters 3 and 4).

I can summarise the central goals of *Bilingualism in Action* as follows:

1) to provide **a unifying account of bilingualism** informed by a) **typological information** about different languages, b) **psycholinguistic evidence** for language processing mechanisms and principles, and for relevant factors that emerge from a variety of empirical studies and c) **sociolinguistic findings** on the long-term outcomes of bilingual interactions and their impact on language change through time;

2) to explain the **effects of bilingualism in different situations** in which bilingual language use occurs, when bilinguals are in action witnessing and reporting events, making judgements or providing professional language services.

We will transcend the confines of one specific methodology or disciplinary approach, which often blocks a comprehensive view of the problems. In other words, I will offer a 'forest view' that is based on broad, general and unifying patterns in bilingual language processing that emerge from very different studies. We will see that similar kinds of linguistic behaviour have been previously labelled using different terminology, just because they involved different kinds of bilinguals (e.g. simultaneous bilinguals vs. L2 speakers vs. heritage speakers). As mentioned earlier, different bilingual groups can and often do exhibit the same kinds of linguistic behaviour. Athanasopoulos (2011: 29) captures this unfortunate phenomenon in bilingualism research by noting that *the same kinds of outputs may be labelled differently just because different bilinguals were producing them.* This is one of the reasons why I will use more unifying terminology here when I discuss all the different bilingual types and their outputs.

I begin by discussing some past and current trends in bilingualism research in order to illustrate how a common platform needs to be found for the interpretation of different results from different methodological perspectives. Our discussion of previous research is not meant to be exhaustive. In fact, there is a vast body of literature that could have been included but is not because the goal is not to provide the most detailed or definitive summary for each relevant factor separately (for exemplary work of that kind, see De Groot, 2011). Rather, I use some key results and findings in order to make connections across fields that have previously gone unnoticed, which can then be further supported by other research findings, past and future.

I must acknowledge here that there is a recent trend in the literature of talking of multilingualism rather than bilingualism. This is because a growing number of people today speak more than two languages and our field is catching up with this development. For example, the acquisition of a third language (L3) is now a subfield in its own right, and there are conferences dedicated solely to it. However, given the goals of this book, using the term 'multilingualism' gives no added value here and we can readily substitute 'multilingualism' for 'bilingualism' in our discussion, adapting our claims and predictions in line with relevant information about acquisition, proficiency and usage of each language.

This book has seven chapters. After this introductory chapter, I present an overview of bilingualism research in Chapter 2, selective as it must be, adhering to our focus on language processing and language effects on memory, judgement and translation and on the sociolinguistic contexts of bilingual language use. Chapter 3 introduces the new model for bilingual language processing, the **Complex Adaptive System Principles (CASP) for Bilingualism** (Filipović & Hawkins, 2018), which captures *bilingualism within and across minds* and shows how different principles of bilingual language processing interact, sometimes competing and sometimes collaborating. Chapter 4 offers a detailed discussion of numerous studies on bilingual lexicon(s) and grammar(s) and shows how CASP for Bilingualism helps us explain the different kinds of bilingual linguistic behaviours reported. In Chapter 5, we see what kind of witnesses bilinguals are in a forensic linguistic context, and whether and how their witness reports and memories of events may differ from those of monolinguals. Chapter 6 illustrates what happens when bilinguals are engaging in translating and interpreting. We see here that the context of bilingual communication creates a communicative environment with very specific restrictions, whereby certain aspects of communication are prioritised (sounding natural in each language) over certain others (expressing an exactly equivalent meaning), with potentially substantial consequences in terms of understanding what was actually said in the original vs. the translation. Chapter 7 connects all the discussion strands, summarises the findings and opens pathways for further investigation.

In summary, theory, empirical research and practice in the field of bilingualism all join forces in this book with a goal of finding unifying generalisations in the many different types of bilingual outputs and interactions reported in the increasingly vast literature. In this way we avoid giving an account of bilingualism that is narrow, partial, or overly complicated by a focus on the apparent extreme variability observed in bilingual language processing and use.

2   Bilingualism Research
What We Know and What We Need to Know

The chapter provides a selective and critical account of some central theoretical and empirical insights into bilingualism, relating to how bilinguals learn, process and store their languages. We look at the similarities and differences between monolingual and bilingual language acquisition and use. I offer a succinct overview of factors that have been studied at length in the field, such as age of acquisition and proficiency, and consider also those that have received rather less attention even though they are equally important for understanding and predicting bilingual language outputs, such as the language profiles of interlocutors and communicative situation type. The chapter ends with a summary discussion of key points in bilingual processing, highlighting the central unanswered questions and challenges in bilingualism research that we take up in the following chapters.

2.1   Who Is Bilingual?

The ability to speak two languages perfectly is usually cited as defining bilingualism (Webster, 1961). In this context, *perfectly* probably means having the ability to use both languages with the fluency of a native speaker in each, which Bloomfield (1935: 56) puts in a nutshell when he states that being bilingual involves having 'native-like control of two languages'. This idea (or rather, ideal) is also possibly entertained primarily by monolingual people who do not have experience of, or with, bilingualism.

In other definitions, 'perfect linguistic ability' in both languages has been replaced by 'the use of two languages'. For instance, R. Ellis refers to bilingualism as 'the use of two languages by an individual or speech community' (1994: 694) and Grosjean (2010: 4) states that 'bilinguals are those who use two or more languages (or dialects) in their everyday lives'. These different definitions illustrate the multidimensionality of the phenomenon. Both psychological factors (e.g. linguistic competence) and social factors (e.g. use in communication within a working environment or at home) are relevant to our understanding of the subject. These two groups of factors reflect the traditional dichotomy in approaches to bilingualism, the psycholinguistic vs. the sociolinguistic. Only rarely have these two perspectives been considered together, and until they are, and until we understand how the features from both areas connect and affect each other, we are unlikely to ever have a coherent, holistic picture of bilingualism. This is what I aim to offer here, an initial attempt to show how it all comes together. In order to understand how I reached the current position that I put forward in this book, we look first at previous research contributions from both psycholinguistic and sociolinguistic perspectives.

One of the problems in the field has been that there are many ways in which bilinguals can be classified. For instance, based on the order in which two languages are acquired, we have 'simultaneous bilingualism' if the acquisition of both is concurrent (Valdés & Figueroa, 1996), and 'sequential bilingualism', if one language is acquired after the other, such that the first one 'is acquired during the age of early syntactic development', and the second 'after the structural foundations of the first language are in place' (Montrul, 2008: 97), when the basic knowledge of the L1 (first-acquired language) has already been established (McLaughlin, 1978; De Houwer, 1995; Genesee, Paradis & Cargo, 2004). What the field cannot agree on is when the cut-off point for simultaneous acquisition occurs; that is, at what age does it become impossible to become a simultaneous bilingual? Simultaneous bilinguals are also referred to as 'early bilinguals', because they have acquired (or rather started acquiring) both languages early in childhood. Late bilinguals are those who started learning the second language after the 'critical period' (when the door apparently closes for simultaneous bilingualism).

A proposal was originally put forward, in the form of the *critical period hypothesis* (Penfield & Roberts, 1959; Lenneberg, 1967), that one reason why children are able to acquire a second language (an L2) relatively quickly and successfully at an early age is biological: humans are most successful at learning a language between the age of two and the early teens. Chiswick and Miller (2008: 16) describe the critical period hypothesis as involving a 'sharp decline in learning outcomes with age', stating that after the critical period, acquisition can be more difficult to achieve (see also Paradis, 2004 for a detailed discussion). The central controversy about this, though, is the total disagreement in terms of the exact age at which this sharp decline is supposed to begin: different authors have very different suggestions, ranging from pre-school age to the late teens, and these contrasting views make it more difficult to compare results across diverse studies. The critical period hypothesis has been both supported and disputed in the literature (see De Groot, 2011: 58–78 for an insightful and comprehensive discussion), and it is not obvious how tenable it is at this point. The purported lack of access later in life to the initial, childhood linguistic sensitivity can often be compensated for by good verbal analytical skills (DeKeyser, 2000). More generally, a number of different studies give reports of late learners achieving native-like standards under different circumstances and in different linguistic domains (Johnson & Newport, 1989; Hakuta, Bialystok & Wiley, 2003; Singleton, 2005; Birdsong, 2005, 2006). Nevertheless, there are some important differences between early child bilinguals and late adult bilinguals that need to be addressed and explained (see Section 2.2.1 of this chapter for more details).

Another classification, into 'balanced' and 'unbalanced', divides bilinguals according to whether their proficiency and competence in both languages are equal or not. Balanced bilinguals are normally those who acquired both languages in childhood and maintained them through adulthood. Late bilinguals with a high level of command in both their first and second language could also be called 'balanced', so sequence of acquisition need not be directly mapped onto the balanced/unbalanced dichotomy. This dichotomy is related to the notion of *dominance*, and bilinguals can have either their first-acquired or their second-acquired language as the dominant one. Thus, the order of acquisition, again, does not map perfectly onto a classification based on dominance (which includes both proficiency and frequency of use; see Silva-Corvalán & Treffers-Daller, 2015). Bilinguals can have their first language deteriorate under the influence of their second language, which takes over, usually due to their educational, living or working environment. This process is called 'language attrition' and the related type of bilingualism is referred to as 'subtractive'. If the bilingual gains competence in another language whilst maintaining the already acquired language, that type of bilingualism is defined as 'additive'. Both language attrition and incomplete acquisition are features of heritage bilingualism (see Montrul, 2008; Polinsky, 2016), whereby immigrant parents may have diminished language skills in their native tongue under the influence of the language spoken in their new country of abode. Their children's acquisition of the parental native tongue is then limited and restricted to the home environment whilst the language of the living and schooling environment becomes their stronger language.

It can be confusing to label languages as L1 and L2 since these can refer to the sequence of acquisition (L1 first acquired, L2 second acquired) or to proficiency (L1 stronger, L2 weaker). In this book I use the latter criterion for distinguishing bilinguals because language proficiency has been shown to be a more reliable predictor of bilingual outputs than some other factors (Abutalebi, Cappa & Perani, 2009; see also Kroll et al., 2008 for the same point), as well as being the reason for some more general benefits of bilingualism (Luk et al., 2011, though this is not a uniformly held assumption; see Section 2.2.2.5 of this chapter). Furthermore, it is hard to make predictions about the language behaviour of bilinguals based solely on age of acquisition: some early bilinguals preserve both their languages equally and some do not. Language use is very different in these two cases, as we shall see throughout this book. When bilinguals are equally proficient in both languages and do not have significant dominance in either one I refer to their two languages as 2L1s. When one language is stronger, regardless of which one was acquired first, I refer to it as L1. The weaker language is an L2. We shall also see that even when the overall proficiency of different L2 speaker groups has been established and verified by the same means (e.g. by a proficiency test), they can exhibit very different behaviours with regard to different L2 features (see Hawkins & Filipović, 2012 for detailed exemplification and discussion). Indeed, some features of a language are more transparent (i.e. easier to 'figure out') whilst others are more opaque (see Gathercole, 2016 for a discussion), and the acquisition pace and related outcomes reflect this throughout the lifespan of a bilingual. A more finely grained scrutiny of bilingual linguistic behaviour is needed, taking into account the *typological information about the specific feature of interest in the relevant languages, the linguistic profiles of the bilinguals, which include proficiency and frequency of use in different contexts, as well as information about what kind of interaction the bilinguals are involved in* (e.g. who the interlocutors are and what the purpose of the communication or of an experimental task is).

Perfectly balanced bilingualism may be something of a myth (Cook, 1995). As Montrul (2008: 18) puts it 'the reality is that most bilinguals are linguistically unbalanced, both functionally (in their language use) and representationally (in their linguistic knowledge)'. In a nutshell, most bilinguals will generally possess a stronger and a weaker language. What needs to be ascertained in this context is *how big the proficiency gap is* between the two languages. We shall return later to this central dichotomy of (almost) equal vs. unequal proficiency, and the role of differences in proficiency and usage frequency in bilingual linguistic outputs, as well as their possible effects on other fronts, e.g. in cognitive tasks such as categorisation and memory (Chapters 4 and 5), and in specialised language use (e.g. translating and interpreting; Chapter 6).

2.2   Monolingual vs. Bilingual Language Processing

What is it that differentiates bilingual speakers from monolinguals, and how are they similar? One of the rare points of consensus in the field is that bilinguals are not two monolinguals in one person (Cook, 1991, 1992; Grosjean, 1992, 1998, 2001). But what are they then?

2.2.1   Similarities: The Age Factor

The learning of either one or two languages happens using the same mental resources, but bilinguals have more information to store and process than monolinguals, and this can exert higher cognitive pressure on bilinguals in certain respects (e.g. more demands on working-memory capacity in the L2; see McDonald, 2006). Early learning of one or more languages is easier (and generally better) than late learning, as discussed in the previous section. If the first language onset is late because of language deprivation (e.g. due to deafness, confinement or no human contact), the language is unlikely to be fully and properly mastered, though other factors of hardship in addition to language deprivation may contribute to poor linguistic performance in these extreme cases of delayed first-language acquisition (De Groot, 2011: 58). Early onset seems to be the key, though late onset can indeed be compensated for to some extent (see De Groot, 2011: 52–9 for a thorough overview of relevant studies in this area). The same appears to be the case when it comes to the learning of a second language. Early and simultaneous bilingual learners seem to have an advantage because some aspects of language are difficult to master perfectly if they are not acquired early (e.g. pronunciation). It seems that children use implicit, unconscious learning mechanisms when acquiring languages early that are not available to adults, who must use more conscious and explicit learning strategies instead when acquiring a second language later in life. This early high sensitivity to linguistic input declines with age for most people, even though we do not know precisely when it starts to do so. After that certain point (the previously mentioned critical period), the door closes on the possibility of complete native-like mastery of either one or more languages (though some bilinguals may come very close). Age, however, is not the sole factor; it does not operate in isolation and it is important not to talk about it as if it did. Children are not always necessarily better second-language learners than adults – such generalisations are misleading at best (see Marinova-Todd, Marshall & Snow, 2000 for a detailed discussion). Late adult learners seem to be better at some aspects of L2 acquisition than early child bilinguals. Filipović and Hawkins (2013) have shown that adult L1 Japanese learners of L2 English do not use head-final structures from their L1 in their L2 production (which would be ungrammatical because English is a head-initial language) even at the earliest stages of L2 acquisition (see Chapter 4, section 4.4.1). On the other hand, Yip and Matthews (2007) do document some head-final Cantonese structures in the L2 English production of child bilingual speakers whose L1 is Cantonese. Adults may be more aware of the communicative cost involved in such cases and they seem to block these kinds of structures early on in acquisition, by a process which Filipović and Hawkins (2013) originally termed the 'communicative blocking of negative transfer' (see also Polinsky, 2016 for a multifactor comparison between child bilinguals and adult heritage speakers).

On the other hand, there are certain aspects of language processing that reveal clear advantages for child learners. McDonald (2000) argues that the decoding ability of language learners decreases with increasing age of acquisition. The later the onset age, the greater the strain on working memory when processing L2 structures. Individual differences in the level of L2 proficiency could thus be due to disparities in working-memory capacity, which some studies have shown to be the case (e.g. Harrington, 1992; Miyake & Friedman, 1998). However, we must also explain why children with still undeveloped cognitive abilities (including working memory) are nevertheless fantastic language learners.

It seems plausible that the learning of a language, just like any other type of learning, favours the young because it is performed using our overall general cognitive apparatus, which is much better at learning when young. Rohde and Plaut (2003) give a reason why this may be so: young children still have largely uncommitted brain resources and the older the learner is, the more mental space (or neural tissue that supports it) is already committed to other forms of knowledge and processes. Ramscar et al. (2017) offer a related explanation that addresses the apparent issue of cognitive ageing and its effect on learning. They argue that it is not ageing per se that leads to the apparent decline in learning among older adults. Rather, those adults are paying the price for greater knowledge: they have an increased experience with the language and this is why they perform worse than younger people, for example, when it comes to associative learning. Older speakers have a lifetime of learning that a cue such as 'jury' is informative for the word 'duty' but not for the word 'eagle'; so if they are trained to associate 'jury' with 'eagle', they are slower in making that association than younger speakers with less exposure and experience with language. Another interesting factor – education – was noticed in this study, confirming that it is increased language experience rather than cognitive ageing that impairs overall associative learning success. Older speakers with doctoral degrees performed significantly worse than did older adults without them. The authors explain that this is due to the fact that better-educated adults are more likely to have more extensive reading experience, which again shows that an increasingly well-discriminated lexical knowledge base leads to higher costs being incurred when it comes to novel learning. Importantly, in a bilingual context, young bilinguals do not show a difference between associative learning in their first and second languages. Older bilinguals do: they are much better associative learners in their second language than in their first and the gap between them and younger bilinguals is significantly reduced in the second language.

Further evidence seems to suggest that the earlier patterns are learned, the more likely it is they will be clearly represented and better stored. Ellis and Lambon Ralph (2000) used computational modelling to devise a learning network and found that over time the network became more committed to representing patterns presented earlier than those presented later, due to a gradual reduction in network plasticity (which reflects age-of-acquisition effects). Therefore, it seems that for both monolingual and bilingual language learning the most important general advantage is the same as in any other type of learning: that of having a young, uncommitted brain.

2.2.2 Differences

2.2.2.1 Processing Speed A number of studies report significant differences between monolingual and bilinguals with respect to processing time. Many of them aimed to establish whether a single processor is in charge of both languages in bilinguals, just as in monolinguals, or whether two separate processors are involved. For instance, Mägiste (1982; 1985) notes that bilinguals took more time than monolinguals to process verbal material in each language and that this was more pronounced with infrequent than with common words, which is interpreted as proof that a single processor was involved. Similarly, Soares and Grosjean (1984) also assume that bilinguals search both their lexicons in monolingual processing, which adds to overall processing time. In syntactic processing, a difference in speed has also been noticed. In a recent study Runnqvist et al. (2013) argue that processing speed in bilinguals is modulated by frequency effects and structural similarity between the bilinguals' two languages (i.e. faster processing in cases of higher frequency and more structural similarity). The differences in speed may also result from different habits of use rather than from the involvement of different processing mechanisms. For instance, Frenck-Mestre (2002) found that bilinguals show the same reading strategies in L2 as in L1 (and as in monolingual speakers), but L2 reading may be slower due to re-reading habits in the early stages of L2 acquisition rather than to the possibility that a completely different processing mechanism is involved.

Crucially, however, language typology may have a role to play here since two typologically close languages can be more conducive to native-like proficiency in late learners than typologically more distant ones (Birdsong & Molis, 2001; Hakuta, Bialystok & Wiley, 2003). In particular, grammatical structures that have no L1 equivalents in the L2 will pose a high load on working memory and this is likely to lead to ungrammatical outputs in the L2. Decoding of utterances has been shown to be slower in an L2 due to the fact that the demands this places on the speaker exceed working-memory capacity, and increasingly so with age. McDonald (2006) has shown that if we tax working memory in a grammatical judgement task, monolinguals perform in their only language similarly to late L2 learners in their L2. Interestingly, this similar performance under experimental conditions taxing working memory indicates that it is general cognitive capacities, rather than some kind of mental device dedicated solely to language learning, that are centrally important in linguistic performance (De Groot, 2011: 76).

2.2.2.2   Preference for Common Ground   Bilinguals differ from monolingual speakers in one major respect that will feature prominently throughout this book. The meanings, structures and usage patterns from one language inspire the use (or creation, if they do not exist) of the same or similar features in the other language. The use of patterns shared in both languages (*maximising common ground*, as we call it; see Chapter 3) thus becomes more frequent, and this can then result on certain occasions in atypical use in one (or both) of the languages. This is because when 'opting' for common meanings and forms in both languages, regardless of which one they are currently using, bilinguals may produce outputs that are more characteristic of one language than of the other (see Nicol, Teller & Greth, 2001; Filipović, 2011, 2018; see also Chapter 4 for numerous examples). The shared pattern may be major in one language but minor in the other, and this makes it obvious that bilinguals are not two monolinguals in one.

It is easy to understand why bilinguals gravitate towards using more of the shared patterns in their respective languages. It is more efficient to use shared representations that come from reducing two linguistic systems to one whenever possible. The more similar the two systems are, the more vulnerable to reduction to a common pattern. This then enables bilinguals to be **multi-language-ready**, prepared to communicate in either language at any point, and it makes their mental representations and 'thinking for speaking' (Slobin, 1987) more efficient as well. This structure-sharing is the essence of **bilingual processing efficiency** (Filipović, 2014), unique to bilinguals, and it differentiates their outputs from those of monolinguals. This point is elaborated and amply illustrated in Chapters 3 and 4, where I also show that, even though bilinguals are not two monolinguals in one, they may come close to being monolingual-like on certain occasions, but not on others. I explain what drives these differences within a single speaker and within different bilingual groups.

2.2.2.3   Greater Tolerance of Ungrammaticality   Bilinguals also appear to differ from monolinguals in terms of their flexibility towards ungrammaticality (discussed in this section) and ambiguity (see the next section), with an interesting contrast between the two: they show higher tolerance of ungrammaticality than monolinguals, but lower tolerance towards ambiguity and vagueness compared to monolinguals. Mack (1986) exemplifies the tolerance of ungrammaticality in one language driven by the fact that a matching structure is grammatical in the other language of the bilingual. French–English bilinguals classified grammatically incorrect English sentences that followed a French word-order pattern as correct more often than did monolinguals for French and English respectively. It seems that bilingualism in French and English has led to more flexibility in decision-making about grammaticality within both bilinguals' languages.

There seems to be some difference in language processing based on relative proficiency in each of the two languages. Highly proficient bilinguals (early bilinguals and very highly competent L2 speakers) seem to access both languages regardless of which they are speaking (Kroll & Bialystok, 2013). This access to both systems may affect how speakers process each language. Fernandez, de Souza and Carando (2017) studied the ways in which bilinguals react to innovations in their L1 coming from the L2 systems. They found that highly proficient Portuguese learners of English accept structures in their L1 (Portuguese) that would be ungrammatical in that language but are grammatical in their L2 (English), which is not the case for bilinguals with low English proficiency (who find the English structures unacceptable in Portuguese, just like Portuguese monolinguals). For instance, the caused-motion construction 'The French captain marched the soldiers to the capital' is grammatical in English but ungrammatical in Portuguese (*'O capitão francês marchou seus soldados até a capital'). The reading times for highly proficient Portuguese speakers of L2 English suggest a tolerance of this caused-motion construction in Portuguese under the influence of English, because another, different construction that is ungrammatical in both languages elicited significantly longer reading times in comparison. It would be worth testing whether early and balanced bilinguals in Portuguese and English also tolerate structures that are ungrammatical in one of their languages, as late and proficient bilinguals did in the Fernandez et al. (2017) study. They could possibly be better at knowing what can be shared and when, and what should not be shared between their two languages. This would enable us to disentangle the role of age and type of acquisition from proficiency: we may find that the way the two languages are acquired (simultaneously, from an early age vs. consecutively, or taught in an L2 classroom – see Chapter 5, Section 5.6.1) may nonetheless result in different outputs regardless of overall high proficiency in both languages. It must be pointed out here that less-proficient bilinguals, such as some L2 adult or child learners, may also not accept meanings and structures in one of their languages *even if they are shared* with the other language because they assume that their languages differ (captured by the notion of psychotypology; see Kellerman, 1983; see also Ben Zeev, 1977 on child bilinguals creating lines of separation between the two languages even when not necessary).

This bilingual tolerance of ungrammaticality, and also tolerance of a breach in usage conventions, is not surprising. The acceptance of unlicensed patterns is just an extreme point on a scale that leads from meaning innovations in one language inspired by the other – that is, affecting usage but not the grammar, such as the lexical expression of evidentiality in Andean Spanish under the influence of Quechua (see Chapter 4; see also Heine & Kuteva, 2005 for details) – to innovations that lead to grammatical changes and the introduction of previously unacceptable patterns in one of the two languages, such as a change in basic word order from subject-verb-object (SVO) to subject-object-verb (SOV) and vice versa (see Ross, 1996, 2001; Gast, 2007). These innovations are prerequisites for language change influenced by bilingualism, which starts within minds and then spreads across minds in the process of historical language change through contact, as attested in numerous sociolinguistic studies (see Heine & Kuteva, 2005; Trudgill, 2010, 2011).

It is interesting to ponder which way an innovation will go, because the result can be either the introduction of a novel, previously ungrammatical construction or the loss of an already existing construction that was grammatical in only one of the two languages. The psycholinguistic processes in bilingual minds that lead to the establishment of new language systems different from either of the two languages are influenced by the specifics of the social contexts in which communication takes place and which prompts bilingual minds to innovate. Either option, adding or discarding patterns, is available to bilinguals and is viable as a solution for reconciling two systems. Both the stronger and the weaker language of the bilingual speaker (i.e. the L1 and L2 respectively) can be the source of innovation, and the effects of these innovations can be detected not just in language production but also in how we think when we speak about objects or events, and how we remember them (see Pavlenko & Jarvis, 2002, and Brown & Gullberg, 2011 for both L1 and L2 as sources of influences on each other in narrative elicitations; see also Wolff & Ventura, 2003 for an example of L2 to L1 influence; Filipović, 2018 for L1 influence on memory when speaking an L2; and Cadierno, Ibarretxe-Antuñano & Hijazo-Gascón, 2016 for L1 effects on categorisation in L2). However, which pattern of innovation will be opted for depends on who the bilinguals are and who they are interacting with in their social environments, and this is why psycholinguistic factors of bilingual language use must be studied in unison with sociolinguistic factors. Before we turn to this in more detail, I explain a further point of contrast between monolinguals and bilinguals, namely bilinguals' apparent lack of tolerance of ambiguity.

2.2.2.4 Lower Tolerance of Ambiguity   Previous research has found that bilinguals appear to have lower tolerance of ambiguity (Benmamoun, Montrul & Polinsky, 2013a, 2013b; Polinsky, 2016). Ambiguity in language is efficient for the speaker and also efficient and tolerable for the hearer as long as the hearer can resolve it in context. The fewer form-to-meaning mappings that must be made, the fewer items there are stored, the more efficient the communication. Speaker and hearer negotiate minimal and less explicit forms and resolve their ambiguities and vaguenesses in communication (see Hawkins, 2004: 38–49 for a thorough discussion; see also Hawkins, 1986, 2009 for more details). However, there is also another apparently general heuristic that is relevant here, namely the intolerance of ambiguity, which is related to an across-the-board desire for a one-to-one mapping between meaning and structure. This tension between the efficiency of ambiguity and the difficulty of dealing with it maps onto the dichotomy between processing and learning. In a nutshell, ambiguity is bad for learners, who would prefer one-to-one form-to-meaning mapping, whilst for the producer and also in significant respects for the comprehender, having fewer form-to-meaning mappings to store and use is more efficient and thus more advantageous in processing terms. Overall, for hearers/comprehenders ambiguity is a mixed bag – it all depends on how quickly meanings can get disambiguated in context.

Knowing what one language regularly disambiguates seems to lead bilinguals to disambiguate in the other language as well. Polinsky (2016), in her discussion on heritage bilingualism, reasons that lack of ambiguity allows heritage bilingual speakers to communicate more effectively, and therefore we can predict that certain ambiguous structures in a language are likely to be reanalysed by heritage speakers of that language. As an example, she considers the well-known ambiguity between the so-called 'strict' and 'sloppy' readings in ellipsis, illustrated in the following English example (from Polinsky, 2016: 14):

1) The linguist promoted his new theory and the logician did too.
  i) The linguist promoted his new theory and the logician promoted the linguist's new theory.
     [strict reading]
  ii) The linguist$_i$ promoted his$_i$ new theory and the logician$_k$ promoted his$_k$ new theory.
     [sloppy (bound variable) reading]

The sloppy reading, in which the linguist and the logician each promoted their own separate theories, is attributed to the presence of a bound variable dependency. The strict reading, on the other hand, represents a simple coreference: the pronoun picks up as its antecedent 'the linguist' and this referent is carried over into the unpronounced verb phrase (VP). Ambiguity under ellipsis has received significant attention in both theoretical linguistics and research on language processing. Within the latter, studies have shown that monolingual speakers prefer the sloppy (bound variable) reading and process it more quickly than the strict reading (Frazier & Clifton, 2000; Koornneef, 2008; Shapiro et al., 2003; Vasić, 2006). For heritage speakers, one might then predict that they will generalise this processing preference and eliminate the ambiguity altogether, assigning only the sloppy reading to the elliptical structure in example (1). This is a testable prediction that can be explored in the contexts of both child and adult heritage language acquisition, with a general expectation that whatever ambiguity is allowed in the baseline will be reduced in the heritage language (see Polinsky, 2016 for further details).

Of particular interest to us are cases in which one language of the bilingual disambiguates within a certain category (e.g. aspect or intentionality) and the other does not. We can make an assumption here that bilinguals will tend to disambiguate in both their languages. This is indeed the case to a certain extent: some bilinguals seem to do it more often than others, and the ones who do it do so more on some occasions than on others. I illustrate and explain what conditions this diversity of outcomes in later chapters (see Chapters 3, 4 and 5).

2.2.2.5 Cognitive Benefits? Further contrasts between monolingual and bilingual speakers have been reported with regard to general cognitive advantages associated with speaking two languages from an early age (Bialystok, 1999; Bialystok, Craik & Ruocco, 2006; Bialystok & Martin, 2004; Costa, Hernández & Sebastián-Gallés, 2008). I have put a question mark in the title of this section because the debate over whether the reported cognitive benefits really exist or not is currently raging, many years since it was first suggested that bilingualism may be beneficial in a number of cognitive tasks. The question is still open.

Since the first important study reporting on the general cognitive benefits of child bilingualism (Peal & Lambert, 1962), we have had numerous research reports claiming that bilingualism is cognitively advantageous because, for example, it can provide 'greater mental flexibility; the ability to think abstractly, more independently of words and providing superior concept formation' (Baker, 2011: 144). Bialystok (2007) summarises the findings of numerous studies in this vein that apparently demonstrate how children gain control of certain cognitive functions earlier as bilinguals compared to monolinguals, have more executive resources available to use in response to especially complex demands, and show a less steep decline in certain respects with age. She emphasises that this is however in no way related to intelligence, as 'there is no evidence that bilinguals are in any measurable sense more intelligent than monolinguals' (Bialystok, 2007: 220). In fact, in some respects, bilinguals are at a disadvantage, according to Michael and Gollan (2005), most likely due to the cost of maintaining two representational systems. Bialystok (2007: 220) notes that bilinguals' performance is worse than that of monolinguals when rapid generation of words is required (e.g. picture-naming tasks; Gollan, Montoya & Werner, 2002). In a nutshell, being bilingual is not completely cost-free, but the gains have been claimed to outweigh the costs.

It seems that early (simultaneous) bilinguals are the ones who benefit the most, since the advantages in cognitive control that they seem to show are not detected in late bilinguals and monolinguals (Luk, De Sa & Bialystok, 2011; though see further discussion below, and also Papp, Johnson & Sawi (2015: 272) for numerous references to studies that did not replicate such findings). Even if the languages are typologically close, such as two different dialects, advantages across the executive control system seem to be detected (see Antoniou et al., 2016). Recent research by Yow and Li (2015) also found a significant effect of balanced bilingualism (balanced usage of, and balanced proficiency in, two languages): a more balanced level of proficiency in two languages resulted in better executive control skills in adult bilinguals. However, there have also been numerous studies that either fail to replicate previous findings of cognitive advantage or they demonstrate experimentally that there are no such advantages to be found (see Papp, Johnson & Sawi, 2016, for critical discussion; see also Gathercole, 2015 for an insightful assessment of the field). The argument against the cognitive advantage of bilingualism has been particularly strongly articulated in the context of the reported presence vs. absence of benefits from bilingualism with respect to executive function. Executive function comprises mental skills that help us monitor behaviour successfully and perform various tasks in order to achieve our goals (e.g. plan, focus attention, remember and juggle multiple tasks). Papp, Johnson and Sawi (2015) examined a wide array of studies that argue in both directions and concluded that executive functioning as reflected in performance on non-verbal tasks is not enhanced by bilingualism. They argue that the previous findings of a positive effect of bilingualism in this domain have various causes, including publication bias (null or negative results are less likely to be offered or accepted for publication) and confounds from different variables.

The debate is far from over and here I only refer to it in order to highlight the importance of bilingualism for the more general study of cognition in various disciplines, including psychology, cognitive science and neuroscience. In the present context our focus is firmly on language processing and on the occasions in which language has to be used or plays some part. Our goal is to find out how much and in what ways language processing can vary for different bilinguals and on different occasions. We are interested in how differences in the type of bilingualism and type of communicative situation affect linguistic outcomes, as well as the outcomes of some other activities that are performed with tacit or explicit access to one or both languages, either habitually or on specific occasions. For example, we will probe for the advantages and disadvantages of bilingualism only with regard to occasions when forms or meanings from one or both languages appear to be invoked in selecting, storing and retrieving information from memory. Before we focus on these instances, we look at the documented effects of bilingualism on how languages change through time (the next section), followed by a detailed discussion of the factors that have been shown to matter in bilingual language acquisition and use (Section 2.4).

2.3   Bilingualism and Long-Term Language Change

We can explain the specific features in bilingual use and make more precise predictions about bilingual outputs if we have information about the social and the historical context of bilingual speakers. Cases of language change that have occurred because of bilingualism are very instructive in this context and can teach us about the importance of social factors in the environments where bilinguals live and interact. For example, it has been noticed that Pennsylvania German has a highly frequent progressive ('be doing') aspect construction, which is not found in Standard German, where such constructions are extremely marginal ('am Tun sein' = 'be at doing'; Heine & Kuteva, 2005: 129). This development is attributed to the influence of English, which is the dominant language of the environment for Pennsylvania German speakers (Heine & Kuteva, 2005: 65). Another example is the creation of a definite article in Sorbian through contact with German and of the indefinite article in Basque through contact with Romance languages (Heine & Kuteva, 2005: 101; though Manterola, 2012 identifies some problems in the way the Basque data have been used in Heine and Kuteva's 2005 contact-induced grammaticalisation explanation). Importantly, Heine and Kuteva (2005: 23) point out that 'article development is a universal process', and in some languages where it has taken place this process might not have been caused by contact with the neighbouring languages; rather, contact has been reported as a contributing or accelerating factor. Language change through bilingual contact is gradual: meaning distinctions are first introduced by bilingual overuse of certain form–meaning mappings, and their use then becomes distinctive later and finally, specialised (see Heine & Kuteva, 2005, for details on these phases in historical language change and for many further examples).

Both socially dominant and socially non-dominant languages can drive language change. The socially prestigious variant is often the source of the innovation in the socially less prestigious variant due to its status in society (e.g. development of evidentiality in Bulgarian under Turkish influence during Ottoman rule; Slobin, 2016). The reverse can also happen, however, namely when the socially non-dominant language becomes the inspiration for innovation in the socially dominant one (as in the development of evidentiality in Andean Spanish under the influence of Quechua and Aymara; Slobin, 2016). A socially subjugated population can introduce an innovation into the language of the socially dominant group if strength in numbers lies with the former and not with the latter (i.e. if the speakers of the socially non-dominant language outnumber the speakers of the socially dominant language in the community). This is a frequent development in former colonies. The language of the socially dominant group changes only locally (e.g. Andean Spanish in Latin America has evidentiality, but Spanish in Spain does not). The number of bilinguals in a community is crucial for such changes to happen – there has to be enough of them regardless of which language is the source of innovation. It is the bilingual speakers who bring about these changes in many instances, because the contact between the two languages takes place in the minds of the speakers who use both languages in communication with other speakers, monolingual and bilingual. This was noticed by Weinreich (1966 [1953]) but somehow the important and widespread phenomenon of contact-induced language change due to bilingualism has not yet made it into the mainstream of historical linguistic research.

For example, in one of the most used textbooks on historical linguistics (Campbell, 2013) the word 'bilingual(s)' is only mentioned once and 'bilingualism' only twice in almost 500 pages. The role of bilingualism has also been labelled as 'minor' in comparison to the 'language-internal' motivations that appear to cause changes in language in all its contact variants (Rosenberg, 2005). We need to acknowledge that not all change is due to bilingualism, but a substantial number of changes are brought about by bilinguals through their learning and use of both languages (i.e. bilingualism is a major cause of language change; see Heine & Kuteva, 2005; Trudgill, 2011, and Chamoreau & Léglise, 2012 for an abundance of examples). Both internal factors and language contact are involved in language change, as was observed many years ago by Meillet (1982 [1906]) but somehow, again, this has not made it into the historical linguistics mainstream until more recently. Thankfully, recent research in language change is re-examining 'multi-causality and the distinctions of the two types of mechanism' (Chamoreau & Léglise, 2012: 9). A clear presentation of factors that appear to be relevant for contact-induced language change is given in Muysken (2013), who discusses the following: similarity factors (lexical similarity/distance, typological similarity/distance), prestige and status factors (L1 prestige, L2 prestige), proficiency factors (low L2 proficiency, high L2 proficiency), contact factors (large/small numbers of L1 or L2 speakers present, type of network), time factors (long/short contact period) and attitudinal factors (low normativity, political distance). Muysken (2013) also calls for more research in order to understand which factors constitute necessary and which constitute sufficient conditions for a particular contact outcome.

Understanding the nature of the contact between populations, which includes the types of their social interactions (close and socially equal vs. distant and socially unequal) and the types of ensuing bilingualism (e.g. balanced vs. unbalanced) is essential for an understanding of why we have some contact-induced language changes but not others. For example, Trudgill (2011) gives the example of Old English, which he argues changed in two different directions due to two different types of bilingualism among its speakers. He observes that Old English was both complexified (gaining new form-to-meaning mappings) and simplified (losing some of the existing form-to-meaning mappings), and this is due, according to Trudgill (2011), to two different kinds of influence: Old Norse and Old British (Celtic) respectively. Old Norse and Old English were in the kind of contact that involved equal status, with much intermarriage taking place and early bilinguals being equally proficient in both. On the other hand, Old British and Old English were in a very different type of contact situation. These two groups were not on equal terms and there was a social distance between the free and landholding Anglo-Saxon aristocracy and the Britons, who were often slaves (Trudgill, 2011: 54; see also Tristram, 2004, 2006).

Trudgill argues that, overall, if two languages are learned simultaneously, as first languages, their speakers (balanced bilinguals) are more likely to add features from one language to another, that is, to complexify, rather than to simplify their languages. When one of the languages is acquired late as an L2, it tends to be simplified according to Trudgill (2011), especially if the social circumstances as such that the communication is very limited (e.g. as in the Anglo-Saxons and Celts master–slave context). In other words, simplification is 'most likely to occur in situations involving language learning by adults, particularly short-term contact' whilst complexification is 'most likely to occur in long-term territorial contact situations involving child bilingualism' (Trudgill, 2011: 34). Trudgill also explains (2010) that the relationships and the nature of contact was different between early Old English and Brittonic speakers (closer and more intimate, leading to 'additive complexification' in Old English) from those of later Old English and Late British speakers (simplification through adult language contact). There are parallel examples of both complexification and simplification in another language, Arabic. There was simplification in Nubi Arabic, spoken as a second language in southern Sudan and northern Uganda (Trudgill, 2011: 44), whilst in different places, Cyprus and Afghanistan, Arabic was complexified as a result of its close sociolinguistic contact with other local languages spoken (Cypriot Greek in the case of Kormataki Cypriot Arabic (Borg, 1985) and Uzbek and Tajik in the case of Afghan Arabic (Ingham, 1994)).

There is still some uncertainty, however, in the literature on the history of English as to who exactly introduced the simplification and complexification changes into English. For instance, McWhorter (2009) argues that Celtic speakers introduced some innovations into English, such as the periphrastic '*do* construction' and that it was actually the Old Norse speakers who simplified English. Perhaps it could have been both Celtic and Old Norse speakers who both simplified and complexified Old English. Trudgill (2010: 34) says that 'the answer to our conundrum of Celtic vs. Old Norse would appear to be that the advocates of the two positions are both likely to be correct'. Old Norse also seems to have influenced Old English in two ways. When it comes to the simplification of the case system in Old English this could as well have been done under the influence of Old Norse. When the Old Norse speakers came to England, they could have been speaking English as an L2 and, in line with Trudgill's thesis about simplification, have simplified some aspects of their L2 (e.g. by keeping the cases in Old English that were the same or similar to those in their L1 and dispensing with those that were not). Then when the social cohesion became tighter and intermarriages started resulting in the balanced bilingualism of new generations, complexification of Old English also started taking place. There is substantial evidence that Old Norse speakers complexified Old English – they introduced many L1-inspired innovations (see Emonds & Faarlund, 2014 for detailed discussion).

The crucial point is that there was more influence on English from Scandinavian than from Celtic sources because there was closer contact and more integration on an equal footing between speakers of Old English and those of Old Norse. Celtic influence was still possible even though Old English was the socially prestigious language because of the strength in numbers that the Celts had. Thus, it seems not impossible that there were simplification and complexification going on in both Celtic and Scandinavian bilingualism with Old English, because bilinguals were trying to maximise common ground (details in Chapter 3) – they would introduce material from their L1 (Celtic or Old Norse) or they would dispense with material from their L2 Old English if it did not match what they had in their respective L1s (see Chapter 4, Section 4.3.2 for a discussion of inflectional loss in Old English).

Nowadays, we can find similar trends in many cases of language contact. For example, L1 Spanish learners of L2 English learn their L2 with the intention of expressing all the meanings they wish to express, just as they do in their L1. In the process, as we shall see, they introduce meanings from their L1 Spanish into their L2 when the L2 does not have them (and this is also the case for many other learners of L2 English with different L1s, see Chapter 4 for examples). These are adult L2 learners but they are not likely only to simplify, and when they do simplify this will be in domains where their L1 lacks a corresponding structure or meaning. The bilingualism in their minds is not driven solely by the goal of basic communication (as it may have been with the Celts) – they are motivated to learn to speak English as well as possible because of the opportunities that speaking English provides. They are not likely, however, to bring about more permanent change to the English language as a whole – for that they would need to live in close proximity with monolingual English speakers and also be demographically strong, i.e. probably more numerous than the monolinguals in English-speaking lands, which is an unlikely scenario in the present day. As Trudgill (2011: 57) emphasises, 'it makes no sense to simply refer to "contact" as an undifferentiated concept' – we must refine our focus and talk about the type of contact instead. In all cases of contact-induced language change there are certain sociolinguistic conditions that have to be fulfilled for changes to have long-term effects: in particular the number of bilinguals must be significant. Our discussion here shows that both psycholinguistic and sociolinguistic analyses are indispensable for understanding the consequences of bilingualism within and across minds.

We shall see in Chapters 3 and 4 examples of both adding and reducing the number of form–meaning mappings in use due to different ways in which the multiple factors involved interact with each other, namely the language types in question, bilingual speaker type and communicative situation types. For instance, L2 speakers can in fact introduce some typological features from their L1 into their L2 and complexify their L2 in one respect, whilst at the same time they may be simplifying the L2 in another respect (e.g. if their L1 does not draw the meaning distinctions that the L2 does). What emerges from the literature on language contact and change reviewed in this section is that there are likely to be multiple factors that are relevant and that operate at one and the same time in bilingual language acquisition and use. This is why *any proposed model of bilingualism must be a multifactor one* (see the next chapter).

2.4   Factors in Bilingual Language Acquisition and Language Use: Internal and External

The factors that impact bilingualism can be divided into essentially two groups, **internal** and **external**. Internal factors include those that determine the potential of a bilingual to operate in each of the two languages and they include age and sequence of acquisition, type of input, proficiency in each language, and language dominance status (which is related to both proficiency and frequency of use). They are labelled 'internal' because they are inherent to a specific individual or to multiple bilingual individuals of the same type. These internal factors are the parameters on the basis of which we are able to categorise bilinguals. We have seen that such classifications are not straightforward (e.g. there is no clear empirical test for when early bilingualism stops and late bilingualism starts). The sharing of just one feature, for example age of acquisition, is not a sufficient basis for placing bilinguals into coherent groups. They could all acquire the same two languages around the same time in their personal acquisition histories, but their usage paths may then diverge, some of them using one language more frequently than another, some experiencing more significant attrition due to lack of use and some maintaining equal or near-equal proficiency throughout their lives.

In this section I will discuss some studies that have focused on one or more of the relevant factors in bilingualism and assess their impact on bilingual language representation and language use. Later I focus in more detail on the importance of these factors for *bilingualism in action:* i.e. on the impact they have on how bilinguals verbalise experience, remember it and make judgements about it (Chapters 5 and 6).

2.4.1   *Internal Factors: Age of Acquisition, Proficiency and Dominance*

Bilingualism research has long been concerned with the effects of age of acquisition on each language, and of relative language proficiency and language dominance on bilingual language processing and use. I consider these three factors together here because they are intertwined and closely related to one another. Early and simultaneous acquisition is usually associated with higher proficiency and no unilateral dominance of one language over the other, except in heritage contexts when incomplete acquisition or attrition affect competence in one of the two languages. On the other hand, later and sequential acquisition is usually correlated with lower proficiency and dominance of the language acquired earlier over the one acquired later in adult second-language acquisition, and with dominance of the language acquired later (that of education and/or living environment) over an earlier one (spoken at home) in the case of child heritage-language bilinguals (see Montrul, 2008, for insightful comparisons between heritage and L2 bilingualism).

Age of acquisition has been one of the most discussed factors in the literature, yet there is no consensus about how to use it consistently in a way that helps us to classify bilingual speakers. There is no agreement on what an 'early' or 'balanced' bilingual is. As pointed out by Hohenstein, Eisenberg and Naigles (2006) for example, an early bilingual in one study can be a late bilingual in another. Myers-Scotton (2006) says that, when it comes to age of acquisition, the situation can be summarised as: many studies, many different conclusions. Abutalebi et al. (2009) argue that proficiency is a more decisive factor than age of acquisition, but then the two factors generally correlate because late acquisition usually equals lower proficiency (Abutalebi et al., 2009: 346–7). What we need to be aware of is that bilingualism is a matter of degree. For example, second-language speakers can be bilingual to very different degrees, just as early bilinguals can. Some late learners can achieve higher proficiency in their second language than early child bilinguals in that same language that they acquired early but as a heritage language. It seems that proficiency is the more reliable predictor in bilingualism and it affects not only differences in linguistic behaviour but also some other non-linguistic aspects of cognition (Kroll & Bialystok, 2013; Luk et al., 2011).

Li (2000: 6) defines a 'balanced bilingual' as 'someone whose mastery of two languages is roughly equivalent' and a 'dominant bilingual' as 'someone with greater proficiency in one of his or her languages and [who] uses it significantly more than the other language(s)'. This definition emphasises the importance of both proficiency and frequency of use for determining dominance. In a recent edited volume dedicated to the construct of language dominance in bilinguals, Silva-Corvalán and Treferrs-Daller (2015: 4) echo Li's view and propose a definition of dominance in bilinguals that is based on both proficiency and the nature of language use. They argue that proficiency refers to a specific aspect of language ability, namely grammatical knowledge, and that different bilinguals could have different proficiency levels whilst having the same combination of stronger–weaker language. They define dominant language 'as that in which a bilingual has attained an overall higher level of proficiency, at a given age, and/or the language that s/he uses more frequently, and across a wider range of domains'. Amount of input and frequency of use of a language are shown to be the determining factors of dominance and proficiency in a number of studies (e.g. Gathercole & Thomas, 2009; Hoff et al., 2012). Overall, proficiency is viewed as a 'component of dominance', but proficiency and dominance are not considered to be absolute synonyms (Montrul, 2015; Silva-Corvalán, 2014: ch. 1).

2.4.2   External Factors: Communicative Situation Types and Interlocutor Types

The other major set of decisive factors that impact the linguistic behaviour of bilinguals, but that are much less frequently and less systematically discussed in the literature, include external factors. They are called 'external' because they are not related to any specific bilingual speaker or bilingual speaker group. They comprise the social and interactional circumstances that serve as a trigger for a bilingual to adjust his or her linguistic behaviour, and their ability to do so is conditioned by the internal factors discussed previously. Namely, success in mastering these external adjustments will depend crucially on the bilingual's level of mastery in each language that is shaped by the internal factors. The same bilingual can behave differently in different situations, just as a monolingual can (e.g. in formal vs. informal discourse). However, the difference is that the bilingual mind needs to achieve this capacity by adjusting the rules and usage habits of two different linguistic systems. Bilinguals also have more different options to consider than monolinguals when it comes to the possible interlocutor types that they interact with in the context of a single communicative situation (e.g. two monolinguals, one in each language vs. two or more bilinguals whose proficiency varies). All of these factors characterising the social conditions of communicative interaction can play a role in determining different bilingual linguistic outputs.

Before I discuss some studies that address these factors empirically, I need to refer to Communication Accommodation Theory, developed by Howard Giles and colleagues in the 1970s. The basic idea behind this theory is that people change their behaviour in order to attune their communication to their partner. This theory is grounded in social psychology and social identity theory (see Giles & Smith, 1979, for details). Although this approach to the study of communication addresses a wider set of issues that concern communication in general and not bilingualism specifically, it is useful to draw a parallel between some of the notions from that framework and our current concerns. Namely, according to Communication Accommodation Theory speakers can employ 'strategies of convergence' whereby individuals adapt to each other's communicative behaviours to reduce social differences. By contrast, 'strategies of divergence' are employed when individuals accentuate the speech and non-verbal differences between themselves and their interlocutors (Giles, Coupland & Coupland, 1991). Too much convergence can lead to over-accommodating that can be interpreted as condescending. This theory has been applied to second-language acquisition by Zuengler (1991), who studied communication between native and non-native language speakers. Interestingly, native speakers have been found to engage in so-called 'foreigner talk' when interacting with second-language learners, adjusting their language by adopting features such as slower speech rates, shorter and simpler sentences, greater pronunciation articulation, and so on.

Bilingual speakers generally accommodate, or make adjustments to, their linguistic behaviour when engaging with different interlocutors. For instance, they will code-switch more when talking to another bilingual speaker of the same two languages than when speaking to a monolingual speaker. By the same token, their code-switching may be kept in check more when talking to other bilingual speakers on a formal occasion compared to informal communicative situations (see examples further below).

The precise mechanisms that control this process of adjustment are debated in the literature. One of the relevant constructs that has been proposed in order to explain this difference in bilingual behaviour under different circumstances is *language mode*. Grosjean's view is that the language system is flexible in a bilingual speaker and that its behaviour depends on the circumstances. He proposed the notion of language mode in order to capture this flexibility (Grosjean, 1992, 1998, 2001) and defined it as the state of activation of the bilingual's language and language-processing mechanisms that can be affected by numerous different factors. It is important to emphasise that proficiency plays the key role when it comes to the level of control that can be exercised over language mode. Bilinguals who are highly dominant in one language may simply not be able to control language mode in both languages in the same way as balanced bilinguals. Although they may deactivate their stronger language in a monolingual environment that requires them to use only their weaker language, their weaker language may simply not be active or developed enough to allow them to stay in a monolingual mode (Grosjean, 2001: 21).

The relevant assumption here is that the bilingual's language system is organised in separate subsets, one for each language, and that these subsets can be activated or deactivated as a whole and independently from each other. The level of activation of each of the bilingual's languages is seen as a continuum ranging from no activation to complete activation, based on factors such as the communicative situation, the form and content of the message being listened to, the function of the language act or the participants involved in the exchange and the conventions between them, which might or might not tolerate code-switching or code-mixing. For example, a Spanish–English bilingual speaking Spanish to a Spanish monolingual is said to be in 'Spanish monolingual mode' (Spanish is the base language and English is deactivated as the mode is monolingual). Grosjean (1998: 140) makes the point that bilinguals will rarely ever find themselves in pure monolingual mode since the other language(s) will always remain active to some degree at least.

However, it is not clear how the different levels of activation can be confirmed with any certainty – it seems they can only be deduced based on the specifics of a communicative situation. Furthermore, the vast evidence for a common store in bilinguals (e.g. Fabbro, 1999; Hernandez, Martinez & Kohnert, 2000; Paradis, 1997, 2000), indicates that identifying activation levels associated with different languages may not even be possible. There has been some further criticism of the notion of language mode and how to determine it, and more importantly, the question has been raised of whether it is the fluctuating language mode that is responsible for variation in bilingual linguistic behaviour or something else; for example, a kind of *conscious output monitor* that regulates the output rather than the language mode per se (see De Groot, 2011: 288, for a discussion and see also De Groot, 2011: 290, on the circularity of attempts to determine language mode). It remains to be seen whether bilingual adaptability to the requirements of different communicative situations concerns changes in the degree of activation of the bilingual's two languages or a change in the 'attentiveness of a mental monitor that watches over the output of the language system' (De Groot, 2011: 294).

As De Groot (2011: 293) observes, being in a bilingual mode need not mean that there would necessarily be a different linguistic output to that in a monolingual mode, for example more language switches between languages when both languages are active in a bilingual mode. For instance, in contrast to the prediction based on language mode, bilingual speakers do not necessarily code-switch more in a bilingual mode than in a monolingual one if the communicative situation is formal (e.g. in official exam contexts). Dewaele (2001) found that students in a bilingual language mode can show very different language behaviour (including code-switching types and instances) depending on the current communicative context (e.g. formal vs. informal). Grosjean (2001) himself mentions that certain situations, like the formality of the communicative occasion, may actually make the mode intermediate rather than fully bilingual. However, the notion of 'intermediate mode' is not very helpful because it is not possible to determine where the bilingual mode stops and the intermediate mode starts, and similarly, when the intermediate mode ends and the monolingual mode begins. Rather, it is only after the fact, when we have observed the behaviour, that we can say what kind of mode we presume the speakers to have been in. It may be more helpful to think in much more specific terms about who is speaking to whom and for what purpose instead of generalising modes as bilingual vs. intermediate vs. monolingual.

Filipović and Hawkins (2018) observe that bilinguals can be in a bilingual mode but behave very differently based on whom precisely they are addressing. There are different occasions when a bilingual speaker will be in a bilingual mode, each of which can result in different linguistic behaviour. For example, our bilingual speaker can be in a fully bilingual mode when he or she is interpreting, speaking to two monolinguals in each language, speaking to a relatively incompetent L2 speaker, speaking formally to a bilingual audience or speaking informally to bilinguals in the same languages. All of these situations are likely to result in *different outputs eventhough the mode is always bilingual*. We need to capture the key differences that stem from the interactions of many factors, including the subtle differences that characterise different types of language modes (see Yu & Schwieter, 2015 on the relevance of language mode for bilingualism research, and recent findings in this regard). Green and Abutalebi (2013: 515–16) argue that it is the *control processes that adapt* to the different demands of different communicative contexts of *single language, dual language or dense code-switching*. They define single-language contexts as those in which each language is spoken in different environments (e.g. home vs. work). Dual-language contexts involve the use of both languages with different speakers, possibly within a single communicative situation but not within an utterance, and dense code-switching occurs when both languages are used within a single utterance, e.g. when speaking to another bilingual with the same language combination (Green & Abutalebi, 2013: 518).

I believe that language mode remains a useful construct that can be used to signal the major distinction between different types of communicative situations that bilinguals find themselves in, i.e. monolingual vs. bilingual. For the purpose of our discussion here, I will refer to situations in which a bilingual is speaking to monolinguals in one of the two languages as monolingual mode (or single-language context, where one language is likely to be significantly more active than the other). When bilinguals are speaking to a bilingual audience (e.g. other bilinguals or two monolinguals, one in each language), I will consider this to be an instance of a bilingual mode (or dual-language context, with or without code-switching, where both languages are highly active, though their levels of activation may vary during the interaction). We have to keep in mind that more precise distinctions are necessary and that different outputs are predicted within the bilingual mode depending on who is talking to whom and why, as explained in this section.

2.5   How Are Bilingual Languages Represented?

Much has been said about whether the two linguistic systems in bilinguals overlap or are kept separate and to what extent they may do so. Paradis (2004:

chapter 7) cites four different options for bilingual storage, all apparently supported by neurolinguistic research, namely the extended system (with no separate storage but rather storing L2 in what is already there for L1), dual system (separate storage, with separate sets of phonemes, rules and words), tripartite system (whereby language-specific elements are stored separately and joint elements, such as cognates, together) and subset organisation (whereby a single-storage system is used and in which links between elements are strengthened through continued use). According to Hartsuiker and Pickering (2008), the variability in research results that support different organisation possibilities for the bilingual mind and brain is illustrative of the variability of bilingual research results in general.

For our purposes here, it is important to note that the two systems in the bilingual mind are intimately connected. Overall, it seems that lexical items are stored separately but that some parts of the lexicon overlap. Some syntactic structures share representations too, namely those present in both languages, but not those that are available in only one of the two languages, as demonstrated in numerous studies that involved cross-linguistic priming (all discussed in more detail below). Importantly, as Myers-Scotton (2006: 297) explains, even if the two systems were stored separately this does not mean that both cannot be activated at the same time. The degree of activation of one or both languages on each individual occasion may vary based on habitual language use (i.e. how often bilinguals activate one vs. both languages in their daily lives) and it may also depend on the requirements of a specific task at hand (e.g. in bilingual vs. monolingual communication or when the choice of language for problem-solving is free vs. restricted to one of the two languages; see Athanasopoulos et al., 2015). It is not enough to know which two languages the bilingual speaks and with what levels of proficiency. We need to capture the *linguistic behaviour of the same bilinguals in different situations as well as the linguistic behaviours of different bilinguals on the same occasion.* Before I illustrate how this can be done in the next chapter, we look in more detail at bilingual language representation by linguistic level.

2.5.1   Bilingual Lexicon(s)

As mentioned in the previous section, it seems that there are different storage options for different types of lexical items. The nature of bilingual representation for specific lexical items may depend on the extent to which there is a match in form-to-meaning mapping. If this mapping is identical or very close, such pairs are so-called 'translation pairs', and this close link is evidenced by the simultaneous translation abilities of bilinguals. De Groot (1993) proposes that the degree of conceptual similarity associated with translation pairs may be the determining factor in their representation (see De Groot, 1993 for further discussion on the cognate status of such pairs). In second-language acquisition these pairs are initially set as *one meaning – two forms* and the bilingual lexicon is 'parsimonious where it is justified to be so: representational space is not wasted by storing the same meaning twice, once for the word in each language' (De Groot, 1993: 46; see also discussion in Field, 2002: 183). An L2 concrete noun is likely to share many perceptual and conceptual features with the corresponding L1 word, whilst more abstract concepts are more likely to have fewer and fuzzier overlapping properties. According to Kroll & De Groot (1997), with growing proficiency more independence is achieved in the meaning representations for each language (but see also Storms, Ameel & Malt, 2015 for discussion of opposing views on the increasing vs. decreasing independence of meaning representations in bilingual acquisition).

Here we have to pause briefly and point out that we need to distinguish between conceptual and semantic store, as noted earlier (Vigliocco & Filipović Kleiner, 2004; see also Kousta, Vinson & Vigliocco, 2008). Kousta et al. (2008) argue that the terms 'semantic store' and 'conceptual store' are used inter-changeably in the literature on bilingualism when language-dependent vs. independent access to the bilingual lexicon is being discussed. They emphasise that if the conceptual store is intended, the claim that there may be two such stores leads to extreme linguistic relativity. In other words, the maintenance of two separate conceptual stores, each resulting from one of the two languages respectively, would mean that language and conceptualisation are linked in a deterministic way. It is more likely that two semantic rather than conceptual stores are intended in such discussions, as Kousta et al. (2008) assume (see Vigliocco & Filipović Kleiner, 2004 on the general importance of *always* distinguishing between the semantic and the conceptual level of representation).

When it comes to learning and remembering word meaning in bilingual contexts, it has been proposed that L2 learning and accessing lexical items both happen via L1 in the early stages and at lower levels of proficiency. In other words, L2 has been thought to be dependent on L1 mediation during the very early stages of L2 learning, as predicted by the Revised Hierarchical Model (e.g. Kroll & Stewart, 1994). According to this model, L1 translations might be involved in processing L2 words but once higher proficiency is achieved in the L2, direct conceptual processing of L2 items becomes possible. More recent research has indicated that L1 translation can remain active even when speakers have achieved high proficiency in the L2 and are able to understand the mean-ing of L2 words directly (Thierry & Wu, 2007; see also Van Hell & Kroll, 2013 for critical discussion). Recent research has also shown, however, that even in the initial stages of second-language acquisition direct access to L2 forms and meanings (not via L1) can be detected. Van Hell et al. (2017) show that child and adult L2 learners have established direct L2 word-to-concept mappings even at a very early stage in L2 learning, in both immersed and classroom-only learning environments. It seems that there is a direct L2 word-to-concept mapping and that L2 meaning representations can be available independent of the L1 from the very early acquisition stages, even when L2 acquisition is happening only through classroom learning (ibid.).

When there is a dependency of representations between the two languages, we can speak of *bilingual accents*. De Groot (2014) discusses bilingual accents in phonology, grammar and semantics. The notion of 'accent' is defined differently there from its usual phonetic sense, in which it refers to speech. It includes grammatical and semantic features of both production and comprehension (see also Lucy, 2014 for a related discussion of semantic accents). For instance, if a French–English bilingual understands the word 'costume' in English to mean 'a man's suit' instead of 'a theatre costume', this would be an example of a semantic accent in comprehension because French is now exerting semantic influence over English (De Groot, 2014: 230).

One of the questions to consider is the nature of these accents. De Groot points out that the most widely held assumption is that these accents are due to 'translation pairs sharing their meaning representation, partly or completely, in the bilingual lexicon' (De Groot, 2014: 250). This is a result of specific learning processes, one of which is 'conceptual transfer' (Pavlenko, 2005; Jarvis & Pavlenko, 2010), whereby an L2 word is paired with its closest translation in L1 in the first instance. The consequence of this process is the use of the L2 word where native speakers may not use it and vice versa: not using the word when native speakers use it. Another process that leads to semantic accents is the gradual convergence or merging of L1 and L2 meanings and combining the representations of L1 and L2 words into a unified single representation (see Chapter 4 for more examples of such instances, which result from the principle of Maximise Common Ground (Chapter 3) in bilingual language processing). De Groot points out (2014: 251) that this process leads to accented semantics in both L1 and L2, since the conceptual representation would contain both L1- and L2- specific information. The key issue here, according to De Groot (ibid.), is whether semantic accents can simply be explained in terms of parallel activation of language-specific memory structures rather than by merger representation (i.e. convergence of representations via restructuring). For instance, bilingual speakers would sometimes encounter 'hat' and sometimes 'chapeau' when talking about the object that covers the head. The consequence of these encounters would be the creation of an associative activation of 'hat' when 'chapeau' is encountered and vice versa. In other words, the name in the non-response language automatically activates its name in the response language. By the same token, Ervin (1961) showed some time ago that, in the domain of colour categorisation, Navajo–English bilinguals labelled a specific colour patch 'tatLqid' ('green') because this is how it would be labelled in English ('green') whilst the monolingual Navajo would label it 'litso' ('yellow'). This is because the Navajo–English bilinguals have both 'litso' and 'green' activated, and immediately, 'green' also activates 'tatLqid' ('green' in Navajo). According to De Groot (2014) this type of semantic accent can be attributed to increased competition between alternative names for specific concepts in bilinguals and not to different concepts in bilinguals and monolinguals. She argues that other studies that apparently feature 'merger representations' in bilinguals (e.g. Ameel et al., 2005; Caskey-Simons & Hickerson, 1977) can in fact be explained in terms of parallel activation (see more on the different strengths of respective linguistic systems and their effects in parallel activation in De Groot, 2011: 121; see also Athanasopoulos et al., 2010, who report on some apparent changes in bilingual conceptualisation such as a permanent shift in the borders between two hues in one language under the influence of the other).

One of the sources of our knowledge about bilingual lexical representation has come from priming studies, which involve testing whether exposure to one language activates meanings or forms in the other. Many studies report that this is indeed the case: accessing a word in one language is known to lead to activation of a related word in the other, both in comprehension and in production (see Costa, Miozzo & Caramazza, 1999; Van Heuven, Dijkstra & Grainger, 1998). There is still no unifying explanation for the precise nature and the extent of this connection. On the one hand, there is evidence which indicates that some aspects of word meaning and access to lexical (and grammatical) information may be independent in the two languages. For instance, Potter et al. (1984) found that the amount of facilitation gained by repeating a word (repetition priming) is much greater and longer-lasting within than between languages, although repetition priming may not actually be tapping into semantic processes. In other studies, some areas of the lexicon have been identified as more likely to be shared than others. For instance, some researchers state that cognate words in particular (i.e. those of common etymological origin such as 'gratitude' in English and 'gratitudine' in Italian) have a special status in the bilingual mental lexicon, and that they are the ones that are located in a shared lexical store (see, for example, De Groot, 1992, 1993; Taylor & Taylor, 1990). The cognate status of words and orthographic similarity between languages are known to have effects on recognition and lexical decision between languages (see Macizo & Bajo, 2006; Van Hell & Dijkstra, 2002) and all this points towards common storage of lexical information.

However, factors like the position of target words in a string, and word frequency, may affect experimental outcomes. For instance, Macizo and Bajo (2006) found that cognate effects were present when both languages were active in their participants (i.e. participants were in a bilingual mode since they were reading for translation) and when the critical words (e.g. 'zebra' in English and 'cebra' in Spanish) were in the final position of the sentence. Ruiz et al. (2008) have also argued that these inter-language effects are not reserved solely for cognate words and that non-cognate words can also cause the elicitation of cognate-like effects. Namely, they detected faster reading for translation in the task when high frequency *non-cognate* words (e.g. 'bridge' = 'puente') were placed at the end of the stimulus sentence. This frequency effect was not found if such words were placed at the beginning of the sentence. The authors argue (Ruiz et al., 2008: 498) that there may be a timing difference between lexical and syntactic processing in bilinguals since syntactic code-switching seems to start from the very beginning of the sentence (see the next section on syntactic processing; see also Ruiz et al., 2008, for more details).

There are other occasions when cognate effects might not be present. Schwartz and Kroll (2006) have shown that speakers of either high or low bilingual proficiency can use context to constrain cross-language lexical competition. They noticed that there was cognate facilitation in low-constraint sentences, which suggests that both languages were active and influencing processing. In high-constraint sentences, there was no cognate facilitation; that is, the cognate effects disappeared. Thus, it seems that specific *types of task demand* can significantly affect the experimental outcome.

This was also the case when gender-marking effects were absent in one study (Kousta et al., 2008) but present in another (Boroditsky, Schmidt & Philips, 2003). Kousta et al. (2008) probed for the semantic effects of grammatical gender (present in Italian but absent in English) in fluent bilingual speakers and compared their performance with that of the respective monolingual speakers. Their results show that Italian–English bilingual speakers behave like monolingual English speakers when the task is in English and like monolingual Italian speakers when the task is in Italian. The authors conclude that Italian–English bilinguals have appropriate (separate) semantic representations for each language and that gender marking does not have a conceptual, non-linguistic effect. They argue further that these results need not be interpreted as evidence against common storage in bilinguals, though lexical access does appear to be independent (Kousta et al., 2008: 855).

But even though some language-specific information in the lexicon can be stored and accessed separately, this does not mean that it will always be *kept* distinct. The results in Kousta et al. (2008), whereby bilinguals apparently kept their two processing patterns separate and mutually unaffected, are not very surprising since their experimental methodology (error induction) tapped into more automated processes in each language and the bilingual participants were in a monolingual mode during the experiment, using only one language on alternative experimental days. If the level of activation for one of the two languages is very low (and especially if one of the languages is blocked; see Athanasopoulos et al., 2015), a competent bilingual may reach a monolingual-like level of performance in certain tasks and inter-language effects do not appear. In addition, the methodological focus in Kousta et al. (2008) was on language-specific morphosyntactic information, and these properties are generally 'non-transferable' across languages (MacWhinney, 2005: 60).

But gender is both a grammatical and a semantic category and in another study on bilingual gender representation, by Boroditsky et al. (2003), grammatical noun gender differences from speakers' L1s resulted in semantic gender differences in L2 English, which does not mark grammatical gender. L2 speakers were presented with objects that have grammatical gender in their L1 (German or Spanish) and were asked to describe these objects in English. Both L1 groups used more masculine or more feminine adjectives with nouns according to the respective noun gender assignment in their L1. De Groot (2011) argues, in relation to the Boroditsky et al. (2003) study, that whilst it may be tempting to talk of conceptual transfer from L1 to L2 in this context, this result can be explained in terms of the non-response language (i.e. Spanish or German) mediating the response during task performance in the L2 (English). For instance, the word 'bridge' automatically activates the word and concept for bridge in L1 and the participants then 'read out' the L1 concept as well as the concept for the word 'bridge' in L2 in order to produce the requested adjectives. So, each noun may map onto meaning in a perfectly native-like way, but the parallel activation of the object's names leads to a competition between alternative names for specific concepts. One of the two competing names, the one marking grammatical gender, produces semantic associations based on grammatical distinctions (masculine & feminine = male & female), which are then used in the other language for the purpose of object categorisation.

Parallel activation and the ensuing sharing of gender categories is not that uncommon. Even monolingual grammatical gender is not purely grammatical but is also conceptual (Bassetti, 2007: 269). It is no surprise that bilinguals who speak one language with, and one without, grammatical gender can introduce gender in the language that does not mark it. For instance, when my husband asked 'where is my handkerchief?', I recall saying 'I saw *her* under the pillow'. 'Handkerchief' is a 'she' (feminine gender) in one of my other languages, Serbian ('maramica'), so I made handkerchief a 'she' in English too on this occasion. Arguably, such outputs are not as frequent with proficient bilinguals as they are with less proficient bilinguals, but they do occur. Since this kind of pronoun usage in English would cause misunderstanding in reference (e.g. as evidenced by my husband's baffled look in reaction to my response about the handkerchief), bilinguals are likely to acquire the different language-specific rules early (see Chapter 4, Section 4.4.1 on incentives for early acquisition and maintenance of language-specific features by adult (but not child) L2 learners if communicative efficiency is in jeopardy).

In fact, parallel activation may also be taking place when both languages mark the category but there is no consistent overlap, as in Italian vs. German gender marking. Bassetti (2007) looked at whether male or female voice would be assigned to objects that were marked by different grammatical genders in the two languages. The subjects included Italian–German bilingual children and Italian monolingual children in an online voice attribution task. The study showed that the Italian monolingual children attributed more female voices to objects whose descriptive nouns were grammatically feminine in Italian, indicating that grammatical gender is used for assigning a male vs. female characteristic to objects, though other criteria in addition to grammatical gender were used in the task as well (e.g. the objects' physical qualities (soft vs. hard or small vs. big); Bassetti, 2007: 265–6). By contrast, the Italian–German bilingual children did not show an Italian or a German bias in gender-based voice assignment: the response by the bilinguals was at chance level.

Bassetti (2007: 268) interprets this finding as evidence that bilinguals 'integrate L1 and L2 concepts and think differently than monolinguals'. The bilingual integration of L1 and L2 on this occasion may result in either in-between concepts that include both L1 and L2 features, or concepts different from those in either language. It may be the case that, regardless of the fact that the experiment was carried out in Italian, habitual use of both Italian and German by the bilingual children activated German nouns and gender information as well (as per De Groot's suggestion earlier). Namely, the bilingual speakers could be activating both gender and conceptual representations from each language, which are competing online and one of which wins at random because each is good enough for resolving the task at hand.

Why do bilinguals tend to activate information in both languages at once when they are speaking only one at a time? It may seem that activation of the second language is redundant, but bilinguals seem to be doing it constantly (see the next section). I will argue in Chapter 3 that it is actually **efficient** to do so. Why should it be efficient to access information in the language that is not currently in use? The answer may be quite simple and obvious.

Even in monolingual processing of information we activate so much more information than is strictly necessary for communication at the present moment as we interact with the world around us. This information is available for us to use even though we do not explicitly verbalise everything. We know that multiple activations occur in the brain during language processing, even in areas not directly related or relevant to linguistic processing. For example, Pulvermuler et al. (2005) and numerous others have shown that there is multi-system activation when processing language. Functional links have been detected between action (motor cortex) and language systems during lexical processing (see also Rizzolatti & Arbib, 1998). This activation is not necessary for language processing per se, yet it does happen. Apparent redundancy is one of the essential features of how the brain (and other search engines) work. Information that may be related or has been known in the past to be related to our current search may be activated automatically even though we may not require it at the very moment of communication. This speeds up communication in the long run, thus making it more efficient, because we have information available *in case* we need it. If we use both systems frequently, the mind learns that we often need both and thus the prompt (and parallel) activation of both lexicons occurs even when just one is in current use.

Crucially, it is more efficient overall from a processing perspective to have a multi-language-ready mind if we know that at any point we may be required to produce outputs in either system. Thus, we want to have all the information required by both systems available and ready at all times, and for all eventualities. Whilst this may be efficient from the perspective of processing, it may not be *communicatively efficient* to provide all the information required by both systems at all times and for every act of communication, for example when only one system is used consistently over time. This will be reflected in different bilingual outputs: there are more shared features in outputs when both languages are active than when only one is. I return to this important issue below when I discuss the different types of linguistic action that bilinguals are involved in.

2.5.2   Bilingual Syntax(es)

When it comes to how bilinguals represent syntax, there is much less experimental evidence and data available than there is for the bilingual lexicon. Some assumptions about bilingual syntax have been made as parts of general theories of language production whereby grammatical encoding (formulating the structure of an utterance) is thought to occur separately for different languages, i.e. speakers access syntactic information associated with the relevant words in two parallel processes (see Levelt, 1989; Vigliocco & Hartsuiker, 2002). However, as Hartsuiker, Pickering and Veltcamp (2004: 410) point out, we cannot address the question of whether bilingual syntactic representations are shared or separate based on 'either a priori arguments or results of studies of the bilingual lexicon'.

A shared-syntax account is supported by a number of priming studies (e.g. Hartsuiker et al., 2004; Loebell & Bock, 2003). Hartsuiker et al. (2004) carried out a syntactic priming study and argued that syntax is shared between the two languages in a bilingual mind, at least for certain aspects of syntax and between certain languages. In a picture-describing task the Spanish–English bilinguals in their study tended to use the same sentence type in English if they had used that type immediately before in Spanish. In particular, English passives were substantially more common following a Spanish passive than otherwise. Thus, we can say that syntactic processing in one language affects the syntactic processing of another, and when the two languages share the relevant syntactic structures, processing is facilitated. This has also been shown by Ruiz et al. (2008). In their reading-for-translation experiment, facilitation was also found upon the presentation of congruent syntactic structures. In this study, activation of the relevant syntactic frames in the second language (i.e. the target language) was detected before the end of the comprehension of the string in the first language used in the experiment (i.e. the source language). Thus, both Hartsuiker et al. (2004) and Ruiz et al. (2008) provide evidence, albeit each using different methodologies, for shared representation of (at least some) syntactic structures and parallel processing in bilinguals, whereby possible linguistic matches are sought in one language whilst processing is ongoing in the other.

There is further recent support for shared syntactic representations in bilinguals. Hatzidaki, Branigan and Pickering (2011) showed that the grammatical systems of both languages were activated during both one-language and two-language production. The effects of the language not currently used were particularly evident in two-language utterances, when the language not used was the bilinguals' stronger language and when both languages were active. Bernolet, Hartsuiker and Pickering (2013) state that between-language priming is stronger for more-proficient than for less-proficient bilinguals, which suggests a shift occurs from language-specific to shared syntactic representations (see also Hartsuiker et al., 2016).

Traxler (2012) points out that reactivating the same syntactic structure representation is easier than activating an entirely new representation (see also Tooley, Traxler & Swaab, 2009; Traxler, 2008; Weber & Indefrey, 2009). Bilinguals reuse as much of the syntax of their L1 as possible when learning and using an L2. Traxler (2012: 427) explains how this happens:

For example, instead of creating an entirely new mental representation to encode the English passive, a native Spanish speaker could simply associate English words that can appear in the passive with the syntactic representation that they acquired for the passive when they first learned the Spanish structure. Doing so could make English easier to learn – new vocabulary can be associated with well-known components of the L1 grammatical system – and could make English sentences easier to comprehend.

The sharing of representations appears to be sensitive to the consistency in the order of elements in a sentence. German and English passives do not appear to prime one another because the passive verb in German appears at the end of the clause, whereas in English it is typically at the beginning of the verb phrase following the auxiliary (Loebell & Bock, 2003). On the other hand, German and English double object/prepositional datives ('X gave Y something' vs. 'X gave something to Y') do prime one another because they have the same types of words in the same order in both languages. Thus, the bilingual mind seems to 'know' what is, and what is not, shared when it comes to the common ground in word-order processing (see also Hartsuiker & Pickering, 2008 on the importance of word order in syntactic priming).

It seems that bilinguals share their syntactic representations and processes as much as possible. The extent to which they do so on different occasions of use needs further examination. Hsin, Legendre and Omaki (2013) were able to prime in children adjective-noun strings from English to Spanish, where, they claim, this word order is ungrammatical. But Spanish does permit adjective-noun order in a number of (minority) cases (e.g. 'la bella Julia'/'the beautiful Julia'), and therefore it is not surprising that Hsin et al. (2013) were able to elicit this structure in a priming setting in Spanish, with children that were heavily exposed to it in English. In another study on adjective/noun ordering, Nicoladis (2006) showed that French–English bilingual children are more likely to depart from the dominant French pattern of noun-before-adjective ordering ('étudiant intelligent' = *'student intelligent') when speaking both French and English. French also permits the adjective-before-noun pattern (i.e. intelligent student), which is the only acceptable pattern in English, although in French it is much less frequent. Therefore, bilingual children who have both languages active use a pattern that works in both, even though it is the less frequent ordering in one of the languages, resulting in less common or even unlicensed patterns compared to those of monolingual French. The key point here is that French allows both patterns, whereas English is more restrictive and allows only one – adjective before noun. The non-shared pattern is therefore avoided, and common ground is maximised using the pattern that is shared. Bilinguals can sometimes stretch common ground beyond its limits and turn partial overlaps between patterns into total overlaps. This can result on occasion in erroneous uses, as with the adjective ordering in the above-mentioned studies. Erroneous uses of adjective ordering by bilinguals seem to be rarer with adult bilingual speakers. For instance, adult French–German bilingual speakers generally avoid erroneous adjective placement in French if their French proficiency is very high and French is their stronger language. If it is not, then they do produce erroneous adjective placement in French, although the errors are restricted to certain specific contexts only (see Kupisch et al., 2013). This is not surprising. Bilingual speakers can indeed perform like monolingual speakers in their respective languages on certain occasions, especially if they are required in experiments to use only one of the languages in which they are highly proficient (see again Kupisch et al., 2013).

Priming effects for ungrammatical structures are not surprising in the context of child bilingual acquisition or in the context of unbalanced adult proficiency. Wolleb (2015) has shown that it was possible to prime a structure that is appropriate in one language but less than optimal in the other. In Norwegian, possessive pronouns can be prenominal or postnominal, which is pragmatically conditioned: possessive pronouns are used prenominally to express contrast, whereas postnominal possessives are neutral, and the possessive relation is information that is *given* as opposed to *new*. In English, possessive pronouns are always prenominal. Wolleb (2015) hypothesised that it should be possible to prime the prenominal possessive from English to Norwegian in bilingual children even in contexts where the postnominal one would be appropriate. She found an overall priming effect, but the effect was stronger for those contexts where the two languages converge, namely in prenominal position, and weaker when they diverge.

Finally, structural priming across the two languages of a bilingual can occur even if the order of arguments is not the same in an otherwise shared syntactic structure. Shin and Christianson (2009) observe cross-linguistic argument-order-independent structural priming in canonical Korean postpositional and English prepositional dative structures. They argue that shared bilingual syntactic processing occurs at the abstract, functional level within a two-stage grammatical-encoding process.

Overall, it seems that the more balanced that bilinguals are, the more they 'know' what can or cannot be shared across their languages and the more they show a clear preference for a shared syntactic processing strategy whenever possible. Namely, there is evidence indicating that bilinguals with equal proficiency in both languages seem to opt for the pattern that exists in both languages regardless of which of the two languages is used during the experiment, and regardless of the fact that the chosen pattern may be more preferred in one but not the other language, thus suggesting that a common processor is involved (see Nicol et al., 2001). When faced with two possible patterns for expressing the same set of concepts or relations, bilingual speakers seem to opt for a *whatever-works-in-both* strategy, as argued by Nicol et al. (2001). Nicol et al.'s early English–Spanish bilinguals opted for the Spanish pattern of conceptual noun phrase (NP) agreement in English, and the authors explain this as being due to the fact that speakers will use whichever agreement mechanism would work in both languages, which in this case is conceptually rather than syntactically based NP agreement. It appears that competent bilinguals share syntactic representations of their respective languages whenever it is possible and to the extent that both language systems allow this.

When either pattern would lead to successful task performance in syntax, bilinguals with equal proficiency in both languages show a random preference for each, similar to the results of the study on the lexicon by Bassetti (2007) discussed at the end of the last section. Fernandez (1995) reports a 49 per cent preference for English-type syntactic attachment in early (balanced) bilinguals when they are speaking English, which means that the Spanish attachment preference was selected 51 per cent of the time when speaking English. Dussias (2001) reports a similar result when Spanish was spoken in the experiment, with a slightly higher score for the Spanish-type preference (56 per cent) than the English type (44 per cent). The apparent lack of a strong preference in bilinguals of equal proficiency in both languages is not surprising, because either pattern leads to ambiguity resolution, and equal proficiency (and equal exposure and frequency of use) would teach them that either pattern is equally good for the task. In the case of unbalanced bilingualism, the pattern of the dominant language seems to guide the attachment preferences regardless of the language spoken during the task (see Dussias, 2001; Dussias and Sagarra, 2007; Fernandez, 2002; see also further discussion in Chapter 4).

A study by Lai, Rodriguez and Narasimhan (2014) showed that early bilinguals used syntactic patterns that were shared in both languages in an event categorisation task, whilst late bilinguals used language-specific, different frames in each language for the same task (see Chapter 4 for further details). The option exercised by competent bilinguals is much more efficient, because if either option is good enough for the task, using one throughout that task is preferable to having to switch between two (see Chapter 3). The late bilinguals in the Lai et al. (2014) study may not have 'figured out' what works in both (i.e. the representations are not shared; see Bernolet et al., 2013).

I can suggest an interim conclusion here: bilinguals are indeed not two monolinguals in one. For bilinguals, the representation of each language is affected by the other and their linguistic outputs in each language will often differ from those of monolinguals. They may not have all the resources and competencies that monolinguals have in both their languages at all times (see Bialystok, 2007), but they do have a *multicompetence* (Cook, 1995) that should not be described by reference to monolingual norms (Silva-Corvalán & Treffers-Daller, 2015), and which enables them to be multi-language-ready. Crucially, the way in which the two languages interact within a bilingual mind is modulated by different factors, and results in different linguistic outcomes for different bilingual types and in different linguistic outcomes for the same bilingual under different circumstances. In the next chapter (Chapter 3) I propose a model that captures the interaction of all the factors referenced here, and I use it in Chapter 4 to account for a palette of different findings in the bilingualism literature.

2.6   Relativity Effects in Bilingualism: Thinking for Speaking in L1 and/or L2

Language is used in various problem-solving tasks by both monolinguals and bilinguals, even when they are not explicitly required to do so. Malt, Sloman and Gennari (2003) term this phenomenon 'language-as-strategy' in the context of monolingual research and they argue that language-specific effects on thinking about objects or events are limited to the task performance in question and have no long-term impact on cognition. However, habitual ways of speaking about objects and events do appear to engender habitual patterns of thinking about them. Dan Slobin found that these repetitive uses of preferred patterns in speech may create corresponding preferences in thought. In other words, when we think in order to speak we do so using the forms and meanings given by the language we speak, i.e. we engage in *thinking-for-speaking*. Thinking-for-speaking 'involves picking those characteristics that (a) fit some conceptualisation of the event, and (b) are readily encodable in the language' (Slobin, 1987: 435). Thinking-for-speaking does not equal conceptualisation per se: rather, it is *conceptualisation necessary for verbalisation*. When we prepare for speech, we first conceptualise our preverbal message (in the Conceptualiser), then we send it to the Formulator to be encoded semantically, grammatically and phono-logically, and it subsequently gets articulated in accordance with the commands specific for individual languages in the Articulator. This is what a general model for speaking looks like as proposed by Levelt (1989), and it has been subse-quently adapted for bilingual speech, in particular by de Bot (1992).

What Slobin (1987) points out, crucially, is that when we learn a specific language, we learn to formulate our thoughts in a certain way based on what that language encodes. The Conceptualiser can become sensitive to those features over time and pay attention to them more than to some others that are not obligatorily encoded (or encoded at all) in our language. This selective attention is driven by differences in the Formulators of the bilingual speaker: English Formulators have different requirements from Dutch Formulators, as Levelt (1989: 71) observed. Thus, our attention is focused on different con-ceptual features in order to meet the requirements of different Formulators. Slobin (2016) explains that a bilingual speaker's two slightly different Formulators are selectively tuned to respective languages. For example, the Turkish Formulator has to attend to the source of evidence for claims, which is marked by evidential morphemes on the verb in Turkish but not in English. If Turkish speakers witness the event they are talking about themselves, they use verbs with the affix '-de', and if their source of information is indirect (so-called hearsay, a third-party source or inference based on what they have heard or seen) they use verbs with the affix '-miş'. When the bilingual speaker switches from Turkish to English, the Formulator looks for a way to express the same information, e.g. if something was not directly witnessed he or she finds that hedging expressions (like 'it seems that . . . ' or 'it looks like . . . ') can be used to signal indirect sources of information that align the English formulation with the Turkish one. In long-term bilingualism we see that this can then lead to contact-induced language change: languages lacking evidential marking create evidential meanings using their own words and constructions (see Chapter 4, Section 4.3.1). Two parallel Conceptualisers are involved in the process of thinking-for-speaking, according to Slobin, and it is no surprise that we often refer to a complete mastery of a language, e.g. an L2, by saying that we are able to think in that language.

This may seem to open up the possibility that different languages engender different conceptualisations, which is the basis of the *linguistic relativity hypothesis*, inspired by the work of Edward Sapir and Benjamin Lee Whorf, though they did not actually formulate it themselves and would not have subscribed to its more extreme form. We do not have to assume an extreme linguistic relativity in this context: conceptualising reality through different Conceptualisers sensitised to a specific language, in the monolingual case, or to two specific languages, in the bilingual case, is flexible, and a matter of more or less habitual emphasis on some aspects of objects and events that a language requires us to express explicitly, over certain others that are not favoured in the relevant language. Thinking-for-speaking does not have a deterministic effect on how we think about the things and events around us, but it does seem to have an effect on how often and in how much detail we describe, categorise or pay attention to some aspects of reality (see so-called neo-Whorfian research on the categorisation of colours, object and events; Bloom et al., 1999; Davidoff, Davies & Roberson, 1999; Gentner & Goldin-Meadow, 2003; Levinson, 2003; Levinson & Wilkins, 2006; Roberson et al., 2005).

Even if we agree that our linguistic attention guides our overall attention and our focus on those aspects of reality that we must express in our language, this does not mean that we focus only on these obligatory notions in the language(s) we speak. Human cognition is characterised by flexibility, and it allows input from various modalities as well as a flexible shift of focus that is not related to language. For instance, our preferred colour on a garment may focus our attention more on the garment than on how tall the person wearing the garment is (for example, I am always and easily distracted by nice clothing items in purple, my 'favouritest' colour). Additionally, if we do not have ready word labels for certain concepts and these concepts do not matter much in our everyday lives, we are likely not to refer to them often. But this does not mean that we have conceptual limitations in the sense of strict linguistic relativity. The limits of our language need not be the limits of our world and of our world view. We can expand our limits at any time by learning new concepts even if we have no words for them in the mother tongue. Our worlds are also enriched by experiences and knowledge that are not verbal, verbalised or verbalisable. Extreme views of linguistic relativity are relics of the past, no longer entertained by anyone in the scientific community, and they were also based on misinterpretation (or simplistic analysis) of the works of some of the greatest philosophical minds, including Humboldt, Sapir and Whorf (see Lee, 1996 for a thorough discussion). We now know enough to be able to say that language does exert some influence on how we conceptualise reality, but the important questions to ask are how much influence exactly, and under what circumstances; questions that are only just beginning to be answered in both monolingual and bilingual contexts.

Slobin uses the thinking-for-speaking hypothesis to explain how speakers get used to 'perspectives that seem to be the obvious and necessary way of framing events and taking stances in interaction' (Slobin, 2016: 106). These habits are 'formed throughout a lifetime of framing utterances in a particular language, that is, through habits of thinking for speaking' (Slobin 2016; see also Slobin 1987, 1996, 1997, 2003, 2006). The thinking-for-speaking hypothesis has played a major role in recent research on language and cognition, in both monolingual and bilingual contexts. Our focus here is on bilingualism, and we need to discover how the two thinking-for-speaking patterns interact in the bilingual mind, and with what consequences for different interactional circumstances. In other words, do bilinguals have two separate thinking-for-speaking mechanisms or just one that contains features of both languages? Do they start out as two but become one, or do they stay separate but get co-activated occasionally? These are very similar questions to the ones posed earlier about bilingual language storage and activation but the emphasis in the thinking-for-speaking paradigm is now on the connection between language and other cognitive functions, such as memory and judgement. These do not depend solely on language, as we shall see (Chapter 5), but language is a relevant factor for both the storage and retrieval of information that is recruited for the formulation of memories and judgements. We shall also see that the influence of different thinking-for-speaking habits on these cognitive domains has been detected in a number of studies (see below and also Chapter 4), and in line with our focus on bilingualism, we will explore bilingual thinking-for-remembering (Chapter 5) and thinking-for-translating (Chapter 6) in more detail.

A number of studies in L2 acquisition and late bilingualism have shown that learning an L2 may be affected by the L1 online verbalisation-driven conceptualisation system, that is, the thinking-for-speaking mechanism as defined and described by Slobin (see, e.g., Cadierno, 2008, 2010, 2017; Cadierno, Ibarretxe-Antuñano & Hijazo-Gascón, 2016; Cifuentes-Férez & Rojo, 2015; Ellis & Cadierno, 2009; Filipović, 2011, 2018; Hijazo-Gascón, 2018). For instance, Cadierno (2010) found strong L1 lexicalisation effects on L2 expressions in a study that contrasted learners of L2 Danish with L1 Russian, German or Spanish. Further, a study by Hasko (2010) on L2 acquisition of Russian by L1 speakers of English showed that L2 online performance provides evidence that surface structures 'mediate our thinking in a non-trivial way' (Hasko, 2010: 57). In the domain of motion events, the differences in the lexicalisation patterns between English and Russian are such that they prevent L2 learners from developing an L2-based thinking-for-speaking pattern, which requires attending to and verbalising different conceptual categories from the ones present in their L1. Hasko concludes that the acquisition of an L2 needs to include not only the internalisation of grammatical and lexical items, but also an adaptation to the 'new ways of attending to, and thinking-for-speaking about, conceptual domains that may be encoded differently in their L1 and L2' (Hasko, 2010: 57).

Some evidence suggests that thinking-for-speaking is not fixed, firm and static. It can change (see, e.g. Han, 2010; Stam, 2010), but not all aspects of it change in the same way and not for all learners equally – there may be a great variability in how this process of change unfolds (see also Han, 2010, on fossilisation in L1 thinking-for-speaking; also Bylund & Jarvis, 2011 on L2 effects on L1 event categorisation). Hendriks, Hickman, and Demagny (2008) detected an increasing attempt to produce target-like expressions of caused motion that nonetheless remained source-like, regardless of the different proficiency levels tested. The conclusion they drew was that learners mastering an L2 may require some reconceptualisation of spatial information (a kind of re-thinking-for-speaking; see Cadierno, 2010, 2017). There are also studies that report an absence of any language effects and only detect universal constraints on perception (e.g. Coventry, Valdés & Guijarro-Fuentes, 2010; Filipović, 2010b). It is worth pointing out that language is only one of the possible strategies that may be used in problem-solving (Tversky, 2011) and it can be more in evidence if the experimental participants are asked to integrate a more demanding quantity of information from the stimuli (e.g. by verbalising and/or remembering details about complex rather than simple motion events; see Fausey & Boroditsky, 2011; Filipović, 2011).

2.7   Conclusion

We have seen in this chapter that bilingualism is affected by numerous factors, both internal, such as proficiency or language dominance in individuals or groups, and external, such as whom the bilinguals are talking to and for what purpose. Depending on these factors and their interactions, linguistic behaviour among different groups of bilinguals can vary substantially, and it can also vary within the same group and even within the same individual over the lifespan or over different concrete contexts of use. Numerous different studies in psycholinguistics and sociolinguistics have identified and documented these factors, as discussed in this chapter.

Classifying bilinguals based on proficiency in each language seems to be the most acceptable criterion in order to enable us to make predictions about what the linguistic behaviour of bilingual individuals will look like. We must also consider all the factors that characterise our bilingual speakers, namely age of acquisition, type of acquisition (e.g. instructed vs. spontaneous) and frequency of use. Importantly, overall equivalence in proficiency in L2 may not result in the same linguistic outputs with regard to a particular linguistic feature for different L1 speakers (see Hawkins & Filipović, 2012, and Filipović & Hawkins, 2013 for more details and a recent overview). Furthermore, even when speakers of the same L1 are grouped at the same proficiency level in the L2, they may exhibit differences in L2 outputs due to individual differences in other respects that may affect their output (e.g. individual differences in spoken vs. written language use). The role of individual differences in bilingualism is only beginning to receive the attention it deserves in the field (see Hulsitjn, 2018 for recent discussion). And then we have the question of how the different communicative circumstances will affect the different outputs predicted based on proficiency. What is clearly needed in the field is a holistic, explanatory account of the way that general principles of language processing and factors relevant for bilingual processing (as discussed here) result in specific kinds of linguistic outputs. What is also missing is a unifying model that captures what all bilinguals are doing vs. what only some bilinguals are doing, and that explains why this happens. In other words, we need *a multifactor model of bilingual learning and processing*, and it is now time to introduce such a model, which is what we will do next.

3   Introducing CASP for Bilingualism

In this chapter I introduce the learning and processing model CASP (Complex Adaptive System Principles) for Bilingualism, which can be used to capture the overall linguistic behaviour of different types of bilinguals. One of the advantages of the proposed model is that it is not limited to any one theoretical framework but is relevant for, and applicable to, many different theoretical approaches. Numerous speaker-specific (internal) and situation-specific (external) factors that we discussed in the previous chapter will be shown to affect the ways in which the proposed general principles interact and affect the outcome predicted in the model. The proposed model will make it possible for us to make predictions that take into account multiple factors. Namely, I will show that the same processing principles operate in all situations, but the manner of their competition or collaboration is driven by the internal and external factors that I referred to, which is what ultimately conditions different outcomes.

3.1   Introduction

After our overview of the field in Chapter 2, the goal of the present chapter is to try to recruit some of the insights and empirical findings into a single coherent model of bilingualism and to explain why we appear to be getting different results in different studies. Unlike the many previous accounts of bilingual processing that are based on limited empirical evidence (e.g. focusing on a single linguistic level, such as syntax, or a single grammatical feature, such as gender marking), the model proposed here encompasses all logically possible outcomes that we may find in any linguistic domain when two different linguistic systems interact in one processor, the bilingual mind.

In the context of *bilingualism in action*, we need to understand better what factors are relevant for the outcomes of bilingual linguistic behaviour when two systems actively collaborate or compete online in different communicative situations. Our central claim is that *all bilingual minds are trying to do the same thing and are guided by the same underlying principles, but that outcomes vary based on who is speaking which language(s) to whom, and why.* The general principles sometimes collaborate with each other and sometimes compete, and their interplay is influenced by the fact that bilingual minds differ with respect to the level of command they have of each language (e.g. equal vs. unequal) and the communicative situations they engage in (e.g. monolingual vs. bilingual interactions), whereby different demands and constraints are imposed on those different bilingual minds. CASP for Bilingualism models and explains the nature of these interactions and the ensuing outcomes and enables us to make many concrete predictions for different language types, bilingual speaker types and communicative situation types.

Bilingualism research, as we have seen, faces numerous difficulties just by the sheer nature of the variability it has to address, in language combinations, acquisition histories, proficiency levels and the social circumstances in which communicative exchanges take place. As mentioned in the Introduction (Chapter 1), the interpretation of the data may vary according to differences between study participants. Athanasopoulos (2011: 29) draws attention to this:

> For example, deviation from monolingual patterns in early bilinguals may be seen as convergence to a unitary form, whereas deviation from monolingual patterns in late bilinguals may be seen as 'failure' to acquire or use the target construction.

In other words, we may be dealing with one and the same set of experimental outcomes, which then get interpreted and labelled differently based on when and how the two languages were acquired by the bilingual populations in individual studies. There is also a growing awareness in the language sciences about the need for different disciplines to look at each other's findings in order to provide a more holistic picture of complex phenomena such as bilingual language processing and language use. One of the central goals in the current chapter is to create a unifying platform for insights about bilingualism in action that come from numerous different sources and that are almost never discussed or considered together (e.g. they come from contact linguistics, heritage linguistics, sociolinguistic typology, translation, language development, bilingual witness memory, etc.). Such a platform is obviously needed, as a number of scholars of bilingualism have argued. For instance, Muysken (2013: 710) emphasises the need for more unification among the many fields of bilingualism research and laments that 'many of the topics listed have been studied in relative isolation from one another'. He points out further (ibid.) that 'in actual academic practice, separate conferences are held for most of these subdisciplines, with different journals and debates, and apparently unrelated conceptual frameworks and terminologies'.

Jarvis and Pavlenko (2010: 234–5) suggest the same direction for the future of the field, saying that 'there is a clear need for more interaction and dialogue between researchers who study "cross-linguistic influence" phenomena in the areas of language contact, childhood bilingualism, child and adult second language acquisition, and first language attrition'. They go on to say that it would be interesting to compare findings on shared phenomena (e.g., syntactic transfer or borrowing) which are studied from the perspectives of different disciplines (e.g. second-language acquisition (SLA) research vs. language contact and historic language change research).

This is exactly what we aim to do here. To begin with, we steer clear of conflicting labels such as 'convergence' vs. 'failure to acquire' that in reality often refer to the same linguistic outputs. Then we establish what the logically possible outcomes are when one mind needs to process two different languages based on the information that language typology has given us. Then we look for empirical evidence for what different bilinguals actually do when they use one or both of their languages. In addition, our CASP for Bilingualism model captures the *malleability of bilingual behaviour*. Of central importance is the insight that the linguistic behaviour of the same bilingual may vary on different occasions. Recent research has shown that bilingualism is a fluid feature that can change over the lifespan (Nicoladis & Montanari, 2016). Bilingualism in action puts the spotlight on the fact that bilingual linguistic behaviour can be very different even from one moment to the next, and is also subject to long-term changes over many years.

The bilingual literature documents the numerous ways in which bilinguals use their two linguistic systems, as we have seen (see again Pavlenko, 2005, 2014 for detailed overviews). There can be 'borrowing' in both directions (L1 to L2 and L2 to L1) of elements that one language has but the other does not. There is also 'restructuring' via 'deletion' or 'incorporation' of elements from one language into the other. 'Convergence' occurs when there is a joining of elements from both languages into a single integrated system, though in practice this term has been used to label quite a few different outcomes. For example, it has been used to refer to some outputs in bilingualism that reflect one language moving closer to the other, as it were, whilst the other stays as it was (Ameel et al., 2005). The term 'attrition' is also relevant here, which refers to loss of elements in one language because of the influence of the other. Sometimes the same authors use more than one term, and it is not always clear why. Pavlenko and Jarvis (2002) refer to both 'borrowing' and 'transfer' in the context of the lexicon, but just to 'transfer' in the context of syntax and discourse. Terms such as 'interference', 'transfer', 'cross-linguistic influence' are also often used to refer to both the process and the product of interactions between two languages in bilingual processing. For example, Muysken (2000: 277–8) describes cross-linguistic influence as interference and notes that 'interference may take several forms, two of which are sharing and convergence'. 'Sharing' is said to involve categories and rules (e.g. subcategorisation frames of functional categories or components of the production systems, such as linearisation), whilst 'convergence' may involve the lexicon ('faux amis') and the syntax ('transfer'). Muysken (2000) also states that sharing is symmetrical and convergence asymmetrical with respect to the language subsystem involved. Slobin (2016) notes that quite a lot can be borrowed or transferred from one language to another; he lists various features, morphological categories, structural patterns, stylistic tendencies, patterns of semantic and pragmatic organisation and language functions, meanings and habits. He states that linguists invoke linguistic form in discussions and use terms such as feature 'diffusion' or 'transfer', but that there is not much specificity when it comes to the processes involved. CASP for Bilingualism *explains the processes behind so-called 'transfer' phenomena.*

The concepts of borrowing or transfer may be useful but are notionally problematic. First, grammatical forms and meanings are not really borrowed or transferred from one language to the other: they remain in the language they originate from and they are expressed in the other language that does not have them using the locally available means. Very occasionally the exact forms of one language may appear directly, as is the case with the interrogative suffix '-mi' being imported from Turkish into Afghan Arabic (Ingham, 1994; see also examples in Comrie, 2008). 'Transfer' has been defined in many different ways by different authors (Jarvis & Pavlenko, 2010; Odlin, 1989; Paradis & Genesee, 1996; Yip & Matthews, 2007). As Siegel (2012: 188) notes of the term, 'it sometimes refers to a process, or sometimes to the outcome of such a process, or sometimes ambiguously to both'. Siegel himself offers a functional definition of transfer, following Færch and Kasper (1987: 112), which can cover a lot of phenomena discussed in the transfer literature, whereby transfer is a 'psycholinguistic process in which the linguistic features of one language are employed by individuals in learning or using another language'. As such, 'transfer can be positive, when the features of the L1 and L2 are similar, or negative, when the features are different' (Siegel, 2012: 189). What gets labelled as negative transfer varies substantially, from differences in frequency distributions between monolinguals and bilinguals, leading to what is still grammatical but perhaps a less typical usage, to a violation of grammatical rules that may seriously impede communication (see Hawkins & Filipović, 2012, for discussion). Namely, negative transfer includes *grammatical errors* (e.g. wrong gender marking, such as using the masculine *'le clé' (m.) instead of the correct feminine 'la clé' (f.) in French because in the other language the word for this same object is masculine, e.g. 'ključ' (m.) in Serbian), *lexical errors* (e.g. using one general term for 'uncle' in both languages even though one of your languages distinguishes between maternal and paternal uncles), *pragmatic infelicities* (e.g. not using language-specific politeness conventions) and *general usage deviations* from the monolingual preference (e.g. opting for a construction that is typical for Spanish but not in English, such as path verb + manner adjunct motion expressions in English, e.g. 'enter running' (see Chapter 2), which is grammatically and lexically correct in English but dispreferred overall).

A further problem with 'the transfer terminology' comes from a possible interpretation of 'negative transfer' to mean that there is something wrong with what the bilinguals are doing, when in fact they may be doing something very positive by exploiting shared patterns in both languages, even though a certain structure can be typical/usual in one but atypical/unusual in the other language. They are optimising their performance rather than incurring higher processing costs from constantly switching between different lexicalisation strategies. Consequently, this 'bilingual-specific language use' should not invite a constant comparison with the monolingual baseline and its ensuing evaluation. It should itself become the norm, and monolingual-like uses would then be seen as a departure from this norm. It makes sense to place bilingualism as the focus of investigations related to language – most of the world's population, after all, is bilingual to some degree. And we need to reconsider our research questions and methodological approaches in order to engage in a '"post-monolingual" psycholinguistic research enterprise' (Vaid & Meuter, 2017: 8) whereby we start with the premise that 'bilinguals are the primary, canonical language users to be theorised [about] and, therefore, the central focus of psycholinguistic inquiry' (see Vaid & Meuter, 2017 for details about what such an enterprise would look like).

One of the reasons for the many apparently different outcomes reported in bilingualism research may be because of the differences between the bilingual populations studied (e.g. early bilinguals, L2 speakers or heritage bilinguals). We have already seen that defining the different bilingual populations and grouping them based on the definitions proposed is not straightforward (e.g. what exactly is an early bilingual?). A variety of outcome types are possible even within one and the same bilingual population depending on the linguistic level being examined (e.g. lexicon vs. grammar), and on variation within a single speaker (in monolingual vs. bilingual mode), in different communicative situations (formal vs. informal) and in different situations of long-term contact resulting in contact-induced language change (e.g. both the simplification and complex-ification of Old English due to different sociolinguistic factors; Trudgill, 2011). It is rare to find a study of bilingualism that controls these many relevant factors, all at the same time, and yet multiple factors are involved on every occasion. In what follows I propose a way to integrate the numerous factors that condition which outcome(s) we can expect, and when, in bilingual interactions.

3.2   CASP for Bilingualism: Theoretical Background

CASP stands for Complex Adaptive System Principles and is a new model for bilingual language processing proposed by Filipović and Hawkins (2018). The model is central to our overarching theme of *bilingualism in action* because it enables us to capture the diversity in bilingual outputs that are evidenced under different conditions. When we use CASP for Bilingualism to analyse data from different studies that employ different types of bilingual speakers, different methodologies and different features of the grammars and lexicons of different languages, we are able to detect some common patterns among the apparently infinite range of possibilities. In fact, there are not that many logical outcomes when we look at a given grammatical or lexical area in two specific languages, and CASP can help us predict which of the few options will be realised and under which circumstances (see further below in Section 3.6 and also Chapter 4 for more details and examples).

The key theoretical underpinning here is the notion of *language as a complex adaptive system* (e.g. in the sense of Gell-Mann, 1992) in which multiple factors interact to produce a range of observable outcomes. Bilingual language systems need to be understood in the same way. Some previous research involved this premise and recognised the need for multiple interacting factors in understanding different kinds of bilingual language acquisition (see, for example, Ellis, 1998; Ellis & Larsen-Freeman, 2009; Mellow, 2008; O'Grady, 2005, 2008). These studies differ in the number and nature of the principles they propose, in their precise formulations, in the predictions they make for interlanguage data and in the range of data on which they have actually been tested. The empirical support has so far been encouraging but is still limited. We need more studies, with many more language combinations spoken by different bilinguals in different types of interactions.

CASP for Bilingualism is an extension of the Filipović and Hawkins (2013) model for second-language acquisition (for comparisons with some other theoretical and practical approaches, such as the Competition Model (MacWhinney, 2005) and Processability Theory (Pienemann, 1998) see the discussion in Hawkins and Filipović, 2012: Ch. 4). It is complex because there are multiple principles involved, and there are multiple possible ways for them to interact with different consequences. Bilinguals vary with respect to their abilities in each of their languages (due to internal (variability) factors) and their outputs differ across a range of communicative situations because of the ability of bilinguals to adjust to different demands from the environment (e.g. different interlocutors or formality levels – external factors). The effects of bilingual variability and adjustability, both short and long term, are well attested in the literature, as we saw in Chapter 2 (see also Section 3.5 of this chapter for more details). I now turn to the general principles of CASP and explain how they work, on their own and in conjunction with one another.

3.3   The Five Principles of CASP for Bilingualism

CASP for Bilingualism is based on five general principles (A) to (E) that underlie bilingual speakers' language behaviour, in terms of both *learning and processing* (Filipović & Hawkins, 2018).

Principle (A): Minimise Learning Effort. Bilingual speakers prefer to minimise learning effort when they learn the grammatical and lexical properties of their languages, just as monolingual speakers do. Learning effort can be minimised in a number of ways. It is minimised when grammatical and lexical properties are shared between L1a and L1b, and pre-existing knowledge of items learned first in one language is then exploited when learning the other. Learning effort is also minimised when properties in both languages frequently occur in the input, which increases exposure to them and with it the ease of learning. It is minimised when structural and semantic properties of the languages are simple rather than complex. There is no suggestion here that learners consciously or intentionally strive to comply with (A), or are taught to comply with it, for this principle or any of the others proposed here.

Principle (B): Minimise Processing Effort. Bilingual speakers prefer to minimise processing effort when using the grammatical and lexical properties of their languages, just as monolingual speakers do. Even when more complex properties have been acquired, bilingual speakers will still prefer to use simpler properties, just like monolingual speakers. Infrequent items in the input are not only harder to learn, but also harder to access and process. Complex grammatical and lexical properties are also harder to both learn and process. This principle is, in essence, a principle of least effort.

Some more specific principles that follow from these general principles are discussed in Filipović & Hawkins (2013, 2018), such as *Maximise Structurally and Semantically Simpler Properties*. We expect simpler forms and meanings to be more readily learned and used in both languages compared to more complex forms and meanings (see also Gathercole, 2016 on the acquisition of transparent vs. opaque language features). Similarly, *Maximise Frequently Occurring Properties* drives the acquisition and use of more frequent forms in both languages more than less frequent ones.

Principle (C): Maximise Expressive Power. Bilingual learners prefer to maximise their expressive power; that is, to be able to formulate in each language whatever thoughts they wish to express, and to perform the same language functions in each language, just as monolingual learners do. This principle stands in partial opposition to principles (A) and (B), since achieving full expressive power requires sometimes more and sometimes less processing effort, for example, more complex as well simpler expressions, and also less frequent, contra (B). Complex and less frequent items are also harder to learn, contra (A).

Principle (D): Maximise Efficiency in Communication. This general principle involves not expressive power per se – that is, expression of meanings – but the efficient delivery of meanings in real time between interlocutors. Bilingual speakers prefer to maximise efficiency in communication with their interlocutors (production and comprehension), just as monolingual speakers do. This principle is also sometimes opposed in its predicted outputs to principles (A) and (B). Hawkins (2004, 2009, 2014) has argued that *efficiency* plays a central role in all communication and that grammars and cross-linguistic patterns show clear evidence for it in their conventionalised rule systems and lexicons. Efficiency, as he defines it, relates to the basic function of language – which is to communicate information from the speaker (S) to the hearer (H) (Hawkins, 2014: 34–5):

1) Communication is efficient when the message intended by S is delivered to H in rapid time and with minimal processing effort.
2) Acts of communication between S and H are generally optimally efficient; those that are not occur in proportion to their degree of efficiency.

There are a number of specific principles that make for efficient communication and for efficiency in grammars in Hawkins' system (see his *Minimise Domains, Minimise Forms* and *Maximise Online Processing*) and that lead to testable predictions for both usage and grammars. These principles are supported by performance and grammatical data showing a clear preference for: *speed* in delivering linguistic properties in online processing; *fine-tuning* of structural selections to frequency of occurrence, accessibility and inferencing; and *few online errors* or garden paths. These efficiency-defining factors interact, sometimes reinforcing, sometimes opposing one another. The main point to be made in the present context is that efficiency is a measure of how quickly, and with how little processing effort and how much online error reduction, the intended message can be delivered by the speaker and understood by the hearer.

There is an interesting relationship between efficiency and complexity in Hawkins' theory (see Hawkins, 2004): efficiency generally results in a preference for structural and grammatical simplicity, and for all linguistic items to be as simple as possible. But sometimes communicative efficiency requires the use of structures that are more complex; for example, when the hearer needs more detailed and explicit information about a referent or event. If the referent is unfamiliar to the hearer, the speaker must use a more complex noun phrase to identify it rather than a simple pronoun; for example, 'the man I talked to last night' instead of a simple 'he'. Efficiency can be maximised by using simple forms when this is possible, and it can also be maximised by using complex forms if necessary. This kind of efficiency-driven model involves considerable hearer-sensitivity on the part of the speaker, in accordance with the insights about co-operation in conversation that have been formulated by Grice (1957) and developed further in neo-Gricean (Levinson, 2000) and post-Gricean theories (Sperber & Wilson, 1986). Speakers are neither always fully altruistic (i.e. adjusting to the hearer; Clark, 1996) nor always fully selfish (i.e. egocentric and not adjusting to the hearer; Wardlow-Lane & Ferreira, 2008).

Rather, they are a bit of both, depending on what they can get away with whilst achieving their goal of being understood (see Traxler, 2012: 308–21 for a contrastive discussion). One thing speakers are likely to be across the board is efficient. I have to point out though that certain uses of language and different genres, such as poetry or narratives, will purposefully delay key information, exploit ambiguity or use certain rhetorical devices, and they will not strive primarily for the typical, everyday kind of efficiency in communication. Their primary goal may be evoking an emotion or creating a certain atmosphere. I would argue that these instances of language use are *efficient in an atypical way* when they achieve their various poetic and rhetorical goals successfully. Grice (1957) explains very clearly that these are departures from normal communicative practice (such as genre-specific uses of language), and that they involve implicatures of various kinds, whereby the hearer recognises the speaker's intention to give too little or too much information or to say something that is only partially true or downright false.

How do we account for redundancy from this perspective and can redundancy ever be explained in terms of efficiency? An explanation is in fact quite simple and almost self-evident. Filipović and Hawkins (2018) argue that the processing system will always aim for optimal efficiency in delivering the intended message in general, but inefficiency and redundancy can indeed be features of communication in certain circumstances. As argued by Aikhenvald (by personal communication, in Trudgill, 2011: 114), redundancy is an attempt 'to clarify what is being talked about'. Namely, efficiency can be said to motivate redundancy as well, since it is based on the speaker's belief that not enough information has been provided for successful communication even though the hearer may have managed to retrieve the message on the basis of less information than the speaker thought necessary. Similarly, inefficiency occurs where assumptions about the success of the message between the speaker and the hearer are mismatched; for example, too little or too much information has been made available. Efficiency is a feature of information exchange from both the speaker's and hearer's perspective, because the communication of a message cannot be deemed efficient if it is just communicated efficiently from the speaker's perspective, with no regard for any demonstration of the intended uptake on the part of the hearer. Therefore, efficiency is maximised incrementally in conversation based on the speaker's production and hearer's feedback. The most efficient way to send a message (i.e. in production) does not always coincide with the most efficient way to get the hearer to understand it. As indicated above, pronominal reference may generally be the most efficient choice for the speaker, but the speaker will not achieve efficient communication if the hearer cannot select the referent based on this information. Therefore, the speaker must often maximise efficiency through complexity and instead of asking 'Where did you buy *it*?' use expressions such as 'Where did you buy *the spectacular dress you wore last week at Nigel's dinner party*?' A longer referential expression, as mentioned before, is more efficient in situations in which the shorter one will not suffice, and when it would lead to the wrong referent being selected or to an inability to identify the referent of the referring expression (Hawkins, 2009).

Therefore, when it comes to what appear to be the deliberately inefficient features of certain genres (which Slobin, in a personal communication, has drawn to my attention), such as narratives aimed at creating a certain atmosphere, seducing or making us laugh, again, we can see that redundancy can still be efficient: it helps to achieve the desired effect. This does not negate the key importance of efficiency: *efficiency is the norm*, and apparent departures from it need special contexts and conventions, which may be efficient in their own right in bringing about the special effect of the contexts.

Principle (E): Maximise Common Ground. Bilingual learners and speakers maximise common grammatical and lexical representations and their associated processing mechanisms in two languages, L1a and L1b, within the grammatical constraints and conventions imposed by each. Specifically:

1) If L1a and L1b share a given construction, grammatical rule or word meaning, and associated processing mechanisms, then these shared entities will be used more frequently in both languages. (These entities may be the preferred or majority pattern in one language and a minority or dispreferred in the other, but they will still be the pattern of choice in the bilingual speaker's use of both languages.)

2) If L1a and L1b do not share a given construction, grammatical rule or word meaning and associated processing mechanisms, then common ground will be created by introducing entities from one language into the other. New shared entities will be introduced wherever possible within the constraints of the grammatical and usage conventions for the relevant language.

3) Any violations of a grammatical or usage convention in L1a or L1b that occurs when maximising common ground will be in proportion to the environmental (i.e. external, sociolinguistic) and psycholinguistic (internal) factors enumerated in Section 3.5.

Maximise Common Ground is a *processing efficiency principle* that advocates as much sharing of resources as possible. Unlike principles (A)–(D), which operate in monolingual speakers as well, *this principle is bilingual-specific.* Processing efficiency as captured in Principle (E) is distinct from the *communicative efficiency* of Principle (D), discussed previously. Even though these two principles often collaborate, they can also be in competition. Bilingual speakers need to alleviate the cognitive load of simultaneously processing two languages, which encourages the maximising of common ground. As Silva-Corvalán (1994: 206) explains: 'in language-contact situations, bilingual speakers develop strategies aimed at lightening the cognitive load of having to remember and use two different linguistic systems'. The relevance of this incentive to maximise common ground is also reflected in the observation by Muysken (2000: 277) that 'it is precisely the simultaneous presence of both languages that favours the searching for parallels between them' and that motivates 'the striving toward congruent lexicalisation'. However, when bilinguals are in a monolingual mode, there will be less incentive for them to maximise common ground and more incentive to be communicatively efficient by using the lexical and grammatical means characteristic of the language spoken at the moment of communication rather than the forms and meanings shared by the two languages. In a bilingual mode, however, and especially when the bilinguals are speaking to two monolinguals, one in each language, we can expect more outputs that are characterised by processing efficiency (and have more instances of maximising common ground) than by language-specific communicative efficiency.

In general, Maximise Common Ground often operates in synchrony with the other four principles because sharing resources means there are fewer items to learn and process, and information in both may be communicated efficiently using certain shared resources (e.g. in the lexicon or syntax). However, our principles can also compete with each other. For instance, Maximise Common Ground can operate against both Principles B (Minimise Processing Effort) and D (Maximise Efficiency in Communication). Speakers sometimes maximise common ground when they do not need to and when it would be more efficient not to do so (e.g. by introducing new meanings from one language into the other), and even when this may add to processing effort and to making communication less efficient (e.g. they could have communicated the message in accordance with the hearer's needs without the additional meanings from their other language). The constant use of both languages encourages the maximisation of common ground as the *most efficient processing strategy*, and it is the go-to option even in cases when there is less pressure to resort to it – some habits are hard to restrain, especially if they are reinforced through frequent positive outcomes!

Maximising common ground can also be achieved by eliminating structures or meanings that are not shared, thus diminishing expressive power in one of the languages (i.e. against Principle (C), Maximise Expressive Power). This is normally discussed as 'avoidance', which can also be seen as a type of 'negative transfer', and is prevalent in populations of unbalanced bilinguals, for example those who have one dominant language (such as heritage speakers or adult L2 speakers) or whose acquisition of one or both languages is incomplete (young children being raised as bilingual). The principle of Maximise Common Ground underlies both of the two processes that take place in order to align two systems, of adding (complexifying) and of omitting (simplifying) information; and examples from both psycholinguistics and sociolinguistics illustrate which outcome is more likely and when (see Chapter 2, Section 2.3 for examples). Overall, going back and forth between two different linguistic systems (i.e. two different thinking-for-speaking mechanisms) is costlier than using one, even when it occasionally involves less than optimal communication efficiency and requires more online processing. In fact, this is what long-term proficient bilingualism encourages. It brings the two Conceptualisers (Levelt, 1989; Slobin, 2016) closer together, and perhaps even merges them to different degrees, depending on how much typological distance there is between languages and how frequently each language is used (equally vs. unequally).

All bilingual speakers try to maximise common ground in order to optimise the processing of two languages instead of constantly switching from one system to another. When two languages have a word or structure in common, the most likely outcome is for it to be used in both. Sometimes this may not happen, as Kellerman (1983) points out: L2 learners may not believe that a word or a structure from their L1 can be mapped perfectly onto a corresponding word or structure in L2. With balanced bilingual speakers this should be less of an issue, because more of the correspondence links between languages will have been made due to equal or near-equal exposure to contexts in which words and structures from both are applicable.

More often, however, a perfect match will not be available between linguistic systems due to a lack of equivalence in meaning, in form or in form–meaning mapping, or due to a difference in general frequency of use (i.e. a given pattern may be dominant in one language but minor in the other). Even similar languages differ in many subtle yet important ways (see e.g. Filipović & Ibarretxe-Antuñano, 2015 for discussion of certain intratypological distinctions and their relevance). In addition, when it comes to frequency of use, we know that bilingual speakers may underuse or overuse certain structures (see Hawkins & Filipović, 2012 for a succinct overview and critical discussion). Such speakers exhibit different linguistic behaviour from monolingual speakers, and this is to be expected because bilingual speakers are not two monolingual speakers in one (Grosjean, 2001). But what are they then, if not two monolingual speakers in one? And how is it that they can be more monolingual-like on some occasions, and not on others?

When bilinguals encounter lexical and grammatical distinctions that are made in one but not the other language, they have two logical options: either maximise common ground, or do not maximise common ground (i.e. keep the two systems separate and keep switching between the two). When common ground is maximised, there are again two options: express the same meaning in both, or do not express the relevant meaning in either. Forms and meanings can be added to the relevant language that does not have them with the result that both languages now have them, or they can be 'lost' in the language that has them with the result that both languages end up not having them.

There are many ways in which common ground can be maximised. Heine and Kuteva (2005) point out that it is generally possible to find at least some minimal common ground between two languages, even in cases where they seem completely different from each other. A very minor pattern in one language can become major when it is in contact with another language in which it exists as the majority pattern. This is why, diachronically, we may witness some apparently extreme changes in domains such as basic word order, for example, from SOV to SVO, and vice versa. Such drastic changes do not happen overnight; they take a long time and they are profoundly influenced by sociolinguistic factors (Heine & Kuteva, 2005; Trudgill, 2011). For the sake of the current argument and the initial illustration of the principle of Maximise Common Ground I define *common ground as items of structure or meaning in both languages that overlap to either a greater or lesser extent*. For example, English and Spanish have common ground when it comes to basic word order because both have SVO as the preferred order, even though Spanish has more freedom in this, and other word-order variants are grammatical that are not found in English. Spanish learners of L2 English maximise common ground even at later stages of L2 acquisition by producing utterances such as *'Yesterday came my boyfriend' (see Filipović & Hawkins, 2013). Clearly, they realise that SVO basic word order is shared and they assume that word order in general is a shared feature (i.e. common ground) between Spanish and English that they can maximise. In English, inverted subject structures like this are very rare, and are found only in restricted syntactic environments and for specific stylistic purposes (e.g. 'Here comes the winner!' or 'I had my feet on my desk and in came the boss!'). The cost to communicative efficiency from this particular ungrammaticality in English is however not very high – the message still gets through with the verb-subject ordering.

Filipović and Hawkins (2013) explain that when the cost to communication is too high, even early L2 learners eschew maximising common ground. This is evident, for example, when Japanese speakers acquire L2 English. In contrast to the Spanish–English combination, English and Japanese are typologically very different; they do not have common ground when it comes to basic word order because Japanese is an SOV language and a mirror image of the English SVO type (e.g. 'Taroo-ga tegami-o kaita' = 'Taroo [subject] a letter [object] wrote'; i.e. 'Taroo wrote a letter' in English). Filipović and Hawkins (2013) found that Japanese learners of L2 English do not use their basic SOV Japanese word orders in their L2 English, even in the very early stages of L2 acquisition. The cost to communication of imposing such a radically different order on English syntax would be too high and communication would be impaired and inefficient, and so it is not done. However, this does not mean that Maximise Common Ground is always trumped in cases of large typological distance. Extreme changes in basic word order have taken place in both directions in the past, SVO to SOV, and SOV to SVO (see Ross, 1996, 2001, Gast, 2007, and Heine, 2008). Bilinguals can bring about more permanent language change such as this through long-term contact, and through the physical proximity of two monolingual or bilingual populations, depending also on demographic factors in the relevant speech communities (numbers of early or late bilinguals, population sizes, etc.) and the nature of the social interactions between them (e.g. equality vs. inequality of the two languages and their respective speakers; Trudgill 2010, 2011; see also Chapter 2).

3.4   Why Maximise Common Ground?

The most important question that needs to be posed here is exactly what drives and underlies all the different outcomes that I refer to as maximising common ground. Muysken (2000) mentions that we may be dealing ultimately with 'principles of economy', a concept assumed by Poplack (1980) as well. These principles are based on equivalence between systems, which Muysken (2000: 273) formulates as: 'when there is equivalence in a switching context, make use of it'. He emphasises that there is pressure towards congruent lexicalisation in bilingual settings. This is very much in line with syntactic priming studies in bilingualism (see Traxler, 2012, for an overview) and also with the findings discussed in this and subsequent chapters (4 and 5).

'Processing economy' (Muysken, 2000: 227) is not, I believe, the most adequate term for what happens in cases where one pattern is used in both languages. 'Economy' normally evokes simple or simplified forms and meanings, and adding constructions from one language into the other would not generally be thought of as 'economical'. So when there is simplification in bilingual outputs (i.e. when certain forms and meanings are dispensed with) it is natural to refer to this as 'economy' in both grammar and processing. But it is more difficult to argue that complexification (creating new lexical and grammatical form–meaning mappings) is also economical. Muysken's overall idea about the advantage of using one single pattern in two languages and the supporting bilingual data he discusses, however, are very much on the right track, and it is this aspect of his theory that we are trying to capture in terms of our Maximise Common Ground principle, which appeals not to economy as such, but to efficiency. Recall our discussion of referential expressions in grammar and usage earlier in this section. The most economical way of referring to an entity ('it') must sometimes be replaced by a less economical option ('the dress you wore'), where there are more items to process, in order to achieve the communicative goal of referring successfully, in a way that enables the hearer to identify the referent clearly and with the least processing effort possible. Efficiency is always goal-oriented and involves expending the least possible effort to achieve the goal in question, be it the goal of successful reference in communication, or of learning and storing two languages and using them successfully in different social circumstances. We cannot say that the referring expressions used for efficient communication are always economical in their grammar and processing, for sometimes they are not; nor that bilingual outputs are more economical in grammar and processing than the corresponding outputs of the respective monolinguals, for again sometimes they are not, as when regular evidential marking is added to a language that does not normally have it. But these outputs are *efficient*, we would argue, and as economical as they can be for the relevant goal to be accomplished; and it is for this reason that I argue in this book for a *general theory of processing and learning efficiency in bilingualism*, and not for processing economy in Muysken's (2000) terms (see further Filipović & Hawkins 2013, 2018; see also Hawkins 2004, 2014).

Categories may be simplified to encompass as many as possible of the shared and more general properties in both languages. New categories may also be created, as in the case of introducing lexical evidentiality or intentionality into one of the bilingual's languages as a match for the grammatical or constructional requirements of the other. For instance, speakers of Quechua Spanish express evidentiality distinctions lexically in Spanish in order to match the grammatical requirements for the expression of evidentiality in Quechua (see Heine & Kuteva, 2005). Similarly, Turkish–English bilinguals also add lexical expressions of evidentiality when they speak English, in line with the grammatical evidentiality of Turkish (Slobin, 2016). Similar observations have been made in the domain of intentionality. Some languages, like English, do not oblige its speakers to say whether an action was performed on purpose or not (e.g. 'He dropped the bag'– on purpose or not?). In languages like Spanish, Italian or Serbian, speakers have to use different verbs or constructions based on whether an action was performed on purpose or not. Bilinguals who speak one language that does and one that does not draw the intentional/non-intentional distinction introduce the means to do so into the language that does not have the distinction (e.g. by narrowing the meaning of certain constructions or by adding adverbs more regularly than is typical for monolingual use; see Filipović, 2018, 2019b).

Some attempts to maximise common ground result in detectable departures from the norms of a certain language, and these departures can come in different degrees, ranging from overuse/underuse of an item or construction to atypical or erroneous (ungrammatical) use. Balanced simultaneous bilinguals, fluent in both languages to the same or a similar degree, are not generally expected to demonstrate ungrammaticalities but may tend to show instances of overuse/underuse and atypical use in one or both of their languages, depending on their specific linguistic profile and usage habits (influenced by their life and work circumstances and environments). Second-language learners or heritage speakers are more likely to exhibit erroneous uses and to allow ungrammaticality because they do not yet have firmly established knowledge and automated intuitions about grammaticality in their weaker language due to incomplete acquisition or attrition. This is when we see the widely different documented effects of 'cross-linguistic influence' (see Jarvis & Pavlenko, 2010 for extensive discussion and examples). Filipović and Hawkins (2018) propose that all the reported cross-linguistic interactional phenomena observed in bilingual processing, diachronic language change and code-switching research are *efficiency-driven phenomena* because bilingual minds adapt to having an efficient representation and storage of both languages and to being multi-language-ready in both.

It is of importance to note that Filipović and Hawkins (2018) put forward the CASP model for bilingualism with the initial premise that both languages in the bilingual mind are readily available and accessible in any given communicative situation. This assumption is supported by substantial evidence from contemporary research on bilingualism, whereby both comprehension and production studies have shown that proficient bilingual speakers 'activate information about both languages when using one language alone' (e.g. Kroll & Bialystok, 2013: 497). Habitual language use (how often each or both languages are used) as well as the concrete communicative situation in question (if it requires one or both languages to be active) determine the activation patterns for a bilingual speaker on each occasion. For instance, if the bilingual speaker is using both languages in daily life or work then the activation of both, even when only one is needed, is more likely than it would be if one of the two languages were rarely used.

3.5   Variability and Adjustability in Bilingualism: The Interplay of Internal and External Factors

One of the fundamental factors in bilingual language processing that must be considered at the outset is the typological factor. Before we start making any predictions about possible bilingual outcomes we must establish what a language has or does not have. This can enable us to make a list of logically possible outcomes when two languages are in contact in the bilingual mind and in contact in general within a broader sociolinguistic perspective. The direction of which pattern may prevail in outputs, for instance, L1 or L2, neither or parts of both, will then depend on the other interacting factors (see Athanasopoulos, 2011: 37 for a succinct list and discussion of these factors). Thus, the point of departure within CASP for Bilingualism is based on *logically possible outcomes when multiple linguistic options, as per the typological characteristics of each language, are 'vying for supremacy' online.* The CASP principles apply in all bilingual language processing, except that the degree to which they are active is modulated by the linguistic profile of our bilingual speaker (which is *variable*; bilingual speakers have different backgrounds and competencies) and who our bilingual is talking to (because bilingual speakers *adjust* to the situation as best they can, depending on their linguistic profile; see further discussion below).

The CASP model for bilingualism explains how the more specific internal and external factors interact with general principles of bilingual language processing, and how they may support or impede these general principles. In other words, the general principles are modulated by both internal and external factors operating at the same time. Specifically, all bilingual speakers can aim to maximise common ground in order to facilitate processing, but they will do so more successfully if their command of both languages is balanced than if it is not (the variability factor), and they will do it to different degrees depending on the demands of the specific communicative situation (as determined by interlocutor type or situation type – the adjustability factor).

As discussed in Chapter 2, internal (*variability*) factors consist of age of acquisition, proficiency and dominance, which may be affected by numerous conditions (e.g. languages spoken at home, the language of primary-school education, the amount of exposure to second languages, the specific language-testing context; further discussion in Bylund & Athanasopoulos, 2014). Bilingual speakers with equal proficiency in both languages can be more successful in output monitoring than those whose proficiency in the two languages is unequal. For example, when it comes to code-switching or code-mixing (see Muysken, 2000, for the distinction between the two), they are expected to occur in line with proficiency: the higher the proficiency, the lower the frequency of switching in monolingual contexts, because it is ineffectual (i.e. monolingual interlocutors will simply not understand the speaker if he/she code-switches) and more proficient bilinguals can control their outputs and block code-switching better than the less proficient ones. Less code-switching is also expected in formal compared to informal bilingual interactions (Dewaele, 2001; see Chapter 2, Section 2.4.2). We can also expect that the same bilingual speaker will produce different outputs under different circumstances. Fluent bilinguals would not code-switch when speaking to a monolingual, as explained above, but they may do so when talking to another bilingual in the same two languages. Language switching can happen for different reasons in fluent bilinguals; for example, the language not currently spoken may have more efficient, or effective, packaging of information than the one currently used, or certain items are more easily accessible in the language that is not being spoken at that moment because they are more frequently encountered or used in that other language. In contrast to adult fluent bilinguals, bilingual children are more likely to code-switch when interacting with monolingual speakers, because they have not yet mastered their languages. Similarly, unbalanced bilinguals such as adult L2 learners may code-switch inappropriately, resorting to their L1 when talking to monolinguals in the L2 since they lack the required means of expression in the L2. These situations are due to incomplete knowledge of the two systems or of rules of usage.

External factors are driven by the inherently *adjustable* nature of bilingual linguistic behaviour, which depends on the interlocutor types involved (i.e. who bilingual speakers are talking to) or the type of communicative situation a bilingual is involved in (e.g. formal vs. informal; see Chapter 2; see also discussion in Muysken, 2013: 714 on different factors that impact outputs in language-contact situations). Interacting with one monolingual interlocutor will exert the least pressure to maximise common ground on bilingual speakers, but this pressure still may occur depending on the bilinguals' habitual language use and the proficiency-driven control of their outputs. When a bilingual is talking to another bilingual with the same languages, there is less pressure to keep the two languages apart than when talking to a single monolingual and it is in effect beneficial to have both of them active because the transition to the other language can happen at any point in the conversation. This will probably be conducive to some instances of maximising common ground due to parallel activation (fewer if there is a lot of code-switching), but the pressure for this to happen is less intense than in a case where communication takes place with two monolinguals, one in each language in a single communicative situation. In that case maximising common ground is highly beneficial in terms of facilitating faster and smoother transitions between the two languages.

Some speakers may be better at output control and be more likely to produce linguistic outputs in line with monolingual norms in each of their languages because of specialised training (e.g. professional translators and interpreters; see Chapter 6 for details). We can also expect that a more formal situation will result in fewer instances of maximising common ground than an informal one because the output monitor (see de Groot, 2011) may be on higher alert in the former than the latter situation and this would result in more controlled and more language-specific outputs. This hypothesised gradual difference in relation to maximising common ground is testable using the CASP platform (see Chapter 4, Section 4.5 for detailed predictions, visually illustrated).

We also need to account for some monolingual-like performances by bilingual speakers. These can occur *when a bilingual speaker is talking to a monolingual speaker in one of the two languages.* Monolingual-like performance is also documented in some psycholinguistic studies. This outcome can be due to the fact that bilingual speakers are kept in monolingual mode (e.g. Kousta, Vinson & Vigliocco, 2008) or may occur when access to one of the two languages is disabled in the experiment (e.g. Athanasopoulos et al., 2015) or when the proficiency is higher in one of the two languages. Monolingual-like performances by bilinguals are one extreme of our cline, modulated by internal factors such as proficiency and external factors such as whether or not there is a need to keep both languages constantly active and accessible throughout the communicative situation. The other extreme of the cline is to maximise common ground excessively even when this is not grammatically licensed in one of the two languages, which is more characteristic of SLA outputs.

The system of CASP for Bilingualism can help us make concrete predictions here, and enables us to explain the relevant processes behind the different outcomes. For example, *Maximise Efficiency in Communication, Minimise Processing Effort* and *Maximise Expressive Power* would go against *Maximise Common Ground* when a proficient bilingual speaker is involved in a monolingual communicative situation, and we can therefore expect fewer instances of common ground here than in a situation where both languages are active to a similar degree. In a bilingual communicative situation, we expect the same conflict among the principles, but with a different outcome because bilinguals would adjust to the communicative situation. The demands of that situation would encourage them to exploit the commonalities of meanings and structures and to have a multi-language-ready-mind, and so be ready to provide the relevant information in either language. This preparedness is ultimately more efficient to have overall even though some sacrifices need to be made elsewhere.

For instance, when both languages are used in communication or habitually (e.g. English and Turkish), bilinguals may express evidential meanings in both even though only one of the languages (Turkish) requires them (Slobin, 2016). On such occasions there will be more processing effort required because there will be more items to process in English with a constant addition of evidentiality-indicating structures such as 'it seems that . . . ' or 'it appears that . . . ', and communicative efficiency may be compromised as a result: evidentiality information is not needed in order to fulfil speed, accuracy and hearer-oriented expectations. The overall common ground and multi-language readiness of the bilingual mind ensures that the speaker has the information required in either language ready for delivery, and this is more efficient overall from a processing perspective (see Filipović, 2014). Communicative efficiency is sacrificed for the sake of overall processing efficiency through adherence to what is clearly the stronger principle in this competition, Maximise Common Ground. The bilingual speaker is most efficient if ready to respond to hearer needs in either language at the drop of a hat.

3.6   How to Make Predictions Using CASP for Bilingualism

How do we then make predictions based on the multiple factors we have outlined and the differences between linguistic profiles, interlocutor or situation types? Many studies of bilingualism focus on proficiency distinctions, which fall under the variability conditions in our CASP model. Variable proficiency results in variable linguistic outputs, as numerous studies have shown (Dussias, 2001; Filipović, 2018, 2019b; Kroll & Bialystok, 2013; Lai et al., 2014). Less attention has been paid to the determinant nature of the adjustability factors, which incorporate information about the communicative situation, i.e. who is talking to whom and why. Because one and the same bilingual speaker can behave differently on different occasions, it is essential that our predictions take into consideration both the linguistic characteristics of the bilingual speaker and the different circumstances of the communicative situation that can affect this behaviour, as illustrated in the previous section. Sociolinguistic research has looked at the products of long-term language contact and bilingualism and has alerted us to the importance of societal hierarchies and demographic structure and to the nature of relationships among the bilinguals and monolinguals in a society, all of which plays a part in the kind of language change that bilingualism brings about (see Chapter 2). We still need more experimental studies and fieldwork data collection of spontaneous language use by bilinguals in order to document the interaction-driven processes that mould bilingual outputs and that may ultimately lead to long-term language change.

In this regard, it is important to point out how our model can be put to use and tested in future research, and more generally to illustrate how it makes testable predictions. Depending on whether proficiency in one language is low or high, or whether the bilingual is interacting with a monolingual or another bilingual, the CASP principles will predict different outcomes. It is crucial, first of all, to identify that subset of factors from the multifactor model that makes predictions for the case at hand, and to assess how they work together. Sometimes one factor will not interfere with the predictions of another. Sometimes it will. Sometimes different factors will cooperate and pull in the same direction; sometimes they will compete. Having multiple factors to consider does not make the overall predictions easy, but it does not make them impossible, as long as we delimit the empirical domain of applicability for each factor and its expected consequences. In any case, we have no choice, in this as in most other area of language sciences. *Any adequate model of bilingualism must be a multifactor one.*

Previous research has drawn attention to the multifactor nature of language processing, in both monolingual and bilingual contexts. Hawkins (2014: ch. 9) provides an insightful general discussion of cooperation and competition among multiple factors in a grammatical and language processing context, and Filipović and Hawkins (2013) offered a detailed illustration of this interaction among multiple factors with specific reference to second-language acquisition. Many papers in the volume by MacWhinney, Malchukov and Moravcsik (2014) discuss and exemplify competing motivations in grammar, processing and learning. The same issues involving the relevance of different factors in any given domain, their relative strength and their cooperation or competition arise in all these studies, and we can use these insights to explain how we can make falsifiable predictions in the CASP for Bilingualism model.

Because there is a lot of possible variation, we need to *first restrict the relevant universe of applicability for our principles*; namely, we need to state what the languages are, who is talking to whom (and why) and with what level of proficiency. It is then that we can start to make falsifiable predictions; these predictions will be relative to the grammatical, social and psycholinguistic universe in which they apply and within which they work together, possibly constraining each other, or not, as the case may be. For instance, English–Turkish bilingual speakers equally competent in both languages who use both languages in their daily life and work, or have Turkish as the stronger language, are more likely to express evidentiality in both English (lexically) and Turkish (grammatically) compared to bilinguals less competent in Turkish or who use Turkish less frequently, or who interact more with monolingual English speakers, and so on, as discussed in the previous section. Expressing evidentiality in both languages is the most efficient way to maximise common ground in grammar and processing and to be communication-ready and able to express all meanings in both languages. But when speakers use one language more than the other habitually (English or Turkish), or when they are speaking to a monolingual person (English or Turkish), these factors will impact the extent to which common ground is maximised. When English is spoken more frequently there will be less frequent manifestations of evidentiality in that language than if Turkish is spoken more frequently, and so on. These hypotheses are straightforward to test within the CASP for Bilingualism framework. CASP can help us test, predict and explain more vs. less likely outcomes in these kinds of cases, per linguistic domain, per speaker or speaker group and per social situation.

Because CASP's predictions are made within the relevant universe of applicability defined by typological features, speaker features and situation features, it is neither plausible nor possible to rank our general principles in the manner of a purely grammatical theory like e.g. Optimality Theory (Prince & Smolensky, 1993). In CASP for Bilingualism the relative strength or applicability of principles does not depend on purely grammatical factors, nor can a relative ordering or ranking of these be stipulated in these terms. We are dealing instead with a much broader and more complex mix of ultimately psycholinguistic, sociolinguistic and grammatical-typological factors which do, nonetheless, enable us to make more gradient, and sometimes even absolute predictions for bilingual outcomes. As we shall see in the next chapter, there are numerous studies that demonstrate how some of our principles interact and what their relevant strengths and rankings are, even though most often not all aspects of the complex system are considered within individual studies. In what follows, we use some of the research findings reported in the field (including our own) in order to demonstrate how the CASP model works in more detail.

4   Action Time

CASP for Bilingualism at Work

In the previous chapter I put forward a framework, CASP for Bilingualism, that can be used to capture the differences in bilingual linguistic behaviour by enabling us to account for when, where and why the outputs of different bilingual minds will differ. In this chapter I look at a number of different reports on bilingual linguistic behaviour from different research areas within bilingualism, and I try to synthesise these reports into a coherent, unifying picture of bilingualism, in spite of the vast diversity of language combinations, data types and methodologies. I shall explain the reasons behind the similarities and differences between results from different studies, and in the process, illustrate the relevant interactions among our general principles and the internal and external factors that play out differently on different occasions of bilingual language use.

4.1   Ways to Maximise Common Ground: The Logic of Bilingualism

Bilinguals are not two monolinguals in one, *because they maximise common ground*. As indicated in the previous chapter, our other general principles within CASP for Bilingualism characterise language processing in general, but Maximise Common Ground *is a bilingual-specific principle* that reflects the overall striving for optimisation in bilingual processing, i.e. *processing efficiency*. The central claim I make here is that bilingual minds are habitually involved in optimising language processing by maximising common ground, that this is their natural state of being and that they become better at it the more they use both languages. When they are not doing so, it is because the requirements in their environment are such that it is not needed (monolingual mode) or is actively blocked (by training, as in professional interpreting; see Chapter 6, or by a particular experimental methodology; see Athanasopoulos et al., 2015). With uneven proficiency, maximising common ground will happen more when the weaker language of the two is spoken because the language-specific conventions of the stronger language will be better known and more frequently used. Furthermore, the patterns of the stronger language are more likely to be commonly used in both languages even though they may be less preferred (or even ungrammatical) in the weaker language. Finally, bilinguals with uneven proficiency can also be expected not to have fully mastered when and how common ground can be maximised, so they may not maximise common ground even when they could, and when it would actually be helpful to do so, e.g. in order to enhance overall efficiency in task performance. Conversely, they may maximise common ground too much, and venture into the realm of ungrammaticality. I discuss these different possible outcomes with illustrations from previous research.

The studies I examine here involve different languages and levels of analysis and also different experimental designs, but they all point to a striving for shared categories in different kinds of bilinguals, in different kinds of testing contexts, and in different linguistic and conceptual domains: in syntactic processing preferences (Dussias & Sagarra, 2007); motion event lexicalisation (Filipović, 2011); aspectuality and event categorisation (Flecken, 2010); lexical categorisation (e.g. Ameel et al., 2009; Gathercole & Moawad, 2010; Brown & Gullberg, 2011); the conceptual representation of colour (Athanasopoulos, 2009) and bilingual memory (Filipović, 2011, 2018; 2019b, see also Chapter 5). Even when common ground is apparently not maximised (see Section 4.4 of this chapter), CASP captures this too because it predicts the circumstances under which it may happen (that is, when driven by those internal and external factors that ensure that bilinguals come closer to monolingual norms in each language).

Let us look first at the ways in which common ground can be maximised and at what conditions the different strategies and outcomes. If two languages have the same possibilities in terms of categories and rules, then bilinguals will use them in both languages (unless they eschew this due to psychotypology – the belief that the similarities are not there; see Kellerman, 1983). Most often there are numerous contrasts between two languages and we need to look at the options available to bilinguals in these cases. The contrasts can be of three different general types:
  i) Contrast due to **partial overlap** in categories and structures (to be illustrated below with examples from various lexical domains, motion constructions, pro-drop rules and adjective ordering)
  ii) Contrast due to **presence vs. absence** of categories or structures (exemplified by evidentials, the affective dative construction and the category of gender)
  iii) Contrast due to **incompatibility** between categories and structures (the 'either-or choice'; e.g. in the cases of basic word order, syntactic attachment and discourse preferences).
There are a number of logically possible outcomes in all three categories. In the case of contrast (i) the bilinguals can opt to:

i.a)   use the shared category or structure more often in both languages,
i.b)   use a different category or structure in line with the main preference of each
         language, or
i.c)   introduce a different category or structure from one language into the other to
         make the overlap complete.

Similarly, in the case of option (ii), when bilinguals do not have a shared
category or structure, they can:

ii.a)   create it in the language that does not have it,
ii.b)   use it only in the language that has it or
ii.c)   lose it (initially via avoidance) from the language that has it.

The last category, (iii), comprises situations in which both languages of the
bilingual have certain categories or structures, but they are mirror-image
opposites of each other because of grammatical differences or usage preferences in each language; e.g. VO vs. OV word order, or a parsing preference for
high vs. low syntactic attachment. It is not possible to completely 'lose' word
order or syntactic attachment, so this category has one possibility fewer than
the other two. Here the possible logical outcomes would be to:

iii.a)   stick to the different pattern of each language, or
iii.b)   use the same pattern in both languages (i.e. change the rule of preference in
         one of the two languages to match those of the other).

It is significant to point out that every single one of these possible outcomes just
mentioned has been attested in the literature on bilingualism! CASP for
Bilingualism can make sense of all these different outcomes by first deriving
them from the same general principles, and secondly showing how competition
or collaboration between them gives different outputs due to different internal
and external factors. Once we establish which two languages are under consideration, and their typological characteristics, as well as the profiles of the
bilinguals and their interlocutors and the social circumstances of their interactions, we are able to account for different outcomes within the same linguistic
domain (e.g. different outcomes in word-order processing or gender processing). We will also see how CASP for Bilingualism makes predictions for what
the reported outputs would have been, had the bilinguals or the communicative
situation been different.

4.2   Maximise Common Ground: Partial Overlap Cases

4.2.1   Partial Overlaps in the Lexicon(s)

Studies of the bilingual lexicon provide us with numerous examples of how
common ground is maximised in cases of partial category overlap, and in this

section we present and critically discuss a number of these studies from different lexical and grammatical domains.

4.2.1.1 What Is in a Container: Object Categorisation   The use of lexical items by bilinguals has often revealed language outputs that are unlike the outputs of the respective monolingual populations. For instance, Ameel et al. (2005) discuss 'lexical convergence' in the bilingual labelling of household objects. The bilingual mind seems to prefer a one-to-one mapping instead of one to many (see Chapter 2, Section 2.2.2.4 on the dispreference for ambiguity), and thus if a category is more finely grained in one language than the other, one of the members of this category 'gets chosen' as an equivalent to the single member of the other language, with the result that the mapping is more straightforward. For example, whilst the referents of Dutch 'fles' are typically differentiated by French monolinguals into 'bouteille' ('larger bottle') and 'flacon' ('smaller bottle'), Dutch–French bilinguals assign most bottles to a general category 'bouteille' and only a few to 'flacon' (Ameel et al., 2005). Conversely, the larger Dutch category 'bus' ('can') has been narrowed down to refer to only spray cans, under the influence of the French label for the same item (ibid.).

Similar findings have been reported by Pavlenko and Malt (2011) for the naming of kitchen objects in English and Russian. Their Russian–English bilinguals, who were all resident in the USA, either extended or narrowed their categories in one language under the influence of the other. For instance, 'chashka' is a Russian label for a narrow category whose central members are small cups with handles used for hot liquids, whilst the English word 'cup' is a much more diverse category. Bilinguals in this study used the Russian category in a broader, English-like way. By contrast, 'stakan' in Russian appears to be a broader category than the English 'glass' but it gets narrowed in bilingual use by increasing the constraint on the material that the 'stakan' receptacle is made of (i.e. glass).

In general, CASP for Bilingualism predicts that the bilinguals will aim to minimise their learning and processing effort by learning and using just one term with the same semantic extensions in both languages. However, the principle of Maximise Expressive Power encourages the learning and use of language-specific meanings, so we see that bilinguals are also able to operate using monolingual-like distinctions in each language, calibrated by how proficient they are in that language and how often they use it. This is a typical push–pull situation in bilingualism where opposite forces operate, as captured by the different general principles of CASP for Bilingualism (see Chapter 3). In this regard, Pavlenko and Malt (2011) detect differences in category overlap between early and late Russian–English bilinguals, whereby with increased proficiency comes an increased ability to represent form–meaning mappings in each language in more independent ways (see also Kroll & De Groot, 1997).

CASP for Bilingualism also predicts that common ground will be maximised more if speakers are in a bilingual mode (during an experiment, and also habitually) than when they are required to speak only the one language, and more so when they are speaking in their weaker or less dominant language (see Pavlenko & Malt, 2011: 34–5 for some relevant proficiency-related comparisons). These are all readily testable hypotheses, which underscore the need to test different types of bilinguals under the same conditions as well as the same types of bilinguals under different conditions (monolingual vs. bilingual mode; see Chapter 5 for some methodological suggestions). It is only through such experimental conditions that we will be able to grasp the full extent of the role that internal and external factors play in determining bilingual outputs. So far, most findings in the field have examined only some of the relevant conditioning factors, but it is necessary to control for multiple factors and determine their cumulative effects and relative strengths.

4.2.1.2 True Blues: Categorising Colour Colour terms are another domain where we see how partial category overlaps lead to bilinguals maximising common ground. In an early study Ervin (1961) found that bilinguals name colours differently from their monolingual counterparts in ways that suggest an influence of the semantic categories of one language on the category boundaries in the other. This finding has been replicated in more recent studies. Athanasopoulos (2009) found that advanced Greek–English bilinguals shift their colour-category boundaries in one language (L1 Greek) under the influence of the other (L2 English). Loss of L1 distinctions within colour categories correlates with frequency of usage: the more the L2 is used, the less the L1 distinctions are preserved (see Athanasopoulos et al., 2010 and Athanasopoulos et al., 2011). Thus, Greek–English bilinguals with longer exposure to their second language (English), in which the relevant colour contrasts are not lexicalised (as they are in Greek: 'ble' = 'dark blue' vs. 'ghalazio' = 'light blue'), distinguish significantly less between the two in a variety of tasks and also display significantly less within-group naming agreement at the ble/ghalazio boundary than bilinguals with shorter L2 exposure. These differences between the two bilingual groups (the long-stay and the short-stay) demonstrate that immersion in the L2-speaking country results in stronger word-to-referent mappings in the L2 than if the L2 is only learned in a classroom (Tokowicz, Michael & Kroll, 2004).

We can pause here and ask when bilinguals would opt for the other logical options, namely behaving like monolinguals in each language, or introducing lexical distinctions into the language that does not have them instead of losing distinctions that are captured by different colour terms? For instance, new colour terms can be introduced through language contact (e.g. 'naranja' (orange) and 'azul' (blue) from Spanish into Mesoamerican languages;

Bricker, 1999; MacLaury, 1997). In some other cases, however, language contact does not seem to lead to either the introduction of colour distinctions in one, or the loss of lexicalised distinctions in the other, language of the bilinguals. Saunders and Van Brakel (1997: 175) cite an example of Kwakw'ala–English bilinguals, who do not distinguish between green and yellow in Kwakw'ala and use the single term available for both (*lhenxa* = yellow + green) even though they 'know perfectly well the difference in English between yellow and green' (ibid.). This is not surprising. We know that bilinguals can sometimes behave like monolinguals in each of their languages. If bilinguals do not have a ready label for drawing distinctions in one of their languages but do have it in the other, they may or may not resort to the category distinctions from their other language. They always have the option to use a modification of some sort in the language that does not have separate labels (e.g. 'warmer (more yellowy) vs. colder (more greeny) *lhenxa*' – I am just using my imagination here!) or they may just stick to the single category label available in the language they are speaking at the moment, e.g. during the task, especially if that category is good enough for the purpose of the task (i.e. it gets the speaker to an acceptable task resolution).

Knowing that bilinguals have and use two terms for a colour category in one language and one in the other does not tell us about the bilingual representation of that category. The Greek–English bilinguals mentioned earlier know the distinction between 'ble' and 'ghalazio' and may still use the two words for blue in Greek and just one ('blue') in English. However, as we saw in Athanasopoulos (2009) and Athanasopoulos et al. (2010), we can obtain experimental evidence about conceptual distinctions that may be gained or lost as a result of language contact within and across bilingual minds, as in the case of the Greek–English bilinguals who appear to be gradually losing their clear conceptual distinctions between the two shades of blue under the influence of English (whilst not necessarily completely losing the Greek terms for the two blues). We do not have information about whether Kwakw'ala–English bilinguals would exhibit a similar or a different trend to the Greek–English bilinguals of this section, but if the language with the single term (in this case, Kwakw'ala) is the dominant one in daily use, it may have the same effect on the English yellow–green distinction as English had on the two blues in Greek – the category border may shift and some distinctions may be lost. If, however, English is the dominant language, then we can expect the yellow–green distinction to persist and be more readily available in Kwakw'ala–English bilinguals than in Kwakw'ala monolinguals. Similarly, if Greek is the dominant language in daily use (e.g. if L1 Greek–L2 English bilinguals are living in Greece), Greek–English bilinguals may be more likely to keep their distinction between the two blues and have more awareness about them when using both languages. Or they may even calque one Greek word into English or signal distinctions with adverbials more often (e.g. light blue vs. dark blue) than an English monolingual would because it is more efficient for the bilingual to maximise common ground even if it involves adding words (see Chapter 3). These hypotheses can be tested empirically in the future, with bilinguals of different proficiency, with different dominant languages and different frequencies of use in the two languages, at different locales, and in different language modes. In other words, we need multifactor studies of bilingualism in the future.

4.2.1.3 Posturing: Verbs of Placement   Verbs of posture/positioning/placement (the terminology appears to be interchangeable in the literature) represent another lexical semantic domain that is good for testing predictions with regard to bilingual outputs, since some languages make more and others less subtle categorial distinctions. For example, the lexically appropriate uses of verbs such as 'zetten' ('to set/stand') over 'leggen' ('to lay') in Dutch is more restricted than it is for the corresponding verbs in English and involves two clearly different scenes depending on the position of the object with respect to the surface (Lemmens, 2002, 2006). In a study of placement verb use by English learners of L2 Dutch, Gullberg (2009) found that the participants employed a number of strategies in order to deal with this distinction which is not available in their L1. They either avoided placement verbs altogether and used constructions with 'doen' ('to do') or other more general non-placement forms or, when they did use a placement verb they overgeneralised one, 'zetten' ('set/stand'), over another, 'leggen' ('lay'), to include both types of posture scenes. A similar finding has been reported in a study of German–Romansh bilinguals in Switzerland by Berthele (2012).

As before, this is what CASP for Bilingualism would predict: Minimise Learning Effort, Minimise Processing Effort and Maximise Common Ground are the principles that ensure this outcome. Maximise Expressive Power would pull in the other direction and would encourage the bilinguals to learn and use the more finely grained distinctions in one of their two languages. If they do not do so, then they may also not be responding to their hearer's needs perfectly in each language because hearers in one of the languages (Dutch) may be used to these lexicalised distinctions, so they would not be Maximising Efficiency in Communication in this case. However, the *cost to communicative efficiency* is low on this occasion (i.e. they probably do not risk any misunderstanding in the great majority of cases) and the *gain to processing efficiency* is considerably higher, so they follow Maximise Common Ground at the expense of Maximise Efficiency in Communication.

Communicative efficiency can win this contest when bilinguals are conversing with monolinguals, in a monolingual mode in the language that makes the subtle distinctions. Depending on whether they have fully acquired the distinctions or not (i.e. if they have fully maximised their expressive power), we can expect bilinguals to make these distinctions more accurately and regularly, though possibly still less consistently than the monolinguals themselves due to the habitual bilingual preference for a shared, more encompassing lexical term.

It is interesting that explicit instruction about distinct lexicalisations for these placement events can be taught and learned in L2 classrooms and then used to enhance memory when using the L2. In a recent study Koster and Cadierno (2018) asked if L1 speakers of German (which lexicalises posture distinctions) and Spanish (which does not) show different recognition memory for object position in placement scenes and whether learning the meaning of L2 German placement verbs can improve memory accuracy. The answer to both questions was yes. Monolingual German speakers were significantly more accurate at spotting changes in object orientation than monolingual Spanish speakers, whose score was close to 0 per cent correct. However, Spanish learners of L2 German were even more accurate than L1 German speakers in spotting changes in object orientation. It would be interesting to see if the enhanced bilingual sensitivity to lexicalised differences in object positions in L2 German is also accessed when speaking L1 Spanish, whereby categories from L2 would be invoked in L1 in explicit verbalisation (e.g. through paraphrase) and/or in memory.

In future research it would be useful to try and capture the variable behaviour of the same bilingual group in partial overlap cases like these depending on the demands of the communicative situation (such as when they are using one vs. both their languages, e.g. in different experimental blocks) and also to compare different bilingual types within a single study: those with equal proficiency and frequency of use of both languages, those with a stronger language with subtle lexical distinctions, and those with a stronger language without these distinctions. CASP for Bilingualism predicts that common ground will be maximised overall, by all bilingual speakers, but to a higher degree in a bilingual than a monolingual mode. Even in the monolingual mode maximising common ground may be in evidence, since bilinguals are not two monolinguals in one and they may have entrenched habits of maximising common ground that pervade their language use and that are present even in the monolingual mode. Common ground would feature less in more fluent bilinguals in the monolingual mode and be more prominently displayed in the outputs of unbalanced bilinguals, especially if they are speaking their weaker language.

4.2.2   Partial Overlaps in Grammar(s)

Maximising common ground occurs also at the level of grammar. In this section we look at different areas of grammar in typologically different language pairs in order to illustrate the different strategies that bilingual minds come up with in order to resolve conflicts of partial overlap between their two grammars.

4.2.2.1 Pronouns: To Drop or Not to Drop   Let us examine the feature of *pro-drop* as our first example of maximising common ground in bilingual grammar. Having pro-drop makes it grammatical in certain languages to omit the subject, typically because the morphology of the verb signals whether the subject is first-, second- or third-person singular or plural. For instance, in Spanish, a pro-drop language, the subject-less sentence 'dormió bien' means that somebody slept well. This sentence does not contain an overt expression of the subject (he or she) but we know, based on the verb, that the subject referred to is third-person singular. It is also possible to use an explicit pronoun in Spanish 'El/ella dormió bien' ('He/She slept well'), but it is most often omitted because the same information is rendered without it and with fewer elements, which is more efficient. The pronoun is normally given in Spanish if a particular kind of distinction has to be made, e.g. because the verb does not tell us the gender of the person who slept well, or for emphasis in the discourse. In some other pro-drop languages (e.g. Slavic ones, like Serbian) verb endings are marked for gender (e.g. 'spavao'– 'he slept'; 'spavala'– 'she slept') so the pronouns are more likely to be habitually omitted, with the exception of cases when special emphasis is needed. In English we always have to use an overt pronoun in order to express these same meanings, e.g. 'He/she slept well', because English is not a pro-drop language. Thus, the feature that is shared between English and pro-drop languages is the option to express the subject explicitly.

So, what happens when a bilingual is acquiring the two language types, pro-drop and non-pro-drop? CASP predicts, in line with option (i.a) for partial overlap categories in the previous section, that the most likely outcome is that the bilingual will use the shared feature, the explicit subject expression in both languages, and the un-shared feature (omitting the pronoun) gets sidelined. However, in line with option (i.b), as given in Section 4.1 of this chapter, bilinguals may stick to the language-specific pattern preferred in each language. We also find examples of bilingual speakers doing what is described in (i.c), namely maximising common ground by introducing a missing feature in the language that does not have it to make the perfect overlap; e.g. using pro-drop structures in the other, non-pro-drop language. We can look at the different strategies for maximising common ground employed by bilinguals and shed light on these differences using our CASP for Bilingualism model.

First, we can note that heritage speakers of pro-drop languages who are immersed in a non-pro-drop-language environment (like English) maximise common ground by using overt subjects in both their languages. Many studies have discussed so-called 'pro-drop resetting' among immigrant communities in the USA (Heine & Kuteva, 2005: 99) including Russian (Schmitt, 2000), Spanish (Silva-Corvalán, 1994; Montrul, 2004; Myers-Scotton, 2006) and Serbian immigrants (Savić, 1995). It has also been documented elsewhere within heritage linguistics research (Polinsky, 1995, for Polish, Tamil and Kabardian; Rappaport, 1990, for American Polish, and Fenyvesi, 1994, for American Hungarian). We have a situation here in which if a shared option exists, it is more likely to be regularly used in both languages. This seems to go against the principle of Maximise Efficiency in Communication because dropping the pronoun whilst achieving the same communicative goal would have been more efficient in one of the two languages. However, bilingual *processing efficiency* is enhanced overall *at the expense of communicative efficiency* by not having to constantly switch between two patterns and by sticking instead to one pattern instead in both languages, as reflected in the principle of Maximise Common Ground. Multi-language-ready minds 'prefer' forms and meanings that can be used in both languages and in this case that option is the non-pro-drop one. We can hypothesise that this is because that makes them more efficient overall, because they then have shared mental representations and are communication-ready in whichever language is required next. This preference is not set in stone, however and there are occasions where other outcomes are detected in bilingual language use.

We can expect a different outcome that does not involve the shared retention of explicit subjects. CASP for Bilingualism operates differently when the pro-drop language is significantly stronger than non-pro-drop one (variability factor); in that case we may find the introduction of pro-drop structures into the non-pro-drop language, as Filipović and Hawkins (2013) have shown for L1 Spanish learners of L2 English, who produce sentences such as *'is a beautiful country' in their L2 English.

It is also possible that speakers may stick to the rules of each language, i.e. behave like monolinguals in each language and not maximise common ground even though there is an easy way to do so. For example, heritage speakers of Italian and Spanish living in Germany have not 'lost' the pro-drop feature from their heritage languages under the influence of German, and the production of pro-drop structures in their heritage languages does not appear to differ from that of comparable monolingual Italian and Spanish populations (Schmitz, Di Venanzio, & Scherger, 2016). This is actually not surprising, because heritage language proficiency of the bilinguals in that study seemed overall quite high, even for participants dominant in German. A heritage language is normally the language of family origin that is either incompletely acquired or has undergone attrition (see Benmamoun, Montrul & Polinsky, 2013b, for a thorough discussion on this topic). In Schmitz et al. (2016) the heritage languages Spanish and Italian were actually the dominant languages for a significant majority of the study participants even though all participants were located in Germany. The authors (Schmitz et al., 2016) argue that overall proficiency in the heritage language did not affect the results (they did have a few participants dominant in German), but it is very likely that their bilinguals said to be dominant in

German were more proficient in, or more frequently exposed to, their heritage Italian or Spanish (and therefore used the pro-drop option) than the speakers of heritage pro-drop languages who participated in the other studies that report opposing results, i.e. the use of overt subjects in pro-drop heritage languages. In most other studies the heritage languages may have been weaker, and the outputs were not as controlled as they may have been in the Schmitz et al. (2016) study, which collected narratives in a monolingual mode (e.g. when only one language was used throughout). Other studies may have been carried out in a bilingual mode (e.g. through interaction with the experimenter). This is plausible because if the task were an elicitation one for grammaticality judgements, and if the heritage language were definitely significantly weaker than the other one (e.g. Polinsky, 1995), then this would skew the preference for overt subjects and even lead some bilingual heritage speakers to consider pro-drop structures ungrammatical even though they were indeed grammatical (see Polinsky, 1995, for examples and discussion). We know that bilinguals are capable of adjusting their behaviour to the demands of the situation (see Chapter 3), and the higher their proficiency in each language the better they are at output control in each, especially in a monolingual mode, which was the case in the narrative elicitation used in Schmitz et al. (2016). As I explained earlier (Chapter 3, Section 3.6), it is in a bilingual mode, not in a monolingual mode, that we expect common ground to be maximised to a greater extent.

As pointed out in Chapter 3, there is no need to maximise common ground at all times, e.g. when a bilingual speaker is speaking to a monolingual who speaks only one of the two languages, as in the experimental elicitation set up by Schmitz et al. (2016). In a monolingual mode, we expect the use of pro-drop to be calibrated to the proficiency scale: bilinguals with balanced proficiency or with unbalanced but stronger proficiency in their pro-drop heritage languages should use pro-drop in a similar way to monolingual speakers of these heritage languages. In a bilingual mode, when both languages are active (e.g. when judging ungrammaticality in a heritage pro-drop language whilst speaking in another, non-pro-drop language), we can expect less support for pro-drop and more overt subjects in the heritage language, even with very proficient speakers, and definitely so with bilinguals whose heritage language is substantially weaker than their other language.

These CASP hypotheses can be readily tested in future research, with different language combinations, and they will be either confirmed or disconfirmed. Proficiency and dominance (which includes frequency of exposure and use) are bound to affect bilingual outputs, as are the circumstances in which bilinguals communicate, when a single language is active (monolingual mode – single-language context) or when they are using both languages in a single conversation or using both when performing in a task (bilingual mode – dual-language context).

4.2.2.2   Bare Necessities: Plurals With vs. Without the Article   It has been noted in the previous literature (e.g. Benmamoun et al., 2013b) that bilinguals seem to be attempting to 'reconcile' different grammatical rules for using definite articles with plural nouns. This is particularly interesting in cases where both languages have articles, but with only partial overlap in the rules for using them in combination with certain nouns. For example, Spanish and English differ in their semantic interpretations for nouns with articles. Generic meanings in English are generally expressed through bare plural noun phrases, as in (1a). If the definite article is used, as in (1b), the noun phrase refers to a specific group of entities (in this case, tigers; though in a limited number of cases where the plural subjects are human, the generic reference can be achieved either with or without the definite article, as in 'Italians/The Italians love pizza'; Hawkins, 1978). In Spanish, on the other hand, one cannot use bare plurals in subject position because this would be ungrammatical, as in (2a), but nouns preceded by the definite article ('los') can have either a generic or a specific reference. Sentence (2b) could either be a generic statement about tigers, or a statement about a specific group of tigers:

1a)   Tigers eat meat. (generic)

1b)   The tigers eat meat. (specific)

2a)   *Tigres comen   carne.
        Tigers eat-PRS.3PL meat

2b)   Los tigres comen   carne. (generic or specific)
        The tigers eat-PRS.3PL meat

Montrul and Ionin (2010, 2012) found that Spanish heritage speakers have a strong tendency to use bare nouns with generic reference in subject position, which as we have seen is ungrammatical in Spanish but grammatical in English. Heritage speakers of Spanish also tend to interpret definite articles in Spanish as specific in generic contexts, in line with the English pattern. The authors presented Spanish heritage speakers with an acceptability judgement task and a truth-value judgement task in English, which showed that the heritage speakers of Spanish accepted bare plurals with generic reference and definite articles with specific reference in English and were indistinguishable from a native-English-speaker group. When given the same tests in Spanish, however, there were significant differences between the Spanish native speakers and the heritage speakers. In fact, the heritage speakers were indistinguishable from L2 Spanish learners in their performance on these tasks, and, unlike the native speakers, who preferred a generic interpretation for plural definites, heritage speakers showed a preference for the specific reading instead. Thus, both L2 learners and heritage speakers exhibited influence from English in the interpretation of definite articles in Spanish (see Montrul, 2008 for more comparative analysis of L2 learners and heritage speakers).

In a similar study Serratrice et al. (2009) looked at the use of articles with generic plurals in English and Italian using monolingual and bilingual populations. English and Italian differ in the same way that English and Spanish do. Plural noun phrases (NPs) in subject position in Italian, as in other Romance languages like Spanish, always require a definite article regardless of their semantic interpretation. By contrast, English plural NPs in subject position can appear with or without a definite article, depending on whether they are interpreted as specific or as generic, as we have seen. The results of this study are said to show 'unidirectional cross-linguistic influence' from English to Italian, and this was interpreted as an 'economical choice'. Even though bare plural NPs with a generic reading in subject position are ungrammatical in Italian, English–Italian bilinguals did accept them as a grammatical option, especially if their community language was English. Whether 'bidirectional cross-linguistic influence' was also possible, and whether structural overlap and economy considerations were viable explanations were open questions awaiting further research, according to this study.

We have to note again here, as I argued in Chapter 3, that it is *efficiency not economy* that is the key driving force. It is not economical for processing to use additional items that are not needed, but it may be efficient to do so. Both options are viable in this case for maximising common ground; namely, either blocking or permitting the bare plural in subject position in both languages. The direction that is taken will ultimately depend on the internal and external factors that I have enumerated (i.e. on whether the speakers have equal or unequal proficiency, or on which language they are using and with whom they are interacting in their environment – monolinguals mainly or bilinguals). In the Serratrice et al. (2009) study it is clear that the language of the environment (English) was the dominant one, which it usually is in the case of heritage speakers. This fact, in combination with the circumstance that the learning of both languages was incomplete in children who were the participants in the Serratrice et al. (2009) study, makes it predictable that the bilinguals were overextending the use of bare plurals in subject position from English into Italian. They had been exposed to a shared option that exists in both languages, namely article + NP in subject position with specific reference, and they used that option for specific meanings, licensed in both languages and predictable in terms of maximising common ground. Nevertheless, they also introduced bare plurals for generic meanings into Italian, which violates the conventions of that language, but creates maximal common ground.

We can expect different bilingual speakers to produce different outputs here even if the same principle of Maximise Common Ground operates on all occasions. This is because internal factors modulate the way in which this key principle operates on each occasion. Balanced adult bilinguals can be expected to know where features are or are not shared, and thus the common ground is more likely to be maximised in the direction of using article + noun in both languages for specific references ('the tigers'), which is the shared option, whilst the non-shared option, bare plural ('tigers') is used only in English and article + noun is used in Spanish for generic reference. Bilinguals with unequal proficiency in their languages might either introduce bare plurals into Spanish and Italian (producing ungrammaticality), as evidenced in the heritage language studies cited above, or lose bare plurals from English, which we can expect in the cases of bilingual children growing up in Italy (with Italian as the dominant language) or L1 Italian learners of L2 English. These are all testable CASP for Bilingualism predictions.

In historical linguistics we have evidence that ungrammatical gains or losses are both viable options that arise under language contact and bilingualism, resulting in either ungrammaticality or in different form–meaning pairings. An example comes from other language pairs, also involving articles. As mentioned in Chapter 2, the definite article was created in the Slavic language Sorbian through contact with German, and the indefinite article in Basque through contact with Romance languages (Heine & Kuteva, 2005: 101). On the other hand, the definite article can also disappear due to bilingual usage, namely in heritage German spoken in Russia (see Rosenberg, 2005: 228–9).

4.2.2.3 Aspect(uality)   Another domain in which bilinguals often encounter a partial overlap between their two languages is that of aspect/aspectuality. *Aspectuality* is used here to refer to the general semantic category that encompasses meanings related to the inner temporality of events and that is expressed in numerous ways across different languages. The term *aspect* refers to a grammatical category, such as the morphologically marked categories of Slavonic languages, i.e. the many prefixes and suffixes that convey perfective and imperfective meanings in addition to their various other meanings and functions (Filipović, 2007b). English does not have this type of morphological marking and aspectual meanings in English are generally distinguished either lexically or through constructions such as the present progressive. One important traditional aspectual distinction is between so-called telic predicates (which are goal-directed/closed; such as 'eat an apple') and atelic (open-ended) predicates (such as 'eat' on its own). There is some overlap in meaning between telicity and perfectivity in the sense that both can mean completeness, but telic predicates can also refer to an action type that would have to be marked as imperfective (incomplete) in Slavonic languages (see Filipović, 2010c, for a detailed account; see also Thelin, 1990 for extensive theoretical discussion); e.g. the telic imperfective 'He read a book all day' = 'Čitao je knjigu ceo dan' (Read-[PTCP.**IPFV**.3SG.M.] COP book all day).

In a bilingual context, Benmamoun et al. (2013b) have noted that lower-proficiency heritage speakers of a Slavic language, Russian, are not consistently sensitive to the sentential aspectual operators that require use of the imperfective in this language, but instead pay more attention to the lexical aspect of the predicate, as English does. They use perfective verb forms when the predicates are telic even if the sentential environment requires the imperfective verb form. Polinsky (2008) argues further that the retention of correct uses of perfective vs. imperfective verbs in heritage speakers of Russian depends also on the frequency of the verbs themselves in different situations to which they apply (see also Filipović, 2007b, for a related discussion on lexicalised aspectuality in English motion verbs). Namely, occurrence of certain verbs in the perfective is more frequent than in the imperfective because of the nature of the actions they depict. Thus, heritage speakers do not preserve the perfective/imperfective opposition as such and the morphosyntactic connection between the two via morphological derivation, as native speakers of Russian would do. In fact, they seem to create forms which are underspecified as to aspect and aspectual interpretations are assigned based on the type of situation they refer to.

Polinsky argues that it is not really possible to say whether the bilingual use of aspect in Russian is due to the influence from English or to some creolisation of Russian that is not directly related to any influence from English. In order to disentangle the two a further source of data from heritage Russian would be required in a different linguistic environment, according to Polinsky (2008: 279), and this was unavailable. She makes a brief reference, however (ibid.), to the rise of the analytical system of aspectual marking in Finnish Russian (heritage Russian spoken in Finland), reported in Leisiö (2001), which suggests, according to Polinsky, that the influence of the host language cannot be the sole determining factor. This is presumably because Finnish is considered a morphologically complex language overall, like Russian and unlike English, and yet we still see the change from morphological complexity towards more analytical structuring of the category of aspect, which might then be explained as being due to some internal factors of language change rather than bilingual contact. The development from more synthetic to more analytic features is often attested in historical language change and is a feature of simplification that need not be due to bilingualism exclusively, though a number of simplification instances (such as, for example, reduction in gender systems) do appear to be 'highly correlated with external contact' (Dahl, 2004: 200). However, the specific way in which aspect changed in Finnish Russian may still point to bilingualism as the cause. In the aspectual marking of Finnish Russian that

Leisiö talks about there is a striking parallel between Finnish Russian and Finnish. Even though Finnish is morphologically complex with an abundance of synthetic morphology, it has an analytical aspectual system that could have affected the heritage (Finnish) Russian spoken in Finland, or at least could have triggered the change (as Heine and Kuteva, 2005 note in other contexts). In fact, Leisiö (2001: 62) herself states that we can hypothesise that heritage Russian–Finnish contact is the reason for the systematic development of the new aspectual meanings in heritage Russian in Finland. Overall, her study of a number of areas of Finnish Russian supports the view that contact-driven bilingualism has a fundamental role in language change (Leisiö, 2001: 246).

It is telling that Russian aspect use by heritage speakers has changed in a different direction under the influence of English (loss of a paradigm) vs. in Finland (rise of the analytical aspectual system), which does indeed point to the likelihood of this being bilingual-contact-induced language change. In order to establish this with more confidence we would need data from heritage Russian spoken in an environment that has an equally (or near equally) complex verbal aspect morphology, exactly on a par with that of Russian, and then see if simplification of the heritage system still takes place (e.g. Serbian–Russian bilinguals living in Serbia vs. in Russia). This has proved difficult, partly because, as Scontras, Fuchs and Polinsky (2015: 3) note, 'the contact language in most of the heritage speakers tested to date is English', which is poor in morphology, and we need more data from more language contact combinations other than with English. We have to be cautious because other processes not due to contact may also be taking place that lead to language change, as highlighted by Rosenberg (2005), albeit with examples from a different area of grammar, namely the reduction of case morphology in heritage German across the world. In particular, in the case of heritage German spoken in Russia, he notes that direct Russian influence is rather unlikely because Russian has a complex case system itself (six cases for nouns, pronouns and adjectives). Rosenberg argues instead that case loss in heritage German is an internally induced change. However, another contact-related explanation may be possible in the case of heritage German in Russia. German and Russian are phonetically and morphologically sufficiently different that even if there is some similarity in case semantics at an abstract level, there are enough differences in form and grammar to inspire heritage speakers of German in Russia, especially the younger generations, to simplify their heritage language, which would be a very common outcome in heritage bilingualism.

Our argument here is not that all language change is due to bilingualism. The crucial point is that when a partial overlap exists in some area of the two languages of a bilingual, such as aspectuality, bilinguals will maximise common ground by adhering to those patterns that work in both languages. This is what the Russian–English and Russian–Finnish bilingual data show. There has been an extension of the past-participle construction in heritage Russian to include perfective aspects more systematically, as is done in Finnish. For Russian–English speakers the common ground is found in the preferred adherence to lexical aspect, whereby telic action types receive perfective interpretation and the atelic ones imperfective in the bilinguals' weaker language, heritage Russian, as a result of the stronger language, English (see Benmamoun et al., 2013a, and Benmamoun et al., 2013b for more discussion and exemplification). The maximising of common ground in L2 is attested in both directions, i.e. both when English is the stronger language (L1) and Russian the weaker (L2), as in the heritage Russian studies discussed above, and when Russian is the stronger language (L1) and English the weaker (L2). Wenzell (1989) found that beginner and intermediate Russian learners of L2 English map the meanings of past forms in English onto the Russian perfective and use all other verb inflections to mark the imperfective aspect. This pattern is probably more characteristic of lower or intermediate L2 English users whose first language was Russian, as Pavlenko and Jarvis (2002) point out. When it comes to bilinguals with two L1s, i.e. balanced bilinguals with equal proficiency in both languages, there would be different predicted outcomes – they would be more likely to use full derivational paradigms of perfective/imperfective verbs in Russian and to rely on lexical aspect when speaking English. The same prediction can also be made for unbalanced bilinguals for occasions when they are speaking their stronger language (either L1 Russian or L1 English).

It would be interesting to test both L1 English/ L2 Russian and L1 Russian/ L2 English unbalanced bilinguals at different proficiency levels in order to see whether and how their outputs differ with regard to aspectuality at different stages of acquisition and to check whether and when they move towards more language-specific use in each language (e.g. if they use full perfective/imperfective paradigm in L2 Russian or if they move beyond the simple mapping of perfective forms onto past simple in L2 English). Language typology is likely to play a significant role here, in particular with respect to the morphosyntactic complexity of L1 paradigms. Filipović and Vidaković (2010) found that trends in L2 acquisition at different levels of proficiency may be different depending on which language is the L1. In their study of the acquisition of Serbian and English as second languages by L1 English and L2 Serbian speakers respectively, they discovered that Serbian L1 speakers master aspectuality in their L2 English at earlier levels of overall proficiency then their L1 English/ L2 Serbian peers master the L2 Serbian aspectual system (see Filipović & Vidaković, 2010 for details). This line of research can be informative for our view of what can and should be expected from learners of different languages as L2s at different proficiency levels, which could in turn benefit L2 teaching and the assessment of L2 proficiency (see Hawkins & Filipović, 2012 for more discussion).

A further systematic study should include a variety of language pairs with typologically different aspectual systems as well as different bilingual speakers (e.g. early vs. heritage vs. L2 bilinguals) interacting under different circumstances (e.g. monolingual vs. bilingual mode). This is needed in order to control for the interplay between internal factors, like proficiency, and external factors, such as demands of the communicative situation, that affect the general processes defined by CASP for Bilingualism. We have seen in this section that proficiency and dominance affect the way bilinguals express aspectuality in their languages, but this may vary additionally based on whom they are talking to, e.g. other bilinguals, one monolingual in either language or two monolinguals, one in each language. Methodologically, we can think of ways to ensure that the mode is bilingual, e.g. by arranging a bilingual dinner table scenario (see Preface) so that the pressure of online competition between two linguistic systems is actively maintained. We would predict that all bilinguals will maximise common ground more in a bilingual mode than in a monolingual mode, and more in an informal situation than in a formal one. Bilinguals with equal proficiency are more likely to maximise common ground within the boundaries of grammaticality in each language whilst those with unequal proficiency (heritage speakers and L2 learners) may stretch the common ground beyond grammaticality in their weaker language. In a monolingual mode, we would predict that bilinguals will come as close to monolingual norms as their proficiency in each and as their language dominance allows. There will be fewer instances of common ground in a monolingual than in a bilingual mode, but common ground may still be in evidence due to habitual bilingual use, which is the reason why bilinguals are not two monolinguals in one.

4.2.2.4 Moving On: Motion Constructions   Motion event lexicalisation has received a lot of attention since the seminal works of Len Talmy and Dan Slobin. Talmy (1985, 1991) proposed a semantic typology of languages, whilst Slobin (1996, 1997, 2003, 2006) examined its effects in different languages empirically. Talmy observed that the world's languages can be classified based on semantic criteria relating to event lexicalisation. Languages habitually express either path or manner in the verb (i.e. English 'run out of the house' vs. Spanish 'salir de la casa corriendo' = 'exit the house running'). The path-verb group includes Romance languages, and also Greek, Turkish and Arabic, whilst the manner-verb group is exemplified by the Germanic and Slavonic families. The consequences of this motion event typology are: (a) that Spanish and similar ('path-verb') languages (e.g. French, Italian, Greek, Turkish, Hebrew) have fewer manner verbs than English (and the English type of languages, such as Germanic, Slavonic, Mandarin Chinese and others in the 'manner-verb' group, see Talmy, 1985); (b) they express manner information in a non-obligatory constituent (e.g. adverbial); (c) they have syntactic restrictions when it comes to manner verbs + path particle combinations (the boundary-crossing constraint; Aske, 1989); and (d) their general narrative preferences are characterised by a lack of information about the manner of motion. Slobin argues that this typological distinction affects the way people 'think for speaking' in their languages. Namely, different areas of language use are affected by this typological preference within a specific language, and language-specific effects on production have been widely attested in various contexts, e.g. spoken and written discourse, translation, metaphorical thinking and memory for events (see Slobin 1996, 1997, 2003, 2006; Filipović, 2007a, 2007b, 2008, 2009, 2010a, 2010b, 2011, 2013a, 2013b; Ibarretxe-Antuñano & Filipović, 2013; Filipović & Ibarretxe-Antuñano, 2015).

The research on motion events has been substantial, both with monolingual and bilingual speakers, and has included both early and late adult bilinguals. The results reported in numerous studies appear at first to be very mixed, with different effects on verbalisation and on cognition more generally, and sometimes with a lack of language-specific effects. We look at some representative studies here and illustrate how CASP for Bilingualism can help us understand where these differences in the results may be coming from and how we can account for them.

For example, Hohenstein, Eisenberg and Naigles (2006) carried out an oral verbalisation experiment where the participants, early and late bilinguals, were asked to describe motion events in both Spanish and English. The participants used primarily Spanish in their personal lives and both English and Spanish in their work or at school. The authors note that the bilinguals differed from monolinguals most obviously when speaking English, displaying 'only L1 (Spanish) to L2 (English) transfer' (Hohenstein et al., 2006: 258). Namely, the bilinguals speaking English manifested lower manner modifier use and bare or path-verb use, 'both properties more typical of Spanish motion event description' (ibid.). They report that bare verbs such as 'go' were used to the same extent in both languages by the bilinguals and that the bilingual participants 'made less of a distinction between the two languages in the grammatical aspect of motion event description'. This pattern (e.g. 'exit running'), whilst not typical or preferred in English monolingual use, is nonetheless perfectly grammatical in this predominantly 'manner-verb' language. Thus, we have a situation here where there is clearly a partial overlap – one pattern that works in both languages ('He entered the house running') and this pattern is the one preferred overall by bilinguals. This is because, I would argue, the bilinguals have evidently 'figured out' what works in both languages, and they are thus being efficient in maximising common ground. Bilinguals with equal proficiency, as well as those with English as their stronger language, can be expected to reduce the preference for this pattern on those occasions when the activation of Spanish is reduced, e.g. when speaking only English to English monolinguals, but they are still likely to use it more than English monolinguals due to the entrenched preference for maximising common ground with their other language, Spanish (thereby maximising the overlap in their mental representations for the two languages and being multi-language ready; see Chapter 3).

There are more studies that confirm this preference for a motion construction frame that works for both languages. Lai, Rodriguez and Narasimhan (2014) asked if bilingual speakers would flexibly shift their event classification preferences based on the language they used to verbalise events presented to them in an experiment. English–Spanish bilinguals and monolingual controls described motion events in either Spanish or English and they also subsequently judged the similarity of motion events in a triad task (i.e. how similar the original event is to two alternatives: one with the same path/different manner and the other with the same manner/different path to the original). They found that late bilinguals (who acquired both language after the age of 6) based their judgements on path similarity more often when Spanish was used to describe the motion events than when English was used, so the language currently in use seems to have guided the classification criteria. By contrast, early bilinguals (who acquired both their languages before the age of 6) categorised events as more similar if they shared the path of motion regardless of the language being used, i.e. in both English and Spanish. It seems that regardless of the language used in the experiment, early bilinguals adhered to the construction frame that works in both their languages. Late bilinguals were less efficient, and possibly less proficient, switching between two different thinking-for-speaking paradigms. Probably, they just had not yet 'figured out' how to maximise common ground. Early bilinguals were more efficient – by using the same mechanism in both languages and being multi-language-ready (see further discussion in the Conclusion section (Section 4.5) of this chapter; see also Chapter 2, section 2.4.2).

Kersten et al. (2010) detect a similar difference in the context of learning novel labels for actions. Late bilinguals are more likely to rely on context when learning new verbs, relating them to the path of motion in a Spanish-speaking context and to the manner of motion in an English-speaking one, as can be predicted by the typological difference between Spanish and English. However, early bilinguals do not rely on context when categorising. The attentional preference of bilinguals may be under 'joint control' of the two languages since they are likely to have been exposed to both in equal or near-equal measure in their early lives. This results in 'attention to attributes that have previously been discovered to be diagnostic of category membership in either language'. Kersten et al. (2010: 652) conclude that:

it is certainly plausible to propose that bilinguals who are exposed to two languages at an early age experience reduced separation of the contexts in which the two languages are heard. Linguistic relativity effects may thus be more difficult to observe in early bilinguals than in monolinguals or late bilinguals, because cognitive performance in early bilinguals may generally reflect the influences of multiple languages.

A different type of motion construction has also been investigated in the contexts of bilingual acquisition and bilingual use, namely the caused motion construction. Engemann, Harr and Hickmann (2012) conducted a bidirectional production experiment whereby caused motion descriptions were elicited in bilingual children, in adult second-language learners and in monolinguals. French has multiple options for expressing caused motion, more than English, which has the typical, habitual pattern of manner verb + path preposition, as seen in Talmy's typology. Engemann et al. (2012: 267) illustrate the lexicalisation possibilities in French with the following examples, which sound rather atypical and even ungrammatical in English:

3a)   Il descends la valise (en tirant).
3b)   *He descends the case (by pulling).

4a)   Il tire la valise (jusq'en bas).
4b)   He pulls the case (to the bottom).

5a)   Il fait rouler la balle (en descendant).
5b)   He makes the ball roll (whilst descending).

English meanwhile has one clearly preferred pattern, with manner expressed in the verb and path outside of the verb, as usual, and with an additional direct object for the transitive verb, as in *He pulls the suitcase down to the bottom* or *He rolls the ball down the hill*. Note that both French and English can use the manner verb in expressions of motion events that do not have any boundaries to cross (e.g. when moving to, from or within a space or a location), but if there is boundary crossing in these events (e.g. moving out of or into a delimited space), French, like Spanish, uses the path verbs instead, as predicted in Talmy's typology (see Aske, 1989 for the original proposal of the boundary-crossing constraint; see also Filipović, 2007b for an overview and thorough discussion of cross-linguistic examples). The difference in lexicalisation strategies between the two languages has profound effects on bilingual acquisition and use. The verbalisations by bilinguals in Engemann et al. (2012) differ significantly from those of monolinguals. Namely, bilinguals overuse cross-linguistically overlapping patterns, and in this case, the strategy available to both English and French is the manner verb + direct object + path preposition (example 4a). This confirms previous findings that there seems to be a general mechanism of 'enhancing convergence between bilinguals' two languages by reinforcing patterns that work in both languages' – i.e. for maximising common ground, in our terms (Engemann et al., 2012; see also Müller & Hulk, 2001; Nicol, Teller & Greth, 2001; Torbio, 2004; Flecken, 2010; Filipović, 2011; Lai et al., 2014).

Sometimes maximising common ground can result in a pattern that is not the shared one. A study by Larrañaga et al. (2012) has shown that the English motion construction (manner verb + path preposition) is used in L2 Spanish even though it is not licensed in that language (e.g. *'corrió en el banco' = 'she/ he ran into the bank'). The authors argue that the reason for this is minimal L2 exposure, and this is to be expected according to our CASP model. Proficiency, as one of the key internal (variability) factors is essential for predicting variation in bilingual behaviour. Less proficient late bilinguals often stretch common ground beyond grammaticality, which early and more proficient bilinguals do not do. Again, bilinguals with late and probably unbalanced proficiency show signs of not having completely mastered how to maximise common ground. In the Lai et al. (2014) study cited above late bilinguals were not maximising common ground when they could have (in contrast to early bilinguals), whilst in the Larrañaga et al. (2012) study the late bilinguals did maximise common ground when they should not have done so. We expect both of these outputs from late and unbalanced bilinguals, who either consider their languages to be too different (in line with psychotypology assumptions; Kellerman, 1983) or simply display incomplete knowledge about grammaticality in their weaker (L2) language.

We can therefore tease apart different processes that have been detected in early and late bilingual processing using three different studies. The fact that the studies discussed used different methodologies does not affect the interpretation of key outcomes, namely the subtle differences in language processing among different bilinguals. Very proficient bilinguals, both early and some late ones, are more likely to maximise common ground and use the most efficient strategy to do so by favouring the shared pattern within the realms of grammaticality in both languages. By doing so, they may be using a pattern that is the majority one in one language and a minority one in the other. They may maximise common ground more in the bilingual mode than in the monolingual. Late and less proficient bilinguals may also maximise common ground, but less often since they may not have figured out what the common ground is, or they do so in ways that are ungrammatical in one of their languages because they have not yet mastered when and how to do so grammatically.

4.3   Maximise Common Ground: Presence vs. Absence

When one language has a category or a structure and the other one does not, then common ground is maximised by using the resources of each language to express equivalent meanings in both, or by avoiding the category or structure that is present only in one of the languages. This may lead to ungrammaticality in the event that the relevant item is obligatory in one of the languages. Again, maximising common ground may not take place at all depending on the communicative situation – it is possible that bilinguals will stick to using language-specific categories and structures in one of their languages, the one that requires them. We need to account for when, how and why maximising common ground may or may not occur, and CASP for Bilingualism enables us to do so. I explore these possible outcomes by looking at a number of different categories and structures in typologically different languages spoken by bilinguals.

4.3.1   Evidentiality: Saying (or Not) Where You Got It From

Evidentiality refers to identification of the source of one's information in linguistic descriptions. Evidentiality is a category that is marked obligatorily in some languages, for example Turkish. In Turkish the inflectional affix ('-di') signals that the reported event was directly witnessed by the speaker, whilst the affix ('-miş') indicates that the reported information was obtained indirectly (e.g. heard from someone or inferred based on circumstances around the event). Several studies have argued that the indirect evidential is the marked term due to its semantic complexity and reference to different information sources (i.e., inferences and reports), whilst the direct evidential is the unmarked form used to refer to actually witnessed past events (Slobin & Aksu, 1982; Aksu-Koç & Slobin, 1986). This distinction in evidentiality can be seen in the following examples (from Arslan, Bastiaanse & Felser, 2015: 3):

6a)   Adam elmayı   yedi.
         man   apple-ACC   eat-DIRECT EVIDENTIAL
         'The man ate the apple.' [witnessed]

6b)   Adam elmayı   yemiş.
         man   apple-ACC   eat-INDIRECT EVIDENTIAL
         'The man ate the apple.' [reported or inferred]

Evidentiality is a concept that can be verbalised in English too, but importantly, the distinction between direct and indirect evidentiality is neither grammaticalised nor obligatory as it is in Turkish. We can say in English 'It seems that the stock market has crashed' instead of 'The stock market has crashed' if we were not in the stockbroker's office to actually witness the crash itself. But we are not obliged by the grammar of English to signal this distinction. Speakers of Turkish have to make this distinction all the time because they need to attach one or the other evidential morpheme to the verb.

CASP for Bilingualism predicts that bilinguals will seek to maximise common ground in this area, either by introducing the evidentiality category from Turkish into the other language that does not have it, or by moving towards not having evidentiality distinctions in both Turkish and their other language. Both outcomes have been reported in the literature. Arslan, Bastiaanse and Felser (2015) report that second-generation Turkish/Dutch early bilingual adults make a large number of substitution errors by inappropriately using direct evidentials in contexts that required an indirect evidential form. They note that there was also a simplification of the Turkish evidentiality system in Turkish heritage grammars among the bilinguals in their study. The direct evidential morpheme '-di' has become the default past-tense marker in heritage Turkish without reference to any specific evidential content. In long-term language contact, evidentiality can also completely disappear (see Section 4.1 of this chapter, option ii.c). A small Turkic population (a Turkish dialect in the Trabzon area on the eastern Black Sea coast) surrounded by non-Turkic speakers has lost the evidentiality system from their grammar altogether (Johanson, 2003).

In addition to disappearing from the language that has it, evidentiality can also appear with consistency under language contact in a language that does not have it (Section 4.1, option ii.a). Aikhenvald (2002) documents the introduction of evidentiality into Portuguese spoken by Tariana-Portuguese bilinguals in Brazil. Tariana is a North Arawak language of north-west Amazonia and it distinguishes four categories of evidentials via the use of clitics (Aikhenvald, 2002: 117–27), namely visual, non-visual, inferred and reported. Tariana Portuguese has corresponding lexical means that are assigned the values for the corresponding Tariana expressions: visual ('eu vi'= 'I saw' or 'eu tenha experiencia' = 'I have experience'), non-visual ('eu senti/ecutei' = 'I felt/ heard'), inferred ('parece' = 'it appears/seems'), and reported ('diz que' = 'it is said that'). Heine and Kuteva note (2005: 74) that evidentiality in Tariana Portuguese is on the way to achieving full category status. They observe further that grammatical change in general, and grammaticalisation in particular, start out with pragmatically motivated patterns of discourse. Once language contact gives rise to major usage patterns, this may lead to a transition from pragmatically motivated to morphosyntactic templates and to the emergence of new grammatical (functional) categories (e.g. the development of articles in Slavic variants under German contact influence; see Chapter 2, section 2.3). Preferential uses that develop as a result of bilingualism within and across minds can gradually become new grammatical categories, but they need not end up being completely grammaticalised since the process can be 'discontinued at any stage of its development' (ibid.).

Slobin (2016) noticed that fluent Turkish speakers of L2 English use expressions like 'apparently' and 'it seems' in abundance which, although 'perfectly grammatical and contextually appropriate', still sounds 'pragmatically unsettling'. A similar thing happened to Slobin himself upon his return from Turkey (Slobin, 2016: 108), where he was sensitised 'to a dimension that is not foregrounded in ordinary English discourse' but is part of habitual language use and processing in Turkish. Slobin (2016) gives examples of cases of language change through bilingualism, whereby both administratively dominant or administratively non-dominant languages can undergo this kind of change, for example Andean Spanish in contact with Quechua and Aymara, and also certain Balkan languages in contact with Turkish. For example, the pluperfect is recruited to mark a non-witnessed past event in Andean Spanish, as in the following examples:

7a)   Hoy día llegó   su mamá de él.
         Today arrive-3SG.PST his mother of him
         'Today his mother arrived (and I saw her arrive).'

7b)   Hoy día había   llegado   su mamá de él.
         Today have-3SG.PST arrive-PTCP his mother of him
         'Today his mother arrived (but I didn't see her arrive)'.

Slobin (2016: 105) explains that 'in the processes of thinking for speaking, speakers attend to dimensions of experience that are available for morphosyntactic and lexical coding, which in situations of long-term language contact results in tendencies, in some conceptual domains, for common patterning across languages'. In order to understand the processes that lead to this contact-induced change it is essential to understand the social factors involved in bilingualism. Addition of new meanings from one language into another normally involves prolonged language contact and simultaneous bilingualism, and the existence of a significant number of speakers who have mastered both systems (Trudgill, 2010, 2011). When evidentiality (or any other feature) is lost, this is more likely to happen due to unbalanced, adult bilingualism in which the dominant (stronger) language in the community, spoken by the great majority, does not have a specific feature or a structure, such as evidentiality, that the other, weaker language does (ibid.). These adult bilinguals will probably be a minority population within the community of monolingual speakers of the language that does not have the feature in question and they would not have enough power in numbers to exert their influence on the monolingual majority. As we saw in Chapter 2, Section 2.3, population numbers, as well as the nature of the social relationships and interactions, affect the kinds of bilingualism that will ensue and consequently the direction of language change resulting from bilingualism (see Trudgill 2010, 2011, for more details and more examples from case studies).

We thus have evidence from both language acquisition and historical linguistics that illustrates the different ways in which common ground is maximised, by either losing the original evidentiality distinctions (in the case of a heritage language) or gaining evidentiality distinctions in change due to bilingual contact. We can explain the processes that lead to these outcomes using CASP for Bilingualism. If expressive power is maximised in both languages, then the correct grammatical forms and rules for evidentiality will have been acquired and used. Maximise Common Ground will then lead to the expression of evidential meanings in both languages even though this sometimes goes against communicative efficiency (because excessive information about the source is not required in English) and it results in more processing effort for the speaker and the hearer, who must produce and comprehend syntactically longer and semantically richer expressions. Maximise Common Ground trumps the pressures in favour of language-specific communicative efficiency and of minimised processing effort here since, I would argue, it is more efficient overall to use the same pattern in both languages than to constantly keep switching between two different ones. If the language without evidentials is the stronger one in a bilingual, then the evidential system may be reduced and ultimately disappear. Social circumstances of use also determine the extent to which evidentiality will be explicitly expressed. For example, in bilingual interactions within a single communicative situation (e.g. chatting at a dinner table simultaneously in Turkish and English) we can expect more maximising of common ground and evidentiality expressions in both languages. In interactions with English monolinguals we can expect fewer instances of common ground by bilinguals if they are equally proficient in both languages and use both with equal frequency, and we expect more if they have Turkish as their stronger language and use Turkish more often. Proficient bilinguals adjust by being more communicatively efficient and reducing production and comprehension effort while matching the different evidentiality expectations of their respective hearers in each language.

4.3.2   Gender: When Bottle Is a She and Wine Is a He

Gender is an interesting category to discuss in the context of bilingualism because it seems that maximising common ground can only go in one direction here, namely towards the loss of grammatical marking in the language that has it. Introducing grammatical morphemes for gender into another language, or any kind of inflectional morphology for that matter, is unlikely (e.g. see MacWhinney, 2005). The introduction of pure morphological forms into a language may be rare, but it does happen (as in the case of the already mentioned Turkish interrogative suffix '-mi' presumably calqued into Afghan Arabic; see Chapter 3, section 3.1 and Comrie, 2008 for some examples of morphological imports). Similarly, using lexical means to express grammatical categories, as is done, for example, in evidentiality, is not an option in this case. It seems that bilinguals will either lose gender distinctions altogether or keep them in the one language that has them and not use them when they speak the language that does not have grammatical gender. Keeping the two languages apart and behaving like monolinguals in each would seem to be the best option in this context, since the other option, losing gender altogether, leads to ungrammaticality in one of the two languages, which can significantly impede communication. This is precisely what the research has found. As discussed in Chapter 2, Section 2.2.5.1, Kousta, Vinson, and Vigliocco (2008) have shown that Italian–English bilingual speakers behave like monolingual English speakers when the task is in English and like monolingual Italian speakers when the task is in Italian.

However, we also saw in Chapter 2 that gender does have a conceptual, non-linguistic effect. Boroditsky, Schmidt and Phillips (2003) have shown that gender categories from the language that marks it grammatically (e.g. Spanish or German) are invoked in the second language (English) that does not mark it for the purpose of grouping objects in a categorisation task. Similarly, Forbes et al. (2008) showed that bilingual speakers can attribute gender-related qualities based on one language to objects in their other language that does not have grammatical gender. Grammatical gender-marking in one language is easily relatable to semantic categories of gender and it is easily accessible as a problem-solving strategy that can be used in any language (see Tversky, 2011 for a succinct critical discussion of 'language as a strategy'). Bilinguals who speak a language with grammatical gender are well aware of this and can easily shift from purely grammatical to semantic reference, sometimes just playfully, as I have done personally many times, by calling a good bottle of wine a 'she' and 'a real beauty' referring to the content of the bottle ('flaša' = 'bottle' and is feminine in Serbian), or when my Italian father-in-law assigns male attributes to a good wine by describing it as 'il signor vino' = 'the gentleman-wine' ('vino'= 'wine' is masculine in Italian). Maximising common ground needs to be kept in check here (see Section 4.1, option ii.b) – we can neither introduce grammatical gender into English nor lose it from Serbian or Italian, because this would lead to misunderstanding. The cost to communicative efficiency would be too high, and by sticking to language-specific patterns in each language (e.g. explicit gender-marking for objects in Serbian and no gender-marking in English) we ensure that communicative efficiency is maximised. Slips like the one mentioned earlier in Chapter 2 (calling my husband's handkerchief a 'she') occur only occasionally because I control my output well, though I can on occasion produce gender-marking via pronouns in English that is not intentional. Somebody with my kind of L1 background and with lower proficiency in English would be more likely to maximise common ground by marking gender for objects in English more often and to confuse interlocutors in the process, who would struggle to identify the intended object-referent (they would look for animate entities instead).

Long term, the drive to maximise common ground in gender-marking may lead to attrition, as Lohndal and Westergaard (2016) argue. They noticed attrition in the gender system of Norwegian spoken as a heritage language in the USA, which resulted in overgeneralisation of the most common masculine gender at the expense of the feminine and the neuter. They state that gender in heritage Norwegian is a vulnerable category due to the lack of transparency of gender assignment in that language. Complete loss of gender is also possible, though this may not necessarily be caused (entirely) by bilingualism. English, for example, lost its grammatical gender system during the Middle English period, which saw the overall decay of inflectional endings and declensional classes. In the case of Middle English, this decay seems to have been 'incipient in the language and accelerated by language contact' (Curzan, 2003: 53). Interestingly, a few authors cite contact with Old Norse as a likely source for the loss of gender in Middle English. Curzan (2003) explains that this is because both Old English and Old Norse were similar enough to be at least partially comprehensible. They had cognate lexicons with different inflectional systems and because they were similar enough both were likely to be used as a lingua franca. The speakers were then facing different inflectional endings being attached to very similar cognate lexical items and this may have led to 'reliance on other means to express grammatical function and the decline in inflectional ending articulation or use' (Curzan, 2003: 52; see also Trudgill, 2010: 33 for the view that inflectional attrition started rather through Late British (Celtic)–Old English contact, and was reinforced by Old Norse).

Unlike evidentiality, which has a clear semantic basis that can be formalised and grammaticalised in one but not the other language, grammatical gender (e.g. masculine vs. feminine) does not have this kind of meaning content, though its relation with semantic gender (male vs. female) can create some parallels for common ground, which as we saw may be useful as classification criteria but which may also lead to ungrammaticality and misunderstanding. The more proficient bilinguals are, the more likely they are to keep their two languages apart when it comes to gender. The cost is too high for common ground to be maximised (e.g. it leads to misassignment or failure to assign reference, or to breakdown of communication) and thus bilinguals will restrain the principle of Maximise Common Ground when it comes to gender, especially bilinguals who are very proficient in both languages.

4.3.3   *Intentionality and the 'Affective Dative' Construction*

Consider the following sentence: 'The man dropped a bag on the floor'. Did the man do it on purpose or not? English does not require speakers to state on every occasion whether something was done on purpose or not, and English sentences are often ambiguous in this regard. In Spanish however, and in many other languages (e.g. Serbian), different verbs or constructions must regularly be used to express the distinction between intentional and non-intentional actions in the cases such as these below:

8a)   *El niño rompió   el juguete.*
       The boy break-3SG.PST   the toy
       'The boy broke the toy'

8b)   *Se   le   rompió   el juguete al   niño.*
       PART PRON.-**DAT** break-3SG.PST the toy   to-the boy
       'The boy broke the toy accidentally.'

9a)   *Dečak   je   slomio   igračku.*
       Boy-NOM.M be-COP   break-PST.PTCP.M   toy-ACC.F
       'The boy broke the toy'

9b)   *Slomila   mu   se   igračka.*
       break-PST.PTCP.F PRON- **DAT**.M PART toy-NOM.F
       'The boy broke the toy accidentally.'

The examples in (8b) and (9b) are *affective dative constructions*, for which there is no exact equivalent in English. Languages provide speakers with different words and constructions for describing different kinds of events. Some languages require speakers to consistently give more details about certain aspects of the events, like intentionality, whilst others do not oblige their speakers to provide these details. English does not require speakers to mark events as intentional or non-intentional and sentences are often ambiguous in this respect, e.g. 'The man dropped the bag' can refer to either intentional or accidental dropping. The distinction can be specified more precisely but it is not obligatory to do so. English verbs such as 'break' or 'drop', are all ambiguous and can be used for intentional and non-intentional events alike. There are more options for describing a causation event in English, and the same event can be described as 'John broke the glass', 'The glass was/got broken' or 'The glass broke', depending on how much information we know or want to reveal about the event (Berk-Seligson, 1983), or how much 'blameworthiness' (Gibbons, 2003) we think should be assigned. However, there are no rules or restrictions in grammar or use for these constructions with respect to intentionality, and each can be used in reference to both intentional and non-intentional events (Filipović, 2013a, 2013b, 2018). By contrast, languages like Spanish and Serbian have means to draw the distinction between intentional and non-intentional events explicitly and habitually through the consistent use of different verbs or different constructions that clearly specify whether an agent did something on purpose or not.

This affective dative construction, according to Pountain (2003: 116), is an extremely frequent construction in Spanish. There is no real equivalent in

English, except perhaps for some marginal examples like 'The car engine died on me'. This construction is possible with only a limited number of verbs and is not really as frequent and as productive as the Spanish affective dative construction. In most cases, this rare and unproductive English construction does not work; e.g. 'X fell on me' or 'X dropped on me' does not mean, as it does in Spanish, that I was non-intentionally involved in a falling or dropping incident; it means that somebody/something landed on me. Thus, we must consider whether constructional options are available and what their frequency of use is, when comparing languages.

How do bilinguals cope with an affective dative construction in one language that is not matched in the other? They maximise common ground by expressing this construction meaning lexically, for example, by adding information on intentionality via adverbs and adverbial phrases. Not all bilinguals do so, however. Balanced bilinguals in both languages and those whose stronger language is Spanish maximise common ground in this way. Those with L1 English do not – they maximise common ground by avoiding the affective dative construction altogether (see Filipović, 2018).

Why does this all make sense from an efficiency point of view? After all, we may be overburdening the processor with more items to deal with in a sentence and, in the long run, complexifying one of our languages when we introduce new constructions or grammatical rules or categories from another language, although the recipient language was apparently doing just fine and serving its speakers well without this influx. This adjustment between grammars may seem counter-intuitive when viewed from a purely monolingual perspective, and it may seem to lead to inefficiency in communication. However, it is still efficient (see Chapter 3).

In bilingual communication, efficiency from maximising common ground becomes particularly evident in cases where speakers appear to be providing too much of what may seem to be unnecessary/unrequired information in one language under the influence of another language in which such information is obligatory (e.g. by constantly adding 'accidentally' vs. 'on purpose' in English). It may appear that these speakers are unnecessarily complicating or complexifying their message, but in fact they are doing something in which an over-arching and stronger efficiency lies elsewhere. Namely, even though distinctions are drawn, and specifications made that are required in only one of their languages, drawing the same distinctions in both is indeed most efficient for their mental representation of both languages, for their thinking-for-speaking routines and for their multi-language readiness in communication, preferable to having to switch constantly between two different patterns.

Avoidance is also a useful mechanism for making common ground when grammaticality is not at stake and only some information loss occurs rather than complete communication breakdown. Avoidance is more likely to happen with some typological contrasts more than others. Whilst avoiding gender-marking may not be possible in languages that mark it without incurring misunderstanding, avoiding the use of the affective dative construction is possible at substantially lesser cost since using other grammatical structures would get most of the message across (apart from the intentionality detail). Filipović (2018) has shown that L1 English/L2 Spanish speakers almost never use the affective dative construction for the expressions of events whereas Spanish monolinguals and Spanish–English balanced bilinguals use it almost 100 per cent of the time when describing non-intentional events. This disparity could be due to incomplete or improper acquisition of the construction itself by L1 English learners of L2 Spanish (see Filipović, 2018). The frequency of this construction is very high in Spanish native use and it is considered typical of the Spanish language, but it has very low overall frequency in Spanish as an L2. A cursory look at the Spanish Learner Language Oral Corpus – SPLLOC (www.splloc.soton.ac.uk/dosearch.php) reveals that there are only a few occur-rences, involving just one verb ('se le cae' = 'to her/him X falls').

4.4   Maximise Common Ground: Incompatibility

Some language contrasts involve opposing and incompatible strategies for structuring information, in grammar or in use. One language may have subject-verb-object word order (SVO) and the other its mirror opposite, subject-object-verb (SOV). One language may prefer one discourse strategy whilst the other prefers a different and opposed one. How do bilinguals deal with contrastive options such as these? Let us look at word order first.

4.4.1   Word Order: Looking in the Mirror

Japanese is an SOV (verb (head of phrase element)-late) language and English an SVO (verb (head of phrase element)-early) language. We have seen that bilinguals strive to maximise common ground when dealing with two systems. It is inefficient to switch from one pattern to the other all the time, but it seems on this occasion that bilinguals have no choice. Adopting Japanese word order in English and vice versa would lead to severe ungrammaticality and to impaired communication – hearers would be confused at best or would not understand English sentences like *'John the book read'. It seems that sticking to the word order of each language is the only option in this case, and this is indeed something that we find in the literature on bilingual adults with such language pairs. We know that for a priming effect to be found across languages, the primed structure has to be sufficiently similar in the two languages. This means that structures with different word orders cannot be primed, as demonstrated by the lack of this effect found for German and

English passive structures, due to German using verb-final word order in passives (Loebell & Bock, 2003). The typological distance between English and Japanese word order means that learners of these two languages as L2s, even at the earliest stages of acquisition, eschew the maximising of common ground and do not try to use one or the other word order in both languages (Section 4.1, option iii.a). Japanese learners of L2 English do not use SOV in their L2, even in the earliest stages of L2 acquisition (see Filipović & Hawkins, 2013; see also Chapter 3). On the other hand, speakers of L1 languages with flexible word order like Spanish do not have the same incentive, because even when they use their L1 word order, which is not licensed in their L2 English, communication is not significantly impaired since the differences between English and Spanish are typologically relatively minor (both are basically SVO languages). When the cost to communication is not so high (because the typological gap is smaller), we do see examples of maximising common ground in word order amongst adult L2 bilinguals. For instance, Filipović and Hawkins (2013) show that Spanish learners of L2 English transfer their pro-drop patterns along with a number of un-English word orders, such as 'Light NP Shift' (*'I like very much sweets') and post-posed subjects (*'Yesterday came my boyfriend').

This difference in the cost to efficient communication can enable us to predict both bilingual behaviours and also more long-term language changes: the smaller the differences between two languages, the easier it will be to resolve them by maximising common ground and with less impact on communicative efficiency.

However, we do see evidence of common ground in word order in bilingual-child language acquisition. Bilingual children have been reported to introduce word order norms from one language into the other in which those norms are ungrammatical. An example is given in Yip and Matthews (2007), where the Cantonese head-final word order in the noun phrase (NP) is also used in the English NP by Cantonese-dominant child. For instance, '*You buy that tape is English?' is used in order to ask 'Is the video tape that you bought in English?' (Yip & Matthews, 2007: 155). This is the direct transposition of Cantonese word order for prenominal object relativisation ('you buy that tape' corresponds to 'the tape that you bought' in English) and the structure is characteristic of spoken Cantonese. This output is not surprising, because these children did not yet know the rules of syntax in their weaker language, English. This has also been found in cases where bilingual children's exposure to SVO word order encouraged them to use it in German more often than German monolingual children do (Döpke, 1998) and on occasions when German requires SOV (see similar findings for Dutch–French in Hulk, 1997 and German–French in Müller, 1998). This is expected especially if the acquisition process is still incomplete so the bilingual children do not yet know how to maximise common ground and preserve grammaticality at the same time in both languages. This knowledge of what can be shared and what is language-specific appears to kick in later, in other domains as well (e.g. language-specific lexical uses; see Field, 2002: 182–3; see also Kroll & De Groot, 1997).

Maximising common ground by adopting the same word order in both languages does happen though even when the word order differences between the two languages of the bilinguals are complete opposites (see Section 4.1, option iii.b). If we look at this diachronically, we can find examples of languages that changed their word orders (from head-initial to head-final and vice versa) due to intense and prolonged language contact in addition to other contributing sociolinguistic factors (see Gast, 2007 for OV to VO shifts through contact in Meso-America and Ross, 1996, 2001, for VO to OV shifts in Papua New Guinea; see also Heine, 2008 for more examples). In West Rumelian Turkish dialects spoken in the Macedonia region populated by Slavic speakers (of Macedonian) the Turkish OV word order changed to VO under the influence of Macedonian VO (see Friedman, 2003, for details and examples). Usually there is some very minor pattern in one language that is similar to the major pattern in the other. Heine and Kuteva (2005) observe that it is often the case that a shared pattern, no matter how infrequent it may be in one of the languages in contact, becomes the one used in both languages. They also note that 'language contact may lead to entirely new patterns' and that 'more commonly there is already some colloca- tion, available for deployment in discourse, even if rarely used' (Heine & Kuteva, 2005: 44). For instance, nominal compounding is common in German but uncommon in Romance languages. German speakers in Eastern Belgium tend to develop a possessive pattern with a genitive instead of the preferred nominal compound. For example, 'Zeit des Herbstes' ('time of the autumn') develops under the influence of the French 'le temps d'automne'. A similar development has been observed in German spoken in northern Italy where speakers use 'das Bündel von Trauben' ('the bunch of grapes') modelled on the Italian construction 'il grappolo d'uva' rather than the preferred German construction ('Traubenbündel'= 'grape bunch'; Heine & Kuteva, 2005: 46).

4.4.2   Discourse Preferences: Painting a Complete or an Incomplete Picture

Languages can have more than one option for expressing certain meanings, and speakers may have different preferences for describing the same scenes in their languages. For instance, both Czech and Russian mark perfective (bound, complete) and imperfective (unbound, ongoing) aspect, but Czech speakers tend to express the end points (which indicate completeness) in motion events more often than Russian speakers do (see Schmiedtová, von Stutterheim & Caroll, 2011). Consequently, Czech seems to direct speakers towards a holistic event perspective that in this case includes the construal of goal-directed motion events (e.g. the equivalent of 'They walked to church'), whilst Russian 'favours' ongoingness (i.e. the equivalent of 'They were walking (to church)'; ibid.). Similar comparisons can be made between other languages. For instance, in English, there is an aspectual marker for ongoingness (the progressive '-ing' form), which is used in narratives about events, whilst German lacks this kind of viewpoint aspect and its speakers' attention is therefore not directed towards motion ongoingness but instead to 'a holistic event perspective in which event end points are included' (Athanasopoulous et al., 2015: 519). Furthermore, as Schmiedtová, von Stutterheim and Caroll (2011) point out, even though there is no automatised grammatical option for expressing ongoingness in German, there is a highly marked construction exemplified by 'Eine Frau ist am Stricken' ('A woman is at-knitting') which can refer to an event as ongoing. Thus, we can say that even though we may indeed have both options available in two languages, different lexical and grammatical options can be preferred for habitual event construal in each language, and this can then affect how the events are categorised and grouped in each language.

Interestingly, Flecken (2010) found that Czech speakers perform very similarly to German speakers when it comes to event construal in discourse, even though Czech has grammaticalised aspect for both boundedness (perfective) and ongoingness (imperfective) in events whilst German does not. The performance of Czech speakers in Flecken's study mirrored the tendencies of German participants to depict events as bounded. It seems that the existence of grammaticalised aspectual forms does not necessarily determine how Czech speakers conceptualise events and that it is more the semantic expressive preferences and discourse conventions that are responsible. Jarvis et al. (2013: 301) note that these discourse conventions in Czech could have been influenced by contact with German.

The event construal tendencies in Czech, Russian and German also play out in an interesting way in an L2 context, where L1 Czech and L1 Russian speakers of L2 German behave differently in the L2: Czech learners of German are more likely to describe events as bounded and mention end points than the Russian learners of German (Schmiedtová et al., 2011). Both learner groups are thereby maximising common ground, but the Czech learners have the advantage of shared event-construal preferences in both their L1 and L2. Note again that the expression of ongoingness in German is not impossible, it is just not a frequent or preferred strategy for event construal, but it can in fact become so in bilingual language use under different circumstances (i.e. under the influence of a majority language). Heine and Kuteva's example of Pennsylvania German cited earlier (Chapter 2, Section 2.3) is relevant here. It illustrates what happens in this domain under long-term contact between heritage German speakers within a majority community of English speakers: the progressive in Pennsylvania German has acquired a much higher frequency of use and is applied to more contexts than in non-contact German (Heine & Kuteva, 2005: 66).

In this section we have seen a discourse preference rather than a grammatical restriction in one or the other language, such as word order, discussed in the previous section (Section 4.4.1). Both Czech and Russian have shared options for event construal with their L2 German. The preferred option in Czech happens to coincide with the preferred option in German (expression of boundedness with end points) whilst the preferred option in Russian maps onto the less preferred option in German (expression of ongoingness and no end points). Either option for maximising common ground is viable in principle (+ bound vs. – bound), with the result that some L1 speakers (Russian) may sound less authentic in L2 (German) than other L1 speakers (Czech). This example also highlights the fact that intratypological distinctions should be studied in a more finely grained fashion and with attention to specific, individual features of a particular language and to the usage habits of its speakers. Just because two languages, Russian and Czech, belong to the same typological group according to one criterion (Slavic family) does not mean that they are similar on every level (e.g. in lexicalisation patterns or discourse preferences; see Filipović & Ibarretxe-Antuñano, 2015 on intratypological contrasts).

4.4.3 Parsing Preferences: How Attachment Works

Let us now look at how speakers of English and speakers of Spanish process syntactic ambiguities. The sentence 'I saw the girlfriend of our neighbour who smokes a lot' is two-ways ambiguous syntactically. The relative clause 'who smokes a lot' could be modifying 'the neighbour' or 'the girlfriend' as its head noun, i.e. either the neighbour or the girlfriend could be the one who is claimed to smoke a lot. However, even though both interpretations are possible in English it seems that there is a preference for so-called low attachment. The closest and most local head is preferred, here the 'neighbour'. By contrast, Spanish speakers seem to favour the other interpretation, or high attachment, and they will more likely understand that 'the girlfriend' is the head and that she was the one who was smoking. This kind of cross-linguistic difference in attachment preferences in parsing has been extensively studied in both monolingual and bilingual contexts, most notably by Dussias and colleagues. In the present context we are particularly interested in what happens when a bilingual is asked to interpret such ambiguous sentences.

Dussias (2001), Dussias and Sagarra (2007) and Fernandez (1995, 2002) carried out a number of experimental studies with Spanish–English bilinguals in both an English-speaking country and a Spanish-speaking country (the USA and Spain respectively). When all other variables were controlled for, the results show that bilinguals do not necessarily adhere to the attachment preferences of the language being spoken in the experiment. For example, early bilinguals proficient in both English and Spanish adhere to either attachment pattern, Spanish or English, when they are tested on English sentences. The preference for the Spanish type, high attachment, is negligibly higher than for that of the English, low attachment: 56 per cent vs. 44 per cent when speaking Spanish (Dussias, 2001) and 51 per cent vs. 49 per cent when speaking English (Fernandez, 1995). It seems that there is no clear or strongly preferred attachment strategy for early and balanced bilinguals because both strategies lead to successful ambiguity resolution. With equal proficiency, the exposure and frequency of use that comes with balanced bilingualism mean that either strategy could be equally effective for disambiguation, thus there is no clear preference. By contrast, bilinguals with unequal proficiency seem to use one and the same processing strategy in both their languages regardless of the language used in the experiments, namely the one from their stronger language (Dussias & Sagarra, 2007; Fernandez, 2002). Similarly, as discussed in Chapter 2, Nicol et al. (2001) showed that conceptual agreement is preferred by Spanish–English bilinguals in both their languages because both have that option, whilst the grammatical agreement that is only available in English is the dispreferred option overall.

To conclude, both early and late bilinguals stick to a single mechanism when it comes to syntactic attachment, with the difference that early bilinguals show no specific preference as to which one (because either is fine in both languages in spite of the different usage preference in each) whilst late bilinguals prefer to use the pattern from their stronger language in both languages (because they are more used to using that one). Late bilinguals prefer to use patterns from their stronger language in both languages, as we have seen in this section, or to keep to a different pattern in each language when they think that common ground cannot be maximised (Lai et al., 2014).

4.5   Conclusion

As we have seen in this chapter, different options are available when languages interact within and across bilingual minds, and different bilinguals may develop different linguistic habits as a result of numerous factors involved even though they are bilingual in the same two languages. The main conclusion to be drawn here is that all bilinguals do nonetheless maximise common ground and that this is the central feature of bilingual efficiency in language use and processing. I have illustrated how different bilinguals bring this about on different occasions, and how its consequences may go beyond language use and discourse and into the grammar per se. Our starting point for any analysis in terms of CASP for Bilingualism is language typology: do certain categories, structures or usage patterns exist in both languages, and do they overlap partially, or not at all; that is, are they in complementary distribution? Fernandez, de Souza and Carrando (2017: 263) make the important point that we should examine the variable of linguistic distance between two systems *not by varying the overall genetic or typological relationship between the languages in question* (since closely related and even typologically similar languages can have very different specific properties) *but rather by examining linguistic distance in a much more finely grained manner: construction by construction.*

We must also note here, based on the evidence of this chapter, that maximising common ground in both the grammar and the lexicon can lead to both addition and loss of form-meaning mappings. Loss seems to occur more commonly in the lexicon than in the grammar: for example, a more general term can take over the relevant lexical space in both languages, whilst subtle meaning distinctions lexicalised in more marginal lexical items within that lexical space are sidelined, possibly disappearing eventually. Another way in which loss occurs is when a more general term is narrowed down under the influence of a similar term in the other language that has a narrower meaning. One reason for greater losses in the lexicon than in grammar is that it is harder for a grammatical property or construction to disappear altogether: a broad range of associated and frequently used meanings may be impaired if it does, thus significantly reducing expressive power and resulting possibly in unintelligible outputs and ungrammaticality. By contrast, if we use one word for all shades of blue instead of many, we are still likely to get our message across in the majority of situations. If we use a more general lexical categorisation rather than a more finely grained one the cost to communication is generally lower than in the case of loss of grammatical forms (though some grammatical paradigms and structures do, of course, get simplified or lost through prolonged language contact; see Sections 4.3.1 and 4.3.2 of this chapter on the loss of evidentiality-marking and gender-marking respectively). Grammatical meanings are often introduced from one language into the other via lexical means and, with time, they may or may not be grammaticalised, but subtle lexical distinctions that are made in one language but not the other rarely receive new, separate lexicalisations (e.g. creating new words for different shades of blue?). This is, again, because the grammatical meanings introduced lexically add a significant amount of new information, for use on many occasions and in many sentence types, whilst possible lexical innovations such as additional shades of blue would be substantially less productive. New, local words are not invented by bilinguals out of the blue (pun intended!), though words can easily be calqued from one language into the other through language contact. Importantly, regardless of the lack of lexicalisation of a colour distinction in one language, having the distinction present in the other language may affect how the colours are represented overall in the bilingual mind (see Section 4.2.1.2 of this chapter).

We have seen that successful maximising of common ground is related to proficiency level, which affects what the outputs of different bilinguals look like. More proficient bilinguals in both languages seem to know better when and how common ground can be best maximised than bilinguals with unequal proficiency. We saw this in the preference for the Spanish motion lexicalisation pattern when early (proficient) bilinguals were speaking either English or Spanish (in the Hohenstein et al., 2006 and Filipović, 2011 studies). Sometimes proficiency may not make a difference: both the lowest-proficiency and highest-proficiency Japanese learners of L2 English have the same outputs of correct L2 English word order (Section 4.4.1). All of this tells us that we have to look at the typological contrasts between two languages in more detail (to assess the communication cost of sharing ungrammatical features), in order to determine when all bilinguals will maximise common ground successfully, when some instances will be successful but others not, and when common ground is not maximised. Maximise Common Ground interacts closely with the principle of Maximise Efficiency in Communication. In some cases, when the cost to communicative efficiency is not very high (e.g. when communication is unlikely to be completely disrupted), Maximise Common Ground can be stretched, even at higher proficiency levels, beyond the realms of current usage or grammaticality in the relevant language (as in *'Yesterday came my boyfriend' in L2 English production by L1 Spanish speakers). If, however, the cost to communicative efficiency is very high and speakers risk being severely misunderstood, then maximising common ground does not occur even at the lowest end of proficiency, as with L1 Japanese learners in their early acquisition of L2 English word order.

Maximising Common Ground can sometimes take a back seat, as it were, and Maximise Efficiency in Communication dominates in the output (there is less common ground and more monolingual-like usage). This is particularly evident in the monolingual mode, when there is less pressure to reconcile the two systems and, depending on the proficiency and level of the language spoken, bilinguals will display different numbers of shared language properties. Speaking to one monolingual is predicted to trigger less maximising of common ground and more language-specific communicative efficiency (i.e. calibrating outputs to the hearer's needs only for one language and not for both).

Maximise Common Ground takes the front seat at the expense of Maximise Efficiency in Communication when bilinguals express information in one language that is not required in that language but is obligatory in their other language. This was the case with evidentiality. On such occasions speakers are being less communicatively efficient in English, which does not require or expect them to signal on every occasion whether they personally witnessed something or heard it from another source. I explained that this happens because the speakers are being multi-language-ready, they have shared thinking-for-speaking habits and mental representations, and constant and consistent use of both languages drives outputs that reflect this advantageous readiness.

Why does the language spoken during experiments matter in some cases but not in others? If bilingualism is balanced, the language used to perform tasks appears not to be the decisive factor. There is now substantial evidence from different linguistic areas (syntactic attachment, motion and intentionality lexicalisation), elicited using different methodologies (verb agreement, sentence completion tasks, paced reading measurement, categorisation and memory-response elicitations), which points to the lack of adherence solely to the language spoken in experiments by early and balanced bilinguals. They seem to rely on whichever pattern works in both languages, if such is available, and if it is not, then they create one using the lexical and grammatical means available to them. When proficiency is unbalanced, the stronger language (e.g. the language of the environment or the language acquired much earlier and spoken for longer and with higher frequency) is likely to be still used in tasks regardless of the fact that bilinguals may be required to use their weaker (L2) language (e.g. see Filipović 2018; see also Fernandez, 2002, and Dussias & Sagarra, 2007 for more examples and discussion). However, we also saw that sometimes bilinguals, e.g. those in Lai et al.'s (2014) study, can categorise in accordance with the pattern of the language spoken during the experiment, though these bilinguals were the late bilingual group and they possibly had less balanced proficiency than early balanced bilinguals would have had. They used the Spanish pattern of motion lexicalisation when speaking Spanish in the experiment and the English one when speaking English. I have argued that in the case of the late bilinguals in Lai et al.'s (2014) study, they may not have internalised the habit of 'figuring out' whether a shared pattern may work in both languages, and if so, which one. They resorted to a less efficient option, that of switching between two patterns and using a different pattern in each language for a categorisation task for which there was a more efficient option, namely the use of the shared, Spanish pattern in both. In contrast, early bilinguals in the Lai et al. (2014) study opted for a more efficient strategy for the categorisation task – they used the Spanish pattern of motion lexicalisation consistently because it enabled the task to be completed in both Spanish and English. It must be noted however that Lai et al. (2014) do not give precise information about any differences in proficiency in English and Spanish between their early and late bilinguals. They only give overall proficiency scores for the whole group in both languages, based on a self-assessment rating and on the experimenter's impression. We can assume that at least some of the late bilinguals in that study (a broad age range for L2 acquisition from 6 to 15 years old) may also have differed in proficiency from the early bilinguals (0–6 years acquisition age for both languages). A precise test would be needed to establish this with certainty. Even if there were small or no proficiency differences in the late bilingual group, the age of acquisition may still on its own have affected the extent to which the habit of maximising common ground is entrenched – more in early and less in late bilinguals.

Overall, the moral of the story here is that we must pay attention to what each language offers speakers in a particular area, whether there is full, partial or no overlap, and whether the restrictions on usage are grammatical (more costly if broken) or only preference-based (less costly for communication if broken). Armed with this essential typological information, we can then begin to address the question of whether and when different bilinguals rely on different patterns when they speak each of their languages or go for the same pattern in both.

Based on the analyses and discussion in this chapter we can postulate a general prediction that: *bilinguals will maximise common ground more in their weaker language (L2) than in their stronger (L1), more when speaking in bilingual than in monolingual mode, more in informal than formal contexts, and more when there is full or partial typological overlap in a domain than when there is hardly any.* This general prediction can be summarised visually in the following graph.

Figure 4.1, which illustrates the predicted relative strength with which the principle of Maximise Common Ground is expected to operate when either a balanced bilingual or unbalanced bilingual is speaking to different inter-locutors (in order from left to right): one bilingual in the L1, one bilingual in the L2, one monolingual in the L1, one monolingual in the L2 and finally to two monolinguals – one in each language. The precise numerical values on

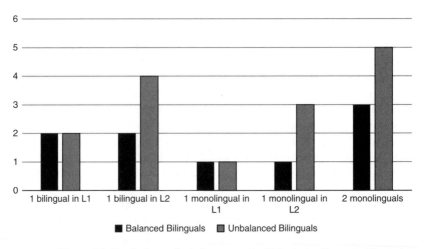

Figure 4.1 Predictions of relative strength of Maximise Common Ground

the y-axis are not relevant because this axis illustrates the *predicted relative activation* of this key principle – precise values can easily be assigned upon empirical verification.

Proceeding from left to right in the Figure 4.1, I discuss the balanced bilinguals first (shown in black columns). For balanced bilinguals L1 equals L2 in proficiency and so the common ground maximised for these speakers is predicted to be at the same level when they are speaking to a bilingual interlocutor in either their L1 or L2, as shown in the first and second parts of columns. Similarly, when balanced bilinguals are speaking to one monolingual in either of their languages, the amount of maximised common ground is the same again, as shown in the third and fourth black columns. Balanced bilinguals are expected to maximise common ground more when talking to another bilingual (black columns one and two) than talking to a monolingual (black columns three and four). This is because the level of activation of the language not currently being used is higher when the other interlocutor is also a bilingual in the same two languages than when the other interlocutor is a monolingual in one of them. Balanced bilinguals can relax their output control and switch from one language to the other seamlessly because their bilingual interlocutor will understand. When conversing with a monolingual interlocutor, however, the output monitor control keeps the other language (the one not currently used) in check because it is not needed or beneficial to have it highly active. Some dual activity due to habitual language use is bound to be there even in balanced bilinguals, thus some common ground may still be detected in the outputs. Finally, I hypothesise that balanced bilinguals are expected to maximise common ground the most when speaking to two monolinguals, one in each language, in the same communicative situation (see the fifth black column in Figure 4.1) because this is the situation that exerts the highest level of pressure and incites heightened efficiency (see Chapter 3, Section 3.5). This dual-language context is not the most frequent (except perhaps in my house!) but it does occur often enough (e.g. in group outings when somebody does not speak the language of the majority).

For unbalanced bilinguals, shown in grey columns in Figure 4.1, I predict that they will maximise common ground more in their weaker language (L2), shown in the second and fourth grey columns, than in their stronger language (L1), shown in the first and third grey columns, and also more when they are talking to one bilingual or one monolingual in their L2 (again, grey columns two and four) rather than in their L1 (grey columns one and three). This is because their knowledge of, and usage habits in their L1 are more entrenched and more likely to be recruited to fill the gaps in knowledge about the grammar and use in their L2. These general predictions are open for empirical testing. Unbalanced bilinguals will maximise common ground the most when they have to use both languages when speaking to two monolinguals, one in each language in the same communicative situation, and they are likely to do this more so than the balanced bilinguals (the fifth grey column) because they lack the precise knowledge about when and to what extent the conventions of grammar and use are shared between their two languages.

I must reiterate here that the principles put forward in Filipović and Hawkins (2018) and in Chapter 3 capture language processing in general, and that Maximise Common Ground is the only one specific to bilingual language processing. We have seen that these principles often co-operate, but sometimes they compete. In acquisition, Minimise Learning Effort and Minimise Processing Effort can come into conflict with Maximise Expressive Power (see Chapter 3, Section 3.3). Once both languages are acquired to the same, similar or a different degree, the crucial competition specific to bilingual language use is that between Maximise Common Ground and Maximise Efficiency in Communication, and how this interaction plays out seems to depend primarily on language typology, on speaker proficiency and on the configuration of the communicative situation. In general, when there is full typological overlap, Maximise Efficiency in Communication will support the outputs of Maximise Common Ground. When there is partial typological overlap, Maximise Efficiency in Communication will often oppose Maximise Common Ground and is more likely to win the contests in the monolingual than the bilingual mode and more in L1 interactions than in L2 contexts. When there is no typological overlap, Maximise Efficiency in Communication will again try to block the principle of Maximise Common Ground and its success in doing so will depend on the relative proficiency of the bilingual (and from a historical perspective, on the specificities of the sociolinguistic situation; see Section 4.4.1). Blocking structures with no typological overlap will be less successful in child bilinguals than in adult SLA learners (see Section 4.4.1 for examples and explanation).

The influence of the Maximise Common Ground principle will be stronger overall in the bilingual mode than in the monolingual, and in the latter case Maximise Efficiency in Communication will only trump Maximise Common Ground in each language if proficiency is high enough and the processing efficiency strategies for each language are adopted (i.e. speakers resort to the grammar and usage patterns of one language only). Maximise Common Ground will never be completely inactive even in very proficient bilinguals, however, and there may be signs of its influence even in the most proficient speakers in a monolingual mode, because, as has been emphasised many times, bilinguals are not two monolinguals in one. The constant use of two languages creates certain habits which necessarily involve maximising common ground. This is also likely to be more evident in informal than formal interactions, because the output monitor (see Chapter 2) may be more relaxed in the former than in the latter.

In terms of CASP for Bilingualism, we can note that, on the one hand, bilinguals minimise learning and processing effort by using the same naming patterns in both languages. Switching between two different categorisation systems is more demanding than using a single system. By maximising common ground and using the same patterns in both languages, bilinguals also achieve greater efficiency in their mental representations for two languages in their thinking-for-speaking habits (Slobin, 1987, 2016) and in their communication readiness for both languages at any moment, as we have stressed. On the other hand, bilingual language acquisition is also driven by the need to maximise expressive power; that is, to be able to express all the meanings that bilingual speakers want to express, just as native speakers do in each language. Bilinguals must also learn and know how to use more semantically or syntactically complex structures and draw the relevant distinctions, and this is what drives language acquisition forward in general (see Chapter 3).

It should be clear that the CASP for Bilingualism model offers a matrix of factors that need to be considered in unison if we are to understand the interplay between general language processing principles and the specific factors related to bilinguals and the situations in which they communicate. In what follows, we look at the consequences of bilingualism for witness memory and judgement (Chapter 5) and then for bilingual professional involvement in language services such as translating and interpreting (Chapter 6).

5   Bilingual Cognition
Language, Memory and Judgement

How do bilinguals remember the events they witness? Does it depend on the type of bilingual they are (i.e. early vs. late)? Is bilingualism helpful for witness memory? In this chapter I will examine bilingualism in action in the context of remembering and making judgements in two languages. Bilingual studies will be contrasted with monolingual studies on memory for witnessed events in order to highlight what is characteristic of interactions between memory and language(s) in the bilingual mind, and whether there are any bilingualism-specific advantages, and if so, of what kind, over monolingual memory. Finally, I will ground a critical discussion of the empirical results in the wider domain of applied bilingualism studies and explain how research into bilingual memory and judgement may contribute to different areas of professional practice, in legal and educational contexts.

5.1   Introduction

Slobin (1996) gave us the insight that we do not only think for speaking, but also for listening, writing, translating and remembering. When we engage in these language-driven activities, we focus on those aspects that a given language requires us to focus on, in both spoken and written modalities and also in memory, with the result that the relevant information is packaged in accordance with the rules of that language for later retrieval. We can think of a language as a chest with many drawers in which we can deposit our experiences and memories for subsequent re-collection. Individual languages may have different numbers of drawers, with different sizes and layouts, and language learners need to learn what (and how much) to put where for later retrieval in communication. This process brings about language-specific habits of recording and retrieving information – the preferred patterns are the top drawers, accessed more easily and more often!

   If bilinguals, like everybody else, think for speaking, listening and remembering, then which of their two languages do they do it in? Do they use different languages on different occasions, for example depending on which language they usually use when they talk about a certain topic? Or do they always think in their stronger language regardless of which one they are speaking?

Language and memory are not isomorphic: not all memory is linguistic. We may have memories that have nothing to do with how we package experience linguistically. For instance, in a Proustian sense, powerful memories of feelings from the past can be formed and evoked by a familiar sound such as a teaspoon tapping on a fine porcelain teacup. Similarly, from another physiological domain, a recognisable scent that we get a whiff of can transport us back to our childhood and bring back memories of things, people or events that we associate with that scent. Our memories can also be visual. Some people are particularly good at having this type of memory, a so-called photographic memory. However, we tend to talk about our memories using language and we know, as a species for whom communication is the defining feature, that language is the main medium for us to relate our experiences to others (although composing a piece of music or painting a picture are also possible media for delivering a message, they are not so for the majority of us and even when they are, they are not used for daily communication). Language is a cognitive tool, as Tversky (2011: 134–5) points out, and like other cognitive tools (our bodies, maps, graphs, design sketches), language can help or hinder thought. Tversky (ibid.) explains that because 'language encodes, encapsulates, emphasises, summarises, organises and transforms certain meanings and relations and not others', it can affect courses of action in some ways and not in others. What language encodes is useful, but what it ignores might have been useful as well, and this is 'true of any tuned and adaptive filtering or processing mechanism' (ibid.).

It seems reasonable to assume therefore that the way in which our memories are formed can have a possible, even significant influence on how something is remembered and retrieved. Similarly, when it comes to making judgements about certain events or situations, can the way in which we acquired our language (as L1 or L2) sway our opinions one way or another? We look at some studies here that address these questions in the context of witness memory and judgements about witness reports and moral dilemmas.

5.2   On Bilingual Memory, Generally and Briefly

Memory has been one of the central foci of cognitive science. A number of models have been proposed with regard to how we process information and store it for later retrieval (see Atkinson & Shiffrin, 1968; Broadbent, 1958; Craik & Lockhart, 1972; see also Craik, 2002 for a critical overview). In this context we focus on a specific feature of memory, namely its relationship to language. Even though memories are not all stored and retrieved in a way that involves language, as already indicated, language is inextricably linked to many, if not most, of our memories and plays a role in their formation and in our access to them.

Bilingual memory has received more scholarly attention in the last few decades as a result of the growing interest in bilingualism generally. Research in this area has included studies of autobiographical memory (how bilinguals remember their personal experiences; e.g. Schrauf & Rubin, 1998; see Pavlenko, 2014 for a recent overview), working memory capacity in different languages (e.g. Ellis & Hennelly, 1980) and the sensory memory of bilingual populations (e.g. Rogers, 2006). A substantial body of work has dealt with memory *for* language itself, that is, how bilinguals remember and retrieve words in their respective languages (Van Hell & Kroll, 2013 for an overview; see also Heredia & Altarriba, 2014). The work presented in this chapter adds another, rarely explored, perspective on bilingual memory, namely the perspective of *bilingual witness memory*. What effects does the online competition between two languages in a bilingual mind have in this area, beyond its effects on the content and form of the linguistic outputs discussed in previous chapters? In other words, our goal here is to explore the effects of the interactions predicted within the CASP for Bilingualism model on other cognitive functions, namely memory.

As with bilingual language processing generally, the degree to which memory storage is language-specific may also vary with language acquisition history, exposure and frequency of use (Chapter 2). That is why it is particularly important to note the precise internal (variability) and external (adjustability) factors in our experimental work. In this chapter I focus on bilinguals with both equal and unequal proficiency in two languages and discuss the methodological issues that ensure both languages are active throughout the experiments – something rarely attempted in the field. This is the most interesting type of situation in that we can discover what happens when both systems are active (bilingual mode or dual-language context; see Chapter 2, Section 2.4.2), since most of the experimental work carried out in the past has been done in a single-language context, where both languages were not kept purposefully active. We know that even in monolingual mode, bilinguals access and use both their systems and shared strategies for task performance, in line with their habits of use and proficiency levels. However, when both languages are equally, or almost equally active, we expect bilinguals to be under more pressure to use shared resources; that is, to maximise common ground more in a bilingual than a monolingual mode. I was intrigued to find out how this fierce online competition between patterns would be resolved. The question was, what would the outputs look like for different proficiency groups, and if and how would this affect their memory of witnessed events?

Just as in bilingual processing, we will see that bilinguals are trying to do the same kinds of things when it comes to memory storage and retrieval: Minimise

Processing Effort, Maximise Efficiency in Communication and Maximise Common Ground. Our other two principles, Minimise Learning Effort and Maximise Expressive Power, are also in operation as constant forces that shape language acquisition through the lifespan. In this context I discuss these two principles only when I assess those aspects of the expressive power of bilinguals in their respective languages that can be an aid to memory (i.e. whether they have acquired all the necessary means of expression that monolinguals have).

One of the fundamental and most controversial issues in bilingual memory research has been whether bilingual memory is organised in one or two storage systems and how items in the two languages are linked. This line of research has been mainly focused on the storage of lexical items. The debate has been ongoing for over half a century, and most current models propose that the two systems are separate but connected (see Jared et al., 2013; Kroll et al., 2010; but see also Brysbaert & Duyck, 2010 for criticism). Namely, bilinguals are assumed to have two separate lexicons but a single underlying conceptual system (see Potter et al., 1984). One of the models that has proposed separate lexicons and a unified conceptual structure is the Revised Hierarchical Model (Kroll & Stewart, 1994; see also Kroll et al., 2010). This model supports the view that bilingual lexicons are linked together bidirectionally, and that each is also bidirectionally linked with the conceptual system. The initial version of this model was revised to take account of different levels of bilingual competence. A direct link between the L2 lexicon and concepts is claimed to be tentative at first and may go through the L1 lexicon instead in the early stages of acquisition. The link to conceptual structure becomes more direct as the proficiency increases.

Empirical support for the Revised Hierarchical Model has come from a number of cross-linguistic priming and translation studies, which have provided evidence for the asymmetries predicted by the model. Cross-linguistic priming was obtained if the prime was an L1 word and the target an L2 word, whilst the reverse (L2 prime/L1 target) resulted in few or no priming effects (see e.g. Altarriba & Basnight-Brown, 2007; Dimitropoulou, Duñabeitia, & Carreiras, 2011). This is because the L1 prime for the L2 target accesses the conceptual system directly, which is necessary for semantic priming, whilst the L2 prime for the L1 target only accesses the lexical level, or seeks a lexical equivalence specifically, and no conceptual store is involved. The model also predicts that L1 to L2 translation will be faster than vice versa because every L2 word is mapped onto an equivalent L1 word but not vice versa (see Kroll & Stewart, 1994). A few studies, however, have demonstrated that both translation directions can be sensitive to conceptual factors (see De Groot, Dannenburg, & Van Hell, 1994; Van Hell & De Groot, 2008) and that priming in both directions is possible if the context is sufficiently constrained (see Basnight-Brown & Altarriba, 2007). And more recently, research including both early and late L2 learners has shown that L2 concepts can be accessed directly and not mediated by L1 regardless of proficiency levels (Van Hell et al., 2017; see also Chapter 2, Section 2.5.1). These findings challenge some of the earlier assumptions of the Revised Hierarchical Model since the direct link between L2 words and concepts may be less tentative than originally assumed. In addition, the type of bilingual acquisition in question (early simultaneous vs. late consecutive) does not seem to be the only important factor here. Other factors, such as typological proximity and the nature of exposure can play a significant role as well, as shown by Van Hell et al. (2017).

Another common distinction that has to be mentioned in this context is the one between semantic memory (i.e. memory for facts about the world) and episodic memory (memory for personally experienced events). Most current models of bilingual memory are essentially accounts of semantic memory whose goal is to explain bilingual lexical access to underlying conceptual referents (Schrauf, Pavlenko & Dewaele, 2003). Considerably fewer deal with bilingual memory for events, where complete lexicalisation frames need to be considered, as well as the lexical and grammatical features of the patterns used to verbalise events that are to be remembered for recognition or recall, which will be the main focus in this chapter.

Another concern in the field has been the extent to which bilingual memory is dependent on specific features of one or the other language. This line of research has tested bilingual memory performance based on whether there was a language match or a mismatch in tasks. Whether the language used for encoding plays a significant role or not varies (see Francis, 1999 for a detailed overview). What interests us here in particular is that episodic memories are especially 'integrative and preserve a large amount of context across modalities' (Bartolotti & Marian, 2013: 10). Thus, the kind of information available for later retrieval may be conditioned in part by the systems used to encode it. Importantly, memory recall seems to be improved if contextual cues at the time of encoding are also present at retrieval (e.g. Danker & Anderson, 2010). One of these cues seems to be the linguistic context of the encoding. When it is the same as that of the retrieval, memories are more numerous and detailed, and also more emotionally experienced (e.g. see Matsumoto & Stanny, 2006).

What is of particular interest for us is to establish which of their two systems bilinguals use when 'packaging' information for memory. CASP for Bilingualism can help us to make and test some predictions. We can check how language and memory interact in different speakers (the variability factor) when both their languages are regularly active vs. when only one of the two is regularly active (or active on a specific occasion). Since we are primarily interested in what happens when both languages compete online, I present experiments here that have kept both languages active (bilingual mode) in different types of bilinguals (with vs. without equal proficiency). Further research is needed to establish whether a monolingual mode also leads to different outcomes (e.g. less maximising of common ground) for the same, as well as different, kinds of bilinguals.

Some features of language typology may be more relevant for witness memories of events than others. For example, we expect that differences in how much information is available about the source of information (as captured in the category of evidentiality in Turkish) or about the intentionality of an actor in an event (as given explicitly in the affective dative construction in Spanish) will matter more than whether, for example, the object comes before or after the verb. Our approach to bilingualism is built on a detailed comparison of languages with respect to the kind of information content that they require their speakers to habitually include or exclude, as a result of their lexical resources, grammatical restrictions and usage preferences. Not all typological contrasts will matter here and those that do are studied within the context of the **Applied Language Typology programme** of Filipović (2017a, 2017b).

Here we are primarily concerned with *bilingual memory for events*, which takes us into the realm of event lexicalisation and well beyond remembering single words. We have known that language can affect memory for events amongst monolinguals at least since the seminal experimental work of Loftus and Palmer (1974). In their study, experimental participants were presented with videos of car accidents and with different descriptions for these events. They showed that if words indicating a stronger impact, like 'crash', were used instead of the more neutral 'collide' in mock witness interview questions, witnesses exhibited false memories, saying that there was broken glass in the video when in fact there was none. If words indicative of weaker impact were used in the interview questions, which were less likely to result in broken glass, the participants did not report any broken glass, which was the correct memory response.

More controversial now is the proposal that there are not only language effects on memory, driven by the use of specific words or constructions, but also *language-specific effects* because of the way individual languages are structured. There are relatively few studies that look at how bilingual memory may be affected by the language used in the experiments targeting memory. One example is from Tosun, Vaid and Geraci (2013), who found differences in memory for event descriptions between Turkish and English speakers and Turkish–English bilinguals due to the presence of evidentiality in Turkish but not in English (recall Chapter 4, Section 4.3.1). Turkish native speakers and bilinguals who have spent less time in English-speaking environments seem to discard sources of information that are marked as second-hand (inferential or indirect, not witnessed first-hand) and they remember the content of event descriptions better if they are marked as first-hand information. This difference in memory for description content is not found in English monolinguals or Turkish–English bilinguals who are more immersed in English-speaking surroundings.

The research programme of Filipović (2011, 2013a, 2013b, 2016, 2018, 2019b) has addressed the possibility that we may be able to detect **language-specific effects on memory** for witnessed events in monolingual and bilingual speakers. It asks: can memory be affected by the particular language used during the encoding of events, or perhaps by the language that is the stronger one of the two (e.g. L1) regardless of the language used explicitly during encoding? One possible outcome here is that the language-specific pattern used in the description of events will also be reflected in the kinds of details that are remembered better. The language used in the experimental task, on the other hand, need not be the guiding pattern. For instance, speakers can still perform in a memory task in line with their L1 even though they are explicitly using an L2 to do so. We also know that the same bilinguals can and do behave differently depending on the situation they are in, i.e. depending on the level of activation of their respective languages, who the interlocutors are and also how formal the occasion is, as discussed in detail in Chapter 3. In the following sections I will discuss when we do and when we do not, find a bilingual advantage for memory, and I will use the CASP model to explain why we may expect different outcomes.

5.3   Memory for Motion

In order to study whether specific languages can exert different kinds of influence on their speakers it is best to select a universal domain of experience and to study languages that carve up that domain differently. The domain of motion events has generated a lot of interest and has inspired numerous studies in language and cognition precisely because it fulfils this condition: it is universal and different languages provide speakers with different means for lexicalising it. The variation is not limitless, however, as Talmy (1985, 1991, 2000) has pointed out. Languages express either manner or path in the verb, and this then conditions what kinds of meanings are expressed elsewhere and how often. Previous research (e.g. Filipović, 2007b, 2008; Slobin, 1996, 1997, 2003) has found that speakers of languages that typically lexicalise path in the verb (e.g. Spanish) are more likely to give less detail about manner or omit manner information altogether because manner is lexicalised in optional constituents such as adverbs or adverbial phrases (e.g. 'salir de la casa *cojeando*' = 'exit the house *limping*'). By contrast, in manner-verb languages such as English, the manner is typically expressed in the obligatory constituent, the verb (as in 'limp out of the house'), and thus most likely to be present in descriptions of motion events by speakers of this language type (see Chapter 4, Section 4.2.2.4 for further details).

As Tversky (2011: 132–3) put it, 'language can select certain features at the expense of others'. She discusses this point in another context, in connection with describing faces, which are 'notoriously difficult to describe' and notes that it may be easier to describe some features (e.g. eye colour) than others that could, in effect, be more useful for discriminating faces. She further points out (ibid.) that 'describing appears to focus attention on features that are easy to describe' and that at the same time this takes attention away from features that are hard to describe. I would argue that exactly the same applies in other perceptual and conceptual domains as well.

Studies that have investigated the interaction of language with other cognitive processes in different cognitive domains, such as the categorisation of objects and events, have largely focused on monolinguals and language-specific effects in categorisation tasks and have been widely documented in different monolingual and bilingual contexts (Lucy, 1992; Lucy & Gaskins, 2003, Malt, Sloman & Gennari, 2003). However, detecting language-specific effects on memory is more controversial because it involves more than just saying that the linguistic system is a strategy for problem-solving. It means that the effects of language are more profound, and that they may have more far-reaching effects on cognition.

Filipović (2011) tested the memory of English and Spanish monolinguals and of English–Spanish bilinguals proficient in both languages, who were deliberately kept in a bilingual mode throughout the experiment. In the first experimental block, the participants were instructed and asked questions in one language whilst they were describing events in the other. They were randomly divided into two groups based on which of the two languages they used for verbalisation during the first experimental block (English-first vs. Spanish-first). Their recognition memory was tested in the second block, again in a bilingual mode, after a distractor task of 120 seconds, which consisted of a search for random letters in a grid. Subsequently, the participants looked at another set of video clips which were similar to the ones originally seen but not identical: one of the three original manners of motion in each clip was replaced with a different one. The interactions in this block took place in the language that was not used in the original verbalisation and the participants were asked to watch a set of videos again and respond with either a plus sign if they thought they had seen an identical event in the first block or a minus sign if they did not see an identical event in the first block. The answer '+' was a recognition error since each target video from the second block differed in one manner component from the corresponding original in the first block. Importantly, in this study the experimental video stimuli depicted complex motion events, with multiple manner components, such as a man *jumping* out of an enclosure, starting to *run* across the road and then *striding* into a garden.

Previous research using simple motion events in the stimuli (i.e. one manner + one path; e.g. a man running into a house) did not detect any language-specific effects on memory (see Filipović, 2010b). The reason may have been the fact that a simple motion event is not difficult to lexicalise in either English ('run into') or Spanish ('entrar corriendo'= 'enter running'). The use of complex motion events increased memory load for the crucial component in the experimental videos, namely, the manner of motion. Spanish speakers would have a substantially bigger difficulty when faced with a requirement to describe multiple manners, because their linguistic resources are more limited in this area and their verbalisation habits typically do not involve provision of information about manner.

Here are some examples of how monolinguals (English and Spanish speakers respectively) described the events they witnessed in the experimental stimuli. The stimuli used in the experiment are listed in Table 5.1.

1a)   She leapt out and marched across the road.
1b)   She limped then swayed across the path.
1c)   She emerged behind a tree, smoothly walked along the path then skipped off.

2a)   Salió despacio cojeando.
        'He exited slowly limping.'

2b)   Caminó dando pequeñitos saltos.
        'He walked with tiny jumps.'

2c)   Cruzó el jardín andando raro.
        'He crossed the garden going in a strange manner.'

2d)   Salió de un recinto haciendo el tonto.
        'He exited from an enclosure behaving silly.'

Table 5.1 *Experimental video stimuli for motion events (Filipović, 2011)*

Block 1	Block 2
X jumps over the wall, <u>walks</u> along the path and skips across the road	X jumps over the wall, <u>skips</u> along the path and hops across the road
X runs out of the garden, <u>walks in very big steps</u> across the road and strolls into the parking lot	X runs out of the garden, <u>runs</u> across the road and strolls into the parking lot
X runs out from behind the wall, <u>marches</u> across the road and strolls into the garage	X runs out from behind the wall, <u>minces</u> across the road and strolls into the garage
X staggers from behind the bushes, <u>stomps</u> across the path and sways into the yard	X staggers from behind the bushes, <u>hobbles</u> across the path and sways into the yard
X limps out of the building, <u>staggers</u> along the path and marches around the corner	X limps out of the building, <u>limps</u> along the path and marches around the corner
X jumps out of the bushes, <u>sprints</u> across the road and strolls through the gate	X jumps out of the bushes, <u>speed-walks</u> across the road and strolls through the gate

And here are examples of the bilingual verbalisations for the same stimuli (Table 5.1) in Spanish (3a–3c) and English (4a–4c):

3a)   Brincó al cruzar la calle.
        'He skipped when crossing the street.'

3b)   Cruzó la calle corriendo.
        'He crossed the street running.'

3c)   Salió movendo el cuerpo de lado.
        'He exited moving the body sideways.'

4a)   She jumped the fence and crossed the street skipping.
4b)   She went out of the building unsteadily.
4c)   She moved slowly across the garden.

The verbalisation and memory performance of English monolingual speakers on the target items (i.e. different manners of motion) was significantly better than that of the control Spanish monolingual speakers. Based on language differences alone, a possible prediction could have been that the bilinguals would behave like monolinguals in each language, providing more detailed manner descriptions and better recognition performance for manner of motion when English was used in the initial verbalisation stage rather than Spanish, prior to the recognition test block; however, the results paint a different picture.

Regardless of the language used during initial encoding, there was no statistically significant difference between the two bilingual groups; that is, between those using Spanish vs. those using English for the original event verbalisation (see Filipović, 2011 for further details and discussion).

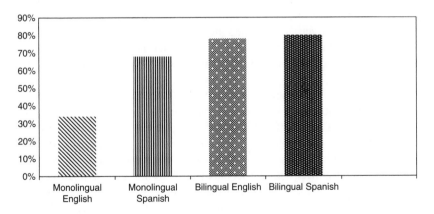

Figure 5.1 Recognition errors for motion events in percentages

Instead, bilingual performance in the recognition task closely resembled that of Spanish monolingual speakers (see Figure 5.1), both when the task was performed in English and when it was performed in Spanish. The bilingual speakers did provide more manner information in Spanish than their monolingual Spanish peers (e.g. by adding adverbials as in (3b) and (3c), or resorting to a particular construction such as 'X ran whilst crossing the street', see example (3a)), but they still expressed manner in substantially less detail than the English monolinguals: both in terms of types and tokens of the manner expressions.

What seems to be going on here is a reliance on a *single set of processing strategies by fluent bilinguals*. There is a common pattern available to bilingual speakers and this was the pattern that they relied on for both verbalisation and memory. In this case, the acceptable pattern in both languages is the Spanish one that involves path verbs (such as 'exit' or 'cross') or basic verbs (such as 'go', 'move' or 'walk') and that does not favour the expression of manner detail. This pattern does not make it easy to express the multiple manners featured in a complex motion event, since the Spanish manner lexicon is more limited. As we saw, manner, if expressed, is normally given in an adjunct, though manner verbs can be used with limitations, in combination with non-boundary-crossing prepositions (e.g. the Spanish equivalent of 'He ran inside (but not into!) the park'). Overall, the bilinguals apparently used the same strategy for verbalisation of motion in both English and Spanish, which did not encourage detailed reference to manner of motion. This strategy is more similar to the Spanish than the English lexicalisation pattern, and it is the one that is acceptable in both languages.

When the shared pattern exists or can be created, it will be favoured. It is less efficient to shift back and forth between two different lexicalisation patterns, especially if both languages are used often and are frequently both active in the same communicative situation. It seems that such shared structural patterns are encouraged in both verbalisation and memory storage as well, though on this occasion the common pattern was a hindrance rather than help when it came to *remembering the manner of motion* because its lexicalisation was not encouraged or facilitated.

In future work it will be important to test what happens when bilinguals are in a monolingual mode (as opposed to the bilingual mode that featured in the Filipović, 2011 study). The CASP for Bilingualism prediction is that there would then be less maximising of common ground and more language-specific communicative efficiency (see Chapter 3). As a result, balanced English–Spanish bilinguals and those with English (but not Spanish) as the stronger language may have better memory for motion events when speaking English in the monolingual mode than when speaking Spanish in the monolingual mode. There is also the possibility that in early and balanced bilinguals constant exposure to, and use of both languages and predilection for shared patterns in both may result in max-imising common ground in both languages to a substantial degree even in a monolingual mode, which would be manifested by higher usage of the Spanish pattern when speaking English than that of English monolingual speakers who can, but do not, prefer to use the Spanish pattern. These hypotheses are worth testing, and one of them will be falsified.

It may be that if we disable the use of language altogether during these experiments, the language effects on memory reported here would not manifest themselves. This is certainly what Trueswell and Papafragou (2010) report in a study on monolinguals, namely that language effects on memory for motion events disappear with the introduction of verbal interference. Visual and audi-tory interference also appear to block language being used as an aid to memory (see Filipović & Geva, 2012; Filipović, Slobin & Ibarretxe-Antuñano, 2013).

Nevertheless, it is important to note that access to linguistic encoding is *normally not impeded in everyday situations* when people witness events, and thus we can conclude that language-specific packaging of information is a force to be reckoned with. In other words, blocking access to overt or covert verbalisation may diminish or completely erase any effects of language on cognition, but that would not then reflect what speakers do in non-experimental circumstances, i.e. in their everyday life and surroundings where they witness events language is always present and accessible.

5.4   Memory for Intentionality

As we saw in Chapter 4, Section 4.3.3, languages differ with respect to how regularly and systematically they require intentionality to be specified, and they provide speakers with different means to express different types of intentionality in events (Gibbons, 2003; Ibarretxe-Antuñano, 2012). English does not generally make an explicit distinction between intentional and non-intentional events (recall 'The man dropped a bag') whilst Spanish, on this occasion, does make this explicit by using two distinct constructions (Chapter 4, Section 4.3.3). It is important to highlight that the more complex these events are, the more likely we are to resort to language as a strategy to organise information about them. We have just seen in the previous section that when motion events are complex, speakers are more likely to resort to language as a system for organising information about these events (Filipović, 2011; Filipović & Geva, 2012). Causation events are also a kind of complex event, as Fausey and Boroditsky (2010: 155) explain:

Observers must integrate information about the basic physics of the event (e.g., whether the person touched the balloon, whether the balloon popped, whether he touched it right before it popped) with more social cues about the individual's state of knowledge and intentions (e.g., whether he meant to touch the balloon, whether he knew the balloon was there, whether he was surprised at the outcome). The need to integrate many different types of information to construe an event may leave some events especially susceptible to linguistic and cultural influences.

Fausey and Boroditsky (2011) argue that language may modulate memory by directing people's visual attention as they witness events, whereby the English speakers would remember an agent better because they typically express it in the subject position in their basic SVO structures, regardless of whether a person is involved in intentional or non-intentional causation (as in 'The man dropped the bag'). Spanish speakers do not express agents in cases of non-intentional causation; they use affective dative constructions instead which refer to affected participants (Chapter 4, Section 4.3.3), and thus their overall attention is less focused on the agents in general. Fausey and Boroditsky (ibid.) state that the exposure to agentive language for English speakers affects their memory for agents positively even offline, in a kind of preparatory fashion, whilst the reverse is the case for Spanish speakers, because they do not use SVO structures with non-intentional agents.

Studies by Filipović (2013b, 2018, 2019b) investigated how monolingual and bilingual speakers remember intentionality, that is, whether a witnessed event contained actions that were done on purpose or by accident. In Filipović (2013b), monolingual speakers of English and Spanish were presented with video clips depicting events in which a person was intentionally causing something (e.g. a girl pushing her Barbie doll off a bed on purpose) and clips in which people were involved in non-intentional causation (e.g. a woman looking for something on a messy desk pushes a water bottle off the desk inadvertently). Speakers watched and described all the videos in the first block and then they performed a distractor task for 120 seconds, whereby they were asked to count how many instances of the letters M, N and Z they could see in a 10 × 10 letter grid. The recall task asked two questions about each of the witnessed events. The questions were unbiased with respect to intentionality (e.g. Did you see a girl with a Barbie doll? Was what happened in that video accidental or on purpose?). They were asked to mark their answers on an answer sheet by circling YES if the action in the video was on purpose (intentional) and NO if it was not on purpose (i.e. it was accidental/non-intentional). They were also told that they should not guess and that they should leave a question unanswered if they were not able to recall the relevant information. Responses were classified as incorrect if the participants circled the wrong answer (i.e. intentional instead of non-intentional), or vice versa, or if they failed to give any response (i.e. they left both options unmarked because they could not recall the crucial piece of information; this was the case in 17 per cent of all responses for all groups). The target videos are listed in Table 5.2 and examples are given as still frames in Figures 5.2 and 5.3.

Speakers of both languages used similar agentive constructions to describe intentional causation (e.g. 'The girl pushed the doll off the bed' in English and

Table 5.2 *Experimental video stimuli for intentionality (Filipović, 2013b)*

Intentional events	Non-intentional events
Girl pops an orange balloon with a needle	Blue balloon pops whilst a girl is playing with it
Girl pushes a Barbie doll off a bed	A cup is pushed off the sink whilst a girl is washing her hands
Woman crushes a plastic cup in her hand	A wooden toy tower gets crushed by a woman falling on it
Woman drops a magazine onto the floor	A pen is dropped during writing
Woman knocks a box off the table using her elbow	A bottle is knocked off the table whilst a woman is rummaging through things located on it

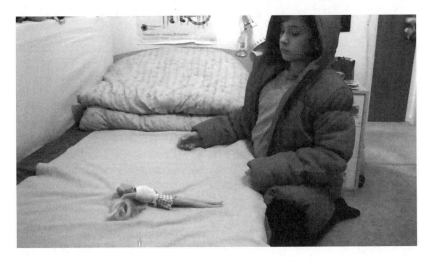

Figure 5.2 Barbie pushed off the bed (intentional)

'La niña empujó la muñeca de la cama' in Spanish), but they differed in their descriptions of non-intentional events:

5a)   The woman knocked the bottle off the table.

5b)   Se le cayó la botella.
         ('To-her-the-bottle-fell.')
         'She dropped the bottle accidentally.'

5c)   The girl popped the balloon.

5d)   Se le rompió el globo a la muchacha.
         ('To-her-the-balloon-burst to the girl.')
         'The girl popped the balloon accidentally.'

Figure 5.3 Balloon pops (non-intentional)

In these examples, the Spanish descriptions give explicit information about whether the action is non-intentional, by using the clearly and unambiguously non-intentional *se*-construction, or intentional, for which the SVO construction is generally (though not exclusively) 'reserved'. Even if SVO structures can sometimes be used in Spanish to describe a non-intentional event, there is almost always an additional specification such as 'rompió un vaso sin querer' ('he broke a glass without wanting to') or a gesture that accompanies the expression and signals that it was done non-intentionally (Ibarretxe-Antuñano, personal communication). Ibarretxe-Antuñano (2012) shows that *se*-constructions involve low intentionality whilst the SVO constructions can involve different degrees of intentionality, based on the *force dynamics* lexicalised *in the specific verbs* (Ibarretxe-Antuñano, 2012: 138–40). The SVO structures in Spanish are more likely to be used for descriptions of intentional events precisely because the *se*-constructions are available for non-intentional events only. English speakers, by contrast, regularly use SVO constructions in descriptions of both intentional and non-intentional events (as Fausey & Boroditsky, 2011, and Filipović, 2013b, 2018 have shown), though Filipović (2019b) points out that some verbs in English may have more inherent intentionality than others (e.g. 'push' vs. 'drop').

The experimental results show that Spanish monolinguals outperformed English monolinguals when it came to the provision of relevant and explicitly verbalised details regarding accidental vs. non-accidental causation (see Figure 5.3). The Spanish participants did indeed always specify whether causation was intentional or not, whilst the English speakers did not. This was expected, since the distinction is obligatory in Spanish and optional in English. Interestingly, Filipović (2013b) found differences in recall memory between English and Spanish monolinguals only with regard to the non-intentional events. Intentional events can be described using the same means in both languages (simple transitive SVO constructions) whilst the unintentional events are described differently in the two languages (typically the same SVO constructions in English vs. *se*-constructions in Spanish). These results support findings from other studies indicating that both verbalisation and memory between English and Spanish participants pertains to the non-intentional event stimuli in particular (Fausey & Boroditsky, 2011; Filipović, 2019b). The reason may be because prototypical transitivity does indeed involve intentionality, as Hopper and Thompson (1980) point out. A transitive agent is normally an intentional instigator or a causer of the action. There is a strong relationship in English between the transitive subject function (and its sentence-initial position) and the agent role, reflected in the fact that subjects are most frequently agents and, as Fausey and Boroditsky (2011) have shown, the focus on agents is more pronounced in English than in Spanish. Thus, even though SVO structures in English are used for both intentional and non-intentional events, these constructions may inspire an agentive (intentional) interpretation more often than the non-agentive (non-intentional) one, and this could have interfered with the recall of non-intentional events for the English speakers.

We may also have to allow for the possibility that the nature of the stimuli is such that they are positively skewed towards the salience of intentionality. What is meant by this is that intentional actions in general may be easier to remember regardless of language, since the depiction of intention is more obvious (e.g. in our stimuli, a girl approaches the bed on which a Barbie doll is positioned, looks at the doll and pushes it off the bed, whereby the intention to perform the action is clear; see Figure 5.2). On the other hand, non-intentional events all had an element of surprise and unexpectedness, which may affect the amount of detail that is recorded, especially if language does not encourage the encoding of certain details (such as whether the action was on purpose or not). In the case of non-intentional event stimuli there was more information to be integrated and there were more inferences to be made in order to encode them fully in memory (e.g. judging the behaviour of the person involved before and after the balloon popped; Figure 5.3). Having clear labels for distinguishing intentional from non-intentional events means that this encoding in language and memory is facilitated for Spanish monolingual speakers.

Now that we have established that there are language-specific effects on monolingual recall for intentionality in events, what about the bilinguals? Filipović (2018, 2019b) carried out two studies using the same materials as those in the previous study with monolinguals (Filipović, 2013b). Bilinguals with equal (2L1s) and unequal (L1–L2) proficiency participated in these studies, and were always kept in a bilingual mode by being addressed in one language whilst performing in the other (see Filipović, 2018, 2019b for details); as a result they heard both their languages throughout the experiment. In the case of balanced bilinguals (Filipović, 2019b) each participant performed half of the experiment verbalising in English whilst hearing the instructions in Spanish and then did the reverse for the other half of the experiment, that is, verbalising in Spanish whilst listening to the instructions in English. They were randomly assigned to English-first or Spanish-first groups. L2 learners performed only in their L2 (English or Spanish respectively) whilst being addressed in their L1 (Filipović, 2018).

The aim of these two studies was to investigate whether the language that is spoken when witnessed events are described affects bilingual memory in a language-specific way. If the language of verbalisation affects memory, then the bilinguals would be expected to perform better in the recall tasks when speaking Spanish than when speaking English because Spanish provides more means as well as more precise requirements for distinguishing between intentional and non-intentional events. If their performance is the same regardless of language, and better than that of English monolinguals, but similar to that of Spanish monolinguals, then they may be accessing both their languages when speaking either language.

CASP for Bilingualism predicts that balanced bilinguals in a bilingual mode will access both their languages regardless of which one is spoken, and they will maximise common ground in both verbalisation and memory (Filipović & Hawkins, 2018). Unbalanced bilinguals are expected to maximise common ground in different ways. If their L1 (dominant language) is Spanish, they will express intentionality distinctions clearly in both languages. If their stronger language is English, they will maximise common ground by not expressing intentionality distinctions consistently in both Spanish and English (see Chapter 4 for the list of ways to maximise common ground).

Filipović (2018) showed that L1 Spanish/L2 English speakers do indeed have better memory for intentionality in causation events when speaking their L2 English than L1 English/L2 Spanish speakers speaking L2 Spanish. The L1 Spanish/L2 English speakers maximised common ground between their L1 and L2 by drawing distinctions between intentional and non-intentional events in their L2, and did so in recall memory as well. They used lexical means, such as adverbial phrases, to make the intentionality distinctions clear (such as 'on purpose' in 'He dropped the glass on purpose', or 'by accident' in 'She pushed it by accident'). English L1 learners of L2 Spanish, on the other hand, used the SVO constructions and the *se-* constructions in L2 Spanish interchangeably for both intentional and non-intentional events, just as they would use the 'X broke Y' or the inchoative 'X broke' in L1 English for either event type depending on whether they wanted to mention the agent (see the earlier discussion in this section about English monolinguals; see also Chapter 4, Section 4.3.3). Filipović (2018) argues that patterns from the stronger language (L1) prevail in memory encoding even when the events that are witnessed are verbalised in the weaker language, the L2. In line with CASP's predictions, both bilingual groups in this study maximised common ground in the L2, but in different ways – driven by the respective L1.

We can draw an important conclusion here: multiple factors are at play, and they affect the general processes of bilingual language processing, and bilingual memory, in different ways. Speakers can be proficient overall in their L2. Some features may be harder to acquire than others, and some meaning distinctions that are only drawn in the L2 may be more opaque to learners; unless taught explicitly, they may never be mastered properly (see Dörnyei (2009: 175) on the need for an explicit component in L2 learning). This seems to be an argument for raising language awareness in L2 learning and teaching about both the similarities and the differences between L1 and L2 (see Filipović, 2016 for a discussion; see also Schmidt, 1990, 1993 on the importance of conscious awareness, and Cadierno, 2008 and Ellis, 2008 on focus-on-form approaches to language learning and instruction). There seems to be an advantage in memory for intentionality if the L1 (Spanish) draws the relevant distinctions systematically, even if the L2 being spoken (English) does not. If the reverse is the case, namely if the L1 does not have distinctive constructions (English) but the L2 does (Spanish), then the benefits for memory are not there even at higher levels of overall proficiency (Filipović, 2018). This finding points to the need to consider both typological information about each language pair as well as relative usage preferences (e.g. by consulting corpora). Recently, Koster and Cadierno (2018) have shown that explicit teaching of lexical distinctions that are present in an L2 (e.g. the different words for describing positions of objects; see Chapter 4 for details) can enhance memory for these distinctions in observed spatial scenes, to the point that the participants' memory becomes even better than that of speakers for whom the L2 in question is an L1.

What happens when the bilinguals have equal proficiency in their two languages? I investigated this (Filipović, 2019b) using the same experimental materials as before (Filipović, 2013b, 2018), and compared the memory recall of balanced English–Spanish bilinguals with English and Spanish monolinguals. The experimental stimuli were distributed between the two bilingual groups (Spanish-first and English-first respectively) in the following way. One list was created for both groups. The Spanish-first group verbalised 4 target items and 6 filler items in Spanish and then 6 target items and 4 filler items in English. The English-first bilinguals did exactly the opposite: 4 target + 6 filler items in English first and then 6 target + 4 filler items in Spanish. The items were randomised for both groups to avoid a recency bias. The verbalisations of balanced bilinguals in both English (6a–6d) and Spanish (7a–7b) are illustrated in the following examples (from Filipović, 2019b):

6a)   The woman threw the magazine down onto the floor. (intentional)
6b)   The girl popped the balloon. (intentional)
6c)   The woman moved something on the table and the bottle fell down, from the table. (non-intentional)
6d)   The girl's balloon popped by accident. (non-intentional)

7a)   Dejó   caer   la revista   al   suelo.
       'She let the magazine fall onto the floor.' (intentional)

7b)   Buscaba algo sobre la mesa   y se le cayó la botella.
       '[She] was looking for something on the table and the bottle accidentally fell.' (non-intentional)

Filipović (2019b) shows that balanced bilinguals did not perform differently based on the language they were verbalising in (see Figure 5.4). During the experiment these bilinguals drew systematic distinctions between intentional and non-intentional events in both languages. In English, they used inchoative constructions such as 'the balloon popped' exclusively for non-intentional events, unlike the English monolinguals, who used both this construction and the SVO structure indiscriminately in descriptions of both intentional and non-intentional events. The bilinguals tended to use the SVO constructions mainly to refer to intentional actions only and they occasionally added an additional adverb there, such as 'She dropped the magazine on purpose' or 'The girl pushed the doll angrily' in order to ensure that the correct meaning was conveyed (see Filipović, 2019b for a detailed list and the statistics for the verbalisation choices). Again, this reluctance on behalf of balanced bilinguals to leave ambiguity unresolved in English, which is typically left unresolved by English monolinguals, indicates that the constraints of the bilinguals' other language, Spanish, are present even when using English. When speaking Spanish, balanced bilinguals used SVO structures for intentional events and se-constructions, including those with the affective dative (se cayó = 'it fell'; se me cayó = 'to me it fell') for non-intentional situations only, just like Spanish monolinguals.

Figure 5.4 shows the recall error results for target items from both monolingual and bilingual groups discussed (balanced and unbalanced). The statistically significant differences are found between monolingual English speakers and L1 English bilinguals, on the one hand, and the Spanish monolinguals, Spanish L1 bilinguals and English–Spanish balanced bilinguals on the other. In sum, monolingual Spanish speakers had better recall than the English monolinguals. Bilinguals had better memory for intentionality if they were balanced in both English and Spanish, or if Spanish was their L1, than if English was their L1.

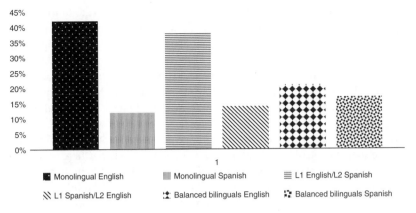

Figure 5.4 Memory of intentionality: recall errors in percentages

It is worth noting that the effect being reported here may be weaker or may disappear altogether if bilinguals are in a monolingual mode, either due to the specifications of the communicative situation (e.g. talking to only monolinguals) or due to experimental conditions (e.g. when access to one language is blocked through interference as in Athanasopoulos et al., 2015). However, when such access is uninhibited and especially when both systems are highly active in a communicative situation or entrenched through habitual and frequent use of both languages, bilinguals are more likely to maximise common ground in both language use and memory. If one language is significantly more active than the other in a specific situation (e.g. through higher output monitoring due to the formality of the occasion) or if one language is stronger in terms of proficiency than the other, then we expect the stronger language to underlie patterns in both verbalisation and memory. More research is needed on memory performance by early balanced bilinguals in a monolingual mode, where one CASP hypothesis is that they may perform more in line with the language used during the task. Alternatively, the same frequency of use in both languages may still lead to maximising of common ground in a monolingual mode similarly to how this is done in the bilingual mode. We need to test also how balanced proficiency interacts with age of acquisition and different frequencies of use and see what happens when these different factors compete in balanced bilinguals. This kind of research is what the CASP for Bilingualism framework leads to and encourages.

5.5   Discussion: Bilingual Memory for Motion vs. Intentionality

It seems that bilinguals minimise processing effort and maximise common ground by using a common linguistic pattern for both storing information and retrieving it from memory. On the other hand, they also want to be able to express all the meanings that are required in each language (i.e. to maximise expressive power) and to maximise communicative efficiency by calibrating their outputs to the hearer in each language whilst also delivering these accurately and fast (NB: remember that efficiency is both speaker- and hearer-oriented). How do these principles interact and how does their interaction affect memory? It seems that the CASP mechanisms lead to different outputs and different consequences for memory in the case of motion vs. intentionality. We can now explain why this is so.

If there is a partial overlap between languages (see Chapter 4, Section 4.3) and one shared lexicalisation pattern can work in both systems, there is no need to switch between two different ones. In the case of memory for motion events, we have one pattern, the Spanish one, which can be used in both English and Spanish verbalisations, and which can consequently lead to bilinguals having the same memory outcomes as Spanish monolinguals. The English pattern would have been more informative since it has a focus on manner of motion and regularly specifies both the manner and the path of motion, but this was not preferred by bilinguals. Why not? Amongst our CASP principles, we are not concerned on this occasion with learning, so Minimise Learning Effort is not relevant, and nor is Maximise Expressive Power, as we can assume that learners have mastered both the Spanish motion lexicalisation pattern (i.e. 'enter running') and the English pattern ('run into'). The three key principles that are battling it out on this occasion are: Minimise Processing Effort, Maximise Efficiency in Communication and Maximise Common Ground. The outcome of the competition is that the shared pattern in both language and memory prevails (Filipović, 2011), but this may be modulated by internal and external factors, as CASP predicts. We have seen in numerous studies (Chapter 2) that bilingual speakers activate information about both languages when they are speaking one of them. The same general principles are in operation. But the success of the outputs may be compromised if bilinguals have unequal proficiency in their languages and lack full knowledge about how to maximise common ground (i.e. knowledge about common forms, meanings and usage preferences in the two systems) and are unable to maximise their expressive power in the weaker language, the L2. As a result, they may maximise common ground even when it is not permitted to do so (e.g. when they use the L1 English pattern of 'run into' in L2 Spanish *'corer en'; Larrañaga et al., 2012).

It is costlier for processing to constantly switch between two structural patterns than it is to use a single common one. In the case of motion events, there is a common pattern that can be used in both English and Spanish (partial typological overlap; see Chapter 4, Section 4.1), and proficient bilinguals seem to opt for it. In the case of intentionality, however, there is no common pattern for distinguishing between different intentionality types (Chapter 4, Section 4.1) and bilinguals have to find a different way to accommodate this gap between the two grammars using lexical means (as in the lexically expressed evidential meanings developed in Andean Spanish; see Chapter 2). This adds some processing effort in the production of the relevant sentences, but the drive to maximise common ground and enhance processing efficiency overall evidently brings more important benefits, namely shared mental representation for the two languages, shared thinking-for-speaking strategies, and multi-language readiness.

The contrast between expression of, and memory for, motion events vs. intentionality is very interesting. When verbalising and remembering motion events there appears to be a *disadvantage* in maximising common ground, because recognition memory responses were less accurate for Spanish monolinguals and for bilinguals in both languages compared with English monolinguals. However, in the domain of intentionality there was an *advantage for bilingual memory* in both English and Spanish for balanced and L1 Spanish bilinguals, as well as for Spanish monolinguals, because the shared pattern involved making the same distinctions in both languages even though they were required only in Spanish. English monolinguals and L1 English bilinguals had comparatively worse memory for intentionality in events. Thus, a mechanism of **whatever-works-in-both** seems to operate in bilingual verbalisation and memory, but its effects are different based on the patterns that are present or not in a language (partial overlap vs. absence of a structure) and on whether they were mastered. As we saw in this chapter, even though Spanish–English bilinguals may add manner adverbials in their motion lexicalisation more than Spanish native speakers do (as Hohenstein, Eisenberg & Naigles, 2006 have also shown in their study) the Spanish lexicalisation pattern still reduces encoding of, and linguistic attention to, information about the manner of motion. This however is compensated for by the processing benefits that bilinguals gain elsewhere from maximising common ground, by the additional meanings and concepts they attend to in other domains and by their readiness to communicate with a much broader audience.

These experimental findings show that multiple factors are involved in determining how common ground is maximised. One factor is proficiency in each language (Filipović, 2018, 2019b). Another is age of acquisition (Lai et al., 2014; although we are not sure if any proficiency differences were also involved there). Another is the typological relationship between the two languages; that is, whether there is or is not a grammatical or lexical pattern with enough shared form and meaning (e.g. in motion vs. intentionality lexicalisation in English vs. Spanish). Finally, another important factor is frequency for different patterns in use; that is, how productive the relevant patterns are. In the case of motion, the pattern that is found in Spanish is available and not infrequent in English. In the case of intentionality, the shared pattern is very infrequent and unproductive in English, so another strategy is employed by bilinguals (creation of a lexical pattern to match the grammatical one in the other language). The choice of strategy for maximising common ground can depend on the sociolinguistic situation as well and we can make interesting predictions in this regard, using evidence from contact-induced language change with respect to how new patterns in languages emerge – caused, triggered or accelerated by bilingualism (see Heine, 2008 for discussion).

For instance, we can predict that if bilingual and monolingual speakers of English and Spanish lived in close geographical proximity and with close social interactions, and the number of bilinguals (balanced or with L1 Spanish) was greater than the number of monolinguals, then intentionality distinctions could develop in English too. Balanced English–Spanish bilinguals and L1 Spanish bilinguals are not likely to 'lose' the affective dative construction of Spanish if they are in the majority, and the English spoken by monolinguals would eventually change towards lexicalised intentionality as in Spanish. This could be achieved either by making the rare construction 'the engine died on me' more productive, or by enhancing the frequency of lexical paraphrases (adverbial phrases) in order to express the relevant intentionality distinctions, which could then spread and become grammaticalised, as has happened in many other areas of grammar in the past (see Heine and Kuteva, 2005 for numerous examples from different lexical and grammatical domains). If English monolinguals and English L1/ Spanish L2 speakers are in the majority in a contact situation, then the loss of the Spanish *se + affective dative construction* would be the more likely outcome. We have already noted, based on learner corpus data, that L2 leaners of Spanish whose L1 is English rarely use this construction (Chapter 4, Section 4.3.3), and we know that L2 learners avoid structures they do not have in their L1, so lexicalised intentionality would then not stand a strong chance of a status upgrade. These differences in demographics can sway the outcome of contact-induced change in completely opposite directions. CASP for Bilingualism accounts for both outcomes, since crucially both would be efficient in different ways, reflecting the internal and external factors governing bilingual behaviour (Chapter 3), and both would reflect the bilingual drive to maximise common ground.

Finally, much of the previous research has shown that verbalisation improves memory performance (see Schooler & Engstler-Schooler, 1990 for an overview and a critical discussion), but there is some evidence that the reverse can also happen: verbalisation may impair memory. Schooler and Engstler-Schooler (1990) showed that negative effects of verbalisation did not result from incomplete encoding of visual detail because this negative effect was recorded in situations where verbalisation occurred post-encoding. This research was carried out in the domains of face and colour recognition, and other cognitive domains may be similarly affected. Schooler and Engstler-Schooler (1990: 62) argue that:

[...] verbalisation of a visual memory can foster the formation of a nonveridical verbally biased representation corresponding to the original visual stimulus. Access of this verbally biased representation can then interfere with subjects' ability to make use of their intact visual code. This interpretation explains why verbalisation impairs memory for a variety of different nonverbal stimuli; in each case the nonverbal stimuli cannot be adequately recalled in words.

This view of verbal interference is driven by the stronger source of information (verbal) becoming dominant over a weaker one (visual). This view is generally consistent with the dual-code theory for visual memory (Paivio, 1986), with one important difference. Many earlier studies used verbalisation that was of some value for visual memory (e.g. providing the word 'apple' when viewing an apple). If the verbal information is not helpful (e.g. because it lacks information about intentionality) then it is more likely to overshadow the information from the other source, the visual.

Filipović (2011, 2013b) included a non-verbalisation condition, but there was no significant difference in the recognition results between the verbalisation and the non-verbalisation group. We can assume that the speakers in the non-verbalisation condition may have been using language anyway, if only tacitly. Verbalisation may have to be blocked in order to stop verbal overshadowing (e.g. Athanasopoulos et al., 2015; Trueswell & Papafragou, 2010;), but we do not normally go around with our language blocked. Whether explicit or tacit, it seems that verbalisation can 'overshadow' the information available through the visual code and affect how we remember what we see.

5.6   Judgements in L1 vs. L2, and Why the Differences Matter

In the last section we saw that bilingual processing efficiency is such that it strongly encourages the drive towards common patterns in language processing and also in memory, regardless of which language is being used at the time of speaking. In this section we will see that judgements made by bilinguals with regard to possibility and likelihood may differ depending on whether the specific language they are speaking when making the judgement is their first or their second. I am referring specifically here to bilinguals who have unbalanced proficiency, and thus a first language that is their mother tongue acquired in childhood monolingually and a second language L2 as the weaker language and acquired subsequently in adulthood. Their second language may be at a high level of proficiency overall, but it is the way in which it was acquired that can impact concrete occasions of bilingual activity. We will look at a less researched area here involving bilingual mock-jury judgements, and I will point to the impact of different levels of emotional involvement in decision-making when speaking an L1 vs. L2.

5.6.1   Bilingual Mock-Jury Judgement

I will ask the same question with regard to bilingual judgements that I asked before, when I discussed bilingual memory – what are the possible language effects here, and in what way(s) can bilinguals be expected to differ from monolingual populations? Interdisciplinary investigations in this area have not been numerous, especially involving bilinguals. We know that even within a single language, different judgements can be elicited based on how things are phrased. Trujillo (2003) has shown that giving English speakers descriptions of violent events that vary in the verbs that are used will elicit different judgements, in terms of severity, depending on the level of intensity in the manner verbs given in descriptions, with greater intensity in the description leading to a more severe judgement for the offence and with neutral manner verbs resulting in less severe judgements. By the same token, Fausey and Boroditsky (2010) have shown, also in a monolingual context, that the use of the clearly agentive structure *X broke Y* to describe an event that witnesses saw leads to more verdicts of the culpability of X than if that offence is described as *Y broke*. Ibarretxe-Antuñano and Filipović (2013) tested judgements made about the severity of violence amongst monolingual English and Spanish speakers and in Spanish–English bilinguals. As explained earlier, the Spanish lexicon is less rich in manner-of-motion verbs and their use is restricted, so the same kinds of violent events described in English (where manner detail is rich and frequent) were judged as being more severe in that language than when they were described in Spanish (where there is typically less rich manner detail).

In this section we ask the question that is most relevant for bilingualism: can a judgement be different based on whether an L1 or an L2 speaker of a language is making it? Filipović (2016) showed that the answer to this question is yes. The study examined judgements made in English by mock jurors who were either L1 or L2 English speakers. All the participants were asked to judge the certainty level of speakers/witnesses and to rate the possibility that the events described actually took place. This was the first study of its kind to investigate whether the way in which a language has been acquired (as an L1 vs. L2) would make a difference in how people use it to make critical judgements in a legal context as jury members. It is very likely that speakers of L2 English will often sit in a jury with L1 English speakers because of the sheer numbers nowadays of L2 English users in English-speaking countries. Whether L1 vs. L2 command of English has consequences for socially important contexts such as this is an important question in our world today, where English is the main second language and an official language in so many countries.

The participants were presented with event descriptions by witnesses containing a variety of English modal verbs, such as 'must', 'could', 'may' and 'might'. One key difference that emerged was the fact that native speakers of English do not make a distinction between the meanings of 'may' and 'might' when it comes to the level of certainty or possibility. Speakers of English as an L2 do, however: for them, 'may' refers to something more probable/likely than 'might'. At issue is the question: does 'The man *may* have dropped the bag by the bushes' refer to an event in which it is more likely that the man dropped the bag by the bushes, compared with 'The man *might* have dropped the bag by the bushes'? For native English speakers it turns out that there is no difference in the degree of possibility or certainty between these expressions with 'may' and 'might'. The non-native speakers, by contrast, judged all the expressions in the experimental stimuli containing the verb 'may' to be referring to events that were much more likely to have happened than those expressed with 'might'. Thus, for L2 speakers of English 'might' clearly seems to refer to less probable situations than those described by 'may'. As a result, the estimated certainty of a witness is significantly higher if 'may' is used and lower for 'might'.

Filipović (2016) argues that this is due to the treatment that 'may' and might' have been given in native-speaker vs. learner grammars and to pedagogical attention. Scholarly grammars of English describing native-speaker usage note that 'might' may be used to describe a lower possibility alternative to 'may', but only on some occasions and for some speakers (Huddleston & Pullum, 2002: 200; Quirk et al., 1985: 223): 'there is a tendency for the difference between may and might (in a sense of tentative possibility) to be neutralised' (Quirk et al., 1985: 234), since there is little or no difference between these words for the speakers involved. In any case, in terms of the degree of perceived possibility (past or future) there is no indication that any distinction is now reliably made in English between these two modals, and nor is this an area to which English grammar pays a lot of attention. In fact, the 'may'/ 'might' distinction is mentioned almost in passing in key grammars of English (or in the case of Quirk et al., 1985 as a footnote). We can therefore conclude that this is not a very salient meaning distinction for native speakers (see also Whitacker, 1987 for a discussion).

By contrast, English L2 grammars and textbooks often highlight that 'might' is more tentative than 'may' and more likely to express a smaller possibility (see Filipović, 2016 for details). L2 speakers, who prefer one-to-one form–meaning mappings rather than one to many or many to one (as discussed before in relation to ambiguity; Chapter 2, Section 2.2.2.4), occasionally latch onto the convenience of remembering that the two distinct forms, 'may' and 'might' express two distinct possibility levels. This is not a surprising strategy for L2 learners to adopt, since the overlap in meaning and use between any two distinct forms is uncomfortable for learners in general and fossilising the 'may'/'might' distinction based on degree of possibility in this way provides welcome relief. In fact, the terms 'flexible rule' and the idea of variable meaning are a learner's worst nightmare at a time when he or she is desperately trying to find some fixed bearings to rely on in the learning process (i.e. unambiguous and steadfast rules to adhere to).

What we can conclude from this is that different bilinguals can exhibit different behaviours under the same circumstances, based on how they acquired the language in question, as an L1 or L2. This contrasts with the finding we have seen earlier in this chapter, that different bilinguals can have the same outputs under the same circumstances (those with equal Spanish–English proficiency and those with L1 Spanish–L2 English in memory for intentionality). Further research is needed for many more typologically different language pairs, in different cognitive domains, and in addition, as has been demonstrated in this section, we must take pedagogical factors into consideration (i.e. what the learners have been taught). It is understandable that second-language tuition cannot cover all the minutiae of L2 grammar and use, but certain aspects certainly deserve more attention than they are currently receiving, on the account of their relevance and practical significance for real-world interactions, as advocated in the Applied Language Typology Programme (Filipović, 2017a, 2017b). Modal meanings in L2 English are one such area. The affective dative construction in L2 Spanish is another. Further research along the lines illustrated here may uncover more features that need a more dedicated focus in teaching and learning, which could lead to additional benefits for L2 learners.

5.6.2   Moral Judgements by Bilinguals

In the last section of this chapter I draw attention to another aspect of bilingual language use: its relationship with emotions, still in the same context of judgement-making. Previous research has shown that there is a strong emotional component associated with the language one speaks, especially when it comes to autobiographical memory (Pavlenko, 2014; see also Altarriba, 2002 for a succinct overview). Our language is part of our identity and of our belief about who we are and where we belong as individuals, culturally and socially. Researchers in psychology have investigated the effects of having more or less emotional distance with regard to the two languages of bilinguals. This assumption was motivated by the evidence that, overall, a foreign language elicits less intense emotional reactions relative to a native language (see e.g. Caldwell-Harris & Ayçiçeği-Dinn, 2009; Dewaele, 2004; Opitz & Degner, 2012). For instance, skin conductance responses and the perceived force of emotional phrases (i.e. reprimands) are more intense and higher if presented in a native language compared to a foreign language of late learners (Harris, 2010). For early learners, no such difference was detected, which means that physiological reaction to emotional language is modulated by relative proficiency. Similarly, loss aversion is reduced when people are asked to use a foreign language when making decisions (Keysar, Hayakawa & An, 2012).

Bilinguals are more likely to make higher-risk choices if these are presented in a language in which they have less emotional involvement, i.e. their weaker language L2. By the same token, Costa et al. (2014) have shown that the use of a foreign (L2) language by bilinguals results in more rational moral judgements than when the first language is used due to the increased emotional distance bilinguals have towards the L2. Costa et al. (2014) argued that reduced emotionality promotes more rational control and leads to a greater likelihood of making 'utilitarian choices' in moral dilemma situations such as the choice between deliberately sacrificing one person in order to save more (the 'footbridge dilemma'; see Costa et al., 2014 for details). There is a need for further research on decision-making in many other contexts, such as medical or judicial, where the choices made could also be affected by the language used to make them, L1 vs. L2. It will also be necessary to test bilinguals with balanced proficiency and see if any reported effects in this area with unbalanced bilinguals can be neutralised. These future studies will have to control for proficiency and the individual language-learning history of speakers in order to ensure that the differences in decisions are indeed driven by the fact that the language in which they are made is an L2 rather than by the lack of a proper understanding of what precisely is stated or requested due to limited L2 proficiency.

5.7   Conclusion

Based on the examples discussed in this chapter, we can agree with Schrauf et al. (2003: 228) that, beyond representing specific pieces of information as the contents of memory, language seems to play a much more active role in online processing and memory. Bilinguals appear to maximise the use of a shared pattern in both verbalisation and memory if there is such a pattern, and if there is not, they will create one, for example by specifying intentionality or evidentiality lexically (see also Chapter 4). If the shared pattern leads to a less frequent or less detailed expression of some of the components of the event (e.g. manner of motion), this component is likely to be less detailed in both language and memory. If on the other hand the common ground is created by adding meanings (e.g. by specifying intentionality), memory recall for this feature improves.

It may be that the differences reported on presence vs. absence of advantages for bilingualism can be due to the fact that bilingualism may produce different effects in different cognitive domains for different speakers, because organising information bilingually may lead to both adding and reducing available information in different circumstances. Regardless, the advantage of having a multi-language-ready mind remains because overall, the resources of two systems when combined, and the control involved in managing them, are ultimately bound to be beneficial for language use and communication with more interlocutors and in more situations. And this is before we even begin to consider the richness of multiculturality that comes with multilingualism. We do need more finely grained, domain-specific and ultimately construction-specific comparisons to detect where the similarities and differences between bilinguals and monolinguals lie, and where the advantages or disadvantages in bilingual language processing and bilingual cognition may reside. The studies selected in this chapter illustrate just the first steps that have been taken in this direction and will hopefully inspire further research.

What we have also seen in this chapter is that having equal proficiency in two languages and using both languages actively in the same situation (actively speaking or having language(s) tacitly present) means that multiple resources for describing or looking at a situation are in place, and these can all be used for verbalisation and other cognitive tasks such as categorising experiences or remembering information about events that have been witnessed. When one language is stronger than the other we see that the access to the resources of each language is not the same and thus we have a greater reliance on the stronger, L1, even though the L2 may be the language being actively spoken. This results in different preferences for maximising common ground: L1 English speakers do not draw the relevant distinctions of intentional vs. non-intentional in L2 Spanish even though they should when speaking that language, whilst L1 Spanish speakers do draw these distinctions in their L2 English even though they do not have to.

We have also discovered that there are benefits for memory in some bilinguals when both languages are kept active in the experiment (and presumably, when they are habitually equally active). CASP for Bilingualism predicts that it is not communicatively efficient to maximise common ground excessively; that is, by always adding meanings from one language when speaking another that does not require them, or by over-using minority patterns in one language just because they are the majority pattern in the other language. This is why bilinguals maximise common ground to different degrees on different occasions (due to external factors such as language mode), and in line with their proficiency and language dominance (internal factors), and both types of factors modulate how much bilinguals can control the output in each language. We need more interaction-based studies, which test to see what happens to the same bilingual speaker under different circumstances (e.g. talking with other bilinguals or monolinguals, in formal vs. informal occasions, to proficient vs. non-proficient speakers of one of their languages, etc.). Further studies in this vein will also enable us to fully understand bilingualism within and across minds and to determine what, if any, online benefits may translate into possibly more permanent, offline benefits, for communication and for cognition.

Finally, we touched upon the differences between bilinguals that stem from how they learned their languages. Both meanings and feelings seem to be affected by the path of acquisition. Classroom English and related pedagogical materials may not capture the usage that is characteristic of native speakers. Whilst the ideal of the 'native speaker' is not necessarily something that I advocate here, an argument can still be made that the consequences of the differences between native and foreign acquisition in terms of making judgements are worth highlighting, especially because it is relevant for contexts other than language learning and teaching, namely legal, and also medical contexts (see Trbojević, 2012). The construct of a 'native speaker' is not to be seen as a norm or an aim or evaluative measure in bilingualism, but it is still a valid concept to have, as Hulstijn (2018) explains in detail.

We have seen that the language used to make a judgement can carry more of an emotional charge, and people asked to make judgements may be more emotionally detached if their attachment to the language in which they are asked to make that judgement is lower (i.e. an L2 as opposed to an L1). The research on moral dilemmas and L1 vs. L2 decision-making discussed in this chapter complements the anecdotal experience that many bilingual parents living in L2 environments have. The parents who speak to their bilingual children using their L2 (the language of daily routine, work and school, and which may be an L1 for their children) most of the time promptly revert to their L1 when emotions run somewhat higher, for example when they are extremely angry or extremely pleased with their children. It is hard to imagine that there can be a balanced bilingual when it comes to emotions and to emotion-affected behaviour in language or with language.

6 Bilinguals in Action as Language Professionals

Specialised Interpreting and Translating

In this chapter the focus of attention is on a specific context of communication in which bilinguals play a vital role: translation. The challenges involved in using both of one's languages in a single communicative situation are particularly high when both languages must be equally active, and when multi-language-readiness is such that it enables a smooth transition from one to the other at each turn. Our focus will be on interpreting in legal contexts. Interpreting is of particular interest to us because it is a highly restrictive context of bilingual action: the competition between two linguistic systems must be dealt with rapidly and accurately and the ultimate goal is to ensure that the translated discourse conveys exactly the same meaning as that of the original. Legal contexts are highly relevant because they provide clear examples of what can happen when the interpreting goal is not achieved: the consequences can go beyond mere misunderstanding or misinterpretation. They impact not only legal outcomes but also the lives of the people involved. At a theoretical level, this gives us insights into the possible ways in which the online competition between two linguistic systems can be resolved and it enables us to suggest ways in which this competition may or may not be generalisable to other instances of bilingual communication in a bilingual mode.

6.1   Introduction

This chapter is not meant to be a general and exhaustive survey of research on translation and interpreting. Rather, our main goal here is to use this context in order to highlight what happens when two languages are fully engaged within a single bilingual mind and in a single communicative situation, and to see how the restrictions of the context impact bilingual outputs. I will refer to a number of studies that have investigated interpreter-assisted exchanges in police or court settings and I will show how typological differences between different languages guide the habits of speakers to include or exclude certain types of information. Entrenched preferences in linguistic expression can then lead to translation and communication difficulties, because the target language may not have the means to accommodate the requirements or preferences of the source language adequately. In other words, perfect translation equivalents often do not exist. It may then fall on the *interpreter to act as a linguistic problem-solver*, for the police, for judges and for jury members.

I also show here how jury judgements can be impacted by grammatical and lexical features of the language used for the presentation of evidence in the original vs. the translation. Using an experimental methodological approach in a translation study enables us to discover what kinds of information detail are likely to be omitted, either from original statements (because the original language makes it difficult to express certain meanings) or from translations (because the target language does not have equivalent means to render the original meanings). These findings can then be applied in professional practice, to fine-tune training for translators and interpreters as well as for legal professionals who work with them.

Translation is something bilinguals do every day: inside their heads, for themselves, or out loud, for the benefit of others. Translators and interpreters are a bilingual population of special interest to us because they are the ones who regularly use both languages to a very similar extent in their daily lives by the nature of the jobs they do. In addition, they use their languages under very specific circumstances: in formal communications to two monolingual audiences.

Even though we must acknowledge that interpreting or translating from one language into another is not the same as free encoding (as discussed in previous chapters), the process of translation is nonetheless a central feature in the daily lives of all bilinguals, who must often engage in translation at least in private (explicitly or implicitly). Some bilinguals make it their profession. As we have seen in previous chapters, bilinguals maximise common ground, which sometimes does indeed resemble what happens in translation but sometimes actually results in outputs that are closer to being 'lost in translation' (e.g. when not all meanings from one language feature readily in the grammar or the lexicon of the other; see Chapter 4).

When speakers have to translate between two languages, whether frequently or not, privately or publicly, translation is bound to play a significant role in engendering certain habits that may impact overall bilingual language use. Previous research has reported that bilingual speakers who habitually engage in translation informally (e.g. as community interpreters) 'show more overlap in the exemplars they generate to a concept when responding in different languages than do bilinguals with less or no translation experience, who show greater divergence in their pattern of response across languages to a given concept' (Lopez & Vaid, 2018: 159). In other words, extensive translation experience involves constant searches for the words in both languages whose semantic representations share the greatest number of features, resulting in 'faster access to similar feature groupings in the other language' (ibid.). Research has shown that prior and extensive experience in translation affects how language is represented and accessed by those bilinguals who have such experience. These bilinguals may be more attuned to shared meanings in the two languages even when they are not required to establish equivalence in a specific task (Lopez & Vaid, 2016; see also Tzou et al., 2012, and Tzou, Vaid & Chen, 2016, for further details and exemplification). Translation is therefore one of the core contexts in which we should examine bilinguals in action.

The act of translating involves an intense and intimate contact between two languages. Being good at it requires considerable skill. It is not an automatic gift granted to any bilingual speaker who has mastered two languages. Bilingual language professionals present us with an ideal testing ground for a number of predictions that stem from our bilingual language processing model as defined and described in Chapter 3. This is because we can be sure that the language contact in the bilingual minds of translators and interpreters is extensive and constant, with a high activation of both languages at the same time on a daily basis. In this chapter I focus specifically on those studies of translation and interpreting that help us understand the outcomes of collaboration and competition between two linguistic systems in conjunction with the relevant internal (*variability*) and external (*adjustability*) factors (as outlined in Chapter 3).

Some important issues discussed in legal translation and interpreting studies will not be considered here because they fall outside the scope of this book, such as matters concerning the outsourcing of interpreter provision, quality of interpreting services, legal requirements for interpreter registration and the professional assessment available in different countries. These are all fundamental areas of importance for professional translation and interpreting practice. Different countries face different problems in this regard, and they have come up with a variety of possible solutions for addressing their problems. Our main focus remains the use of language itself, and its consequences for a very specific, high-risk communicative context. Other contexts of translation are also not in focus here because they are not necessarily restricted to meaning equivalence. For instance, poetic or literary translation may be directed at achieving and creating the same kind of atmosphere or provoking the same reaction in the target text audience as the source text (which makes the translation dynamic; Nida, 1964). Therefore, it may be necessary to alter some of the original meanings in order to adjust the source text to the cultural or conceptual preferences of the target audience in order to achieve the same audience response. This kind of approach would not be acceptable in the context of legal translation, where no alteration of the original information content is appropriate.

Legal contexts therefore represent an ideal testing ground for forensic linguistic analysis of the kind of issues we may encounter, which stem from language contrasts that go beyond differences in formulation and that can impact the content of the message, with potentially important consequences for access to justice, legal decisions and equality. In other words, this inter-disciplinary research has relevance for real-life outcomes such as whether a person is found innocent or guilty, or deemed to be telling the truth or lying. Here we go beyond mere detection of the language contrasts that cause difficulties in translation and document what their wider social relevance can be.

Translation is an activity that has been practised since antiquity, but translation studies as an academic discipline is a relatively novel field that is fast becoming a progressive interdisciplinary area of research, informed by the latest findings in psycholinguistics, sociolinguistics, philosophy of language, language typology and cognitive and forensic linguistics. Rojo (2015) provides extensive illustration of how research on translation can inform cognitive science, and vice versa: multiple methodologies and insights from a number of approaches within cognitive science can help us address the complex phenomena that are involved in the translation process. Adopting new meth-odologies from other disciplines (such as the use of electronic corpora and experimental approaches to data elicitation) means that translation studies has been able to move beyond impressionistic assessments of small, limited, individual samples and could offer significant new insights into how bilingual minds process language.

Translation itself is most often considered an art, and successful translations of creative narratives or historical accounts are awarded prizes. Translated legal (and also medical) texts are not up for translation awards. This kind of translation is not considered an art because these contexts do not afford the same kind of freedom of expression available to translators of literature, for example. In fact, taking the artistic licence that may result in including or excluding something in translation can sometimes be potentially fatal for people impacted by legal (or medical) documents and procedures. It is easy to understand why this is so. As indicated before, when translating novels or poems, some information can be added or omitted for the purpose of maintaining the rhetorical style, the flow or the general atmosphere and imagery of the original narrative. If this happens, some meanings may have to be lost in translation, but nobody is likely to die as a result (except maybe figuratively). However, if this is done in a legal or medical context, somebody might die for real. Non-literary contexts are therefore the most restrictive, and they oblige translators and interpreters to resolve the conflicts between their two systems, the source and the target language, in an optimal way so that no meaning is lost or distorted. They create active online pressure, and thus they represent a key area for studying the clash of linguistic patterns in the bilingual mind. CASP for Bilingualism is useful here because it can help us predict and account for the outcomes in these clashes between patterns.

The pressures on language professionals such as translators and interpreters are manifold, and the pressures impact linguistic outputs. Mulayim, Lai and Norma (2015) give a succinct summary of what is expected of a translator in general, and of a legal translator/interpreter in particular. It is not easy to navigate one's way through this professional context as an interpreter, because expectations can vary from situation to situation. Some legal professionals expect interpreters to be little more than neutral conduits that transform texts from one language into the other, whilst others expect interpreters to be cultural mediators and to provide relevant information in this regard in addition to their language renditions (see Berk-Seligson, 2002 [1990] for a thorough discussion). The legal context restricts the overall freedom that the translator or interpreter may have, and its sole purpose is to render the meaning from the original in such a way that it stays the same in the translation. Accuracy is the key priority and it is essential to bridge differences between languages in order to avoid misunderstandings or misinterpretations that could have serious consequences for speakers or those being talked about. We will see, however, that absolute accuracy is not always achieved when there is also a drive for naturalness and when the general goal in translation is to sound authentic in the target language. We are faced with competing motivations here, pulling in different directions, just as in other domains of language processing and use (see Chapter 3).

I will focus here mainly on the way language contrasts have been resolved in situations involving interpreting. I use the term 'translation' to refer to the products of both translating and interpreting, but I must note that translating is an offline activity, which it involves longer decision-making processes and potentially more changes to initial outputs. Thus, it is interpreting that takes centre stage at present.

6.2   Legal Translation and Interpreting: Some Contextual Background

Bilinguals play a crucial role in legal systems, increasingly so with the prevailing multilingualism worldwide. Not only are they responsible for rendering meaning from one language into the other, but they can sway opinions and judgements and affect the perception of the original speakers. Legal interpreting has been investigated extensively, for example in multilingual court-rooms (e.g. Berk-Seligson, 2002 [1990]); Hale, 2004, 2014), in police investiga-tions (Berk-Seligson, 2009; Filipović, 2007a, 2013a, 2013b, 2019a; Filipović & Hijazo-Gascón, 2018; Hijazo-Gascón, 2019; Kredens & Morris, 2010) and in community interpreting (Hale, 2007). All types of legal communication, spoken or written, if relevant for the law, can be studied within the field of *forensic linguistics*. A sample of language is relevant for the law if it has a role to play in a legal process, such as a criminal investigation or court proceedings, be it a contract, a personal letter or a recorded conversation. Police interviews and interview transcripts as well as court transcripts and court examinations are all examples of forensically relevant texts. It is not always enough to study just the written transcripts – there are other types of interactions that are relevant in communicative exchanges and that are often not well recorded.

Berk-Seligson (2002 [1990]) lists a number of features that characterise court interpreting (e.g. hedges, insertions, hesitations, etc.). These features underlie the perception of witness testimony style as either powerful or power-less. Interpreters sometimes add markers of powerless speech when these were not present in the original, or omit them in translation when the original did contain them. Thus, they can change the characteristics of the original speech from powerful to powerless and vice versa and affect the perception of the speaker by listeners (e.g. by a judge or jury members). Therefore, it is crucial to have an accurate rendering of the original speech in translation, involve only professional interpreters, and record everything that was said as well as *how* it was said (e.g. whether there was hesitation or hedging or not).

Professional interpreting may not always be available or chosen. On some occasions there is no time to get a professional interpreter to the site and police officers need information urgently, which can be provided by bilin-guals within a community or by community interpreters (see Hale, 2007 for detailed investigation of community interpreting). More problematic are occasions when bilingual police officers, who are usually heritage bilinguals, also act as interpreters. Firstly, the ethical dimension for such situations is questionable at best, especially in serious crime investigations and when interviewing suspects. Access to justice has been shown to be endangered in such cases (Berk-Seligson, 2011; Filipović & Abad Vergara, 2018). Secondly, the quality of interpreting is poorer with non-professional inter-preters. As mentioned earlier, bilinguals are not necessarily good interpreters, especially if they are heritage speakers, who normally have much lower proficiency in one of their two languages (usually the heritage language). Hayes and Hale (2010) have discovered that, unfortunately, appeals on the basis of inadequate interpreting rarely succeed, because courts are unlikely to be convinced by linguistic arguments about the impact of poor interpretation on the outcome of the case.

In a law enforcement context, it is of the utmost importance to have an interpreter who is neutral and accurate when rendering information into the target language, because the life of 'a suspect [. . .] may depend on what he is understood as having said' (Berk-Seligson, 2011: 30) at the investigative stage. Related concerns have been voiced in my own research (Filipović 2007a, 2013b, 2019a). Non-native speakers are at a disadvantage from the very beginning, first in the interviews with law enforcement and then further on in the judicial process in courts, where the statements they make in their language are never recorded. These findings are very hard to come by because in most jurisdictions throughout the world bilingual police interview transcripts are not available, or if they are, they are likely to be transcribed as monolingual and non-verbatim (e.g. as in the UK; Filipović, 2019a). The excellent practice in the United States of making bilingual transcripts of police interviews is extremely helpful for the purpose of revealing the kinds of disadvantages that non-native speakers face (Filipović, 2007a; Filipović & Hijazo-Gascón, 2018; Hijazo-Gascón, 2019).

6.3   Unbalanced Proficiency, Unprofessional Interpreting

Forensic linguistic evidence, such as bilingual transcripts, can be a window into bilingual language processing more generally as well as being an invaluable exemplification of how important bilingualism is for both theory and professional practice. In a recent study of police interpreting Filipović and Abad Vergara (2018) drew attention to the ways in which linguistic inaccuracies and the lack of impartiality on the part of an interpreting officer had contributed to blame attribution and a lack of neutrality that is required of an interpreter, as a result of the officer's assumed dual role (as both interpreter and police officer). For further details regarding ethical issues related to the biases of officer-interpreters see Filipović and Abad Vergara (ibid.). On this occasion the focus is on the communicative consequences of the fact that the interpreter was a heritage speaker of Spanish, with English as his stronger language.

The police interview analysed by Filipović and Abad Vergara (ibid.) was carried out with a Spanish-speaking suspect charged with a serious offence (sexual assault). One of the two officers was acting as interpreter throughout the interview. It was evident that the police officer's command of the heritage language (Spanish) was not adequate in many respects, even though he appeared to be fluent overall. The problems became clear upon more detailed scrutiny of the transcript. One example involved the use of the two different verbs ('ser' and 'estar') in Spanish for which there is only one equivalent in English, *to be*. English does not distinguish between these two different meanings of the verb 'to be', which distinguish between the temporary and the permanent ('she is a teacher (at the moment)' as opposed to 'she is a woman'), and which are distinguished by 'estar' and 'ser' respectively in Spanish. For instance, in example (1) the bilingual police officer should have said '¿cómo estaba ella?' not '¿cómo era ella?' because he was inquiring about the state of the victim at a specific time rather than her essence (i.e. permanent personality characteristics). The use of 'ser' instead of 'estar', was out of context and confused the suspect (Filipović & Abad Vergara, 2018: 72):

(1)   Police officer-interpreter: Cómo era ella?
        Translation: 'What was she like?'
        Suspect: [inaudible/unclear; does not understand the question]

On another occasion, the officer-interpreter produced some grammatically unlicensed structures in Spanish, which would have been perfectly grammatical in English:

(2)   Police officer-interpreter: * Cuando usted la caminó para la escuela . . .
        Translation: 'When you walked her to school . . . '

Again, the suspect's response was a muffled confusion due to lack of understanding caused by the use of the ungrammatical structure (2) in Spanish. As Fernandez, de Souza and Carrando (2017) observe (see Chapter 2, Section 2.2.2.3 for more details), bilinguals have higher tolerance/acceptance than monolingual speakers for ungrammatical structures if they are grammatical in their other language. Using motion verbs (such as 'walk') transitively ('to walk somebody somewhere') is not grammatical in Spanish. Example (2) is a construction calqued from English, and as it stands in Spanish it may be tolerable for a bilingual who can figure out its meaning based on its English counterpart, but it causes confusion and is hard to process for a monolingual speaker of Spanish. The police officer-interpreter used this construction type on more than one occasion during the same interview. In our terms, he was maximising common ground beyond grammaticality, which the monolingual Spanish-speaking suspect found utterly confusing. The suspect hesitated and faltered each time, asking for clarification when this construction was used by the officer-interpreter (i.e. by saying '¿Cómo?' = 'What?' or similar). When we consider that pauses and hesitations have negative consequences on communication in general (Dingemanse & Enfield, 2014; Roberts, Margutti & Takano, 2011), and in judicial contexts in particular (Berk-Seligson, 2002 [1990]), we can conclude that the suspect is more likely to be judged negatively with regard to his apparent lack of co-operativeness and confidence when responding.

There were numerous other instances when the officer-interpreter displayed inadequate command of Spanish (Filipović & Abad Vergara, 2018). Heritage speakers are not appropriate interpreters in formal and high-risk contexts. Even though they may be able to communicate in each language, their knowledge of the heritage language is not adequate for the purpose. Crucially, interpreter training develops specific and necessary skills that get honed through professional experience, and these are not available to untrained interpreters.

6.4   Balanced Proficiency, Professional Interpreting

In the remaining part of this chapter we shall focus on cases of professional interpreting by speakers with equal competence in both languages, and who have been professionally trained, as our central group of interest. We will examine how this specific context influences the operation of our CASP for Bilingualism mechanisms. Since interpreting in this context requires the highest possible standards of accuracy and precision, we do not expect interpreters to add to or omit information from the original. However, there is also the general expectation that interpreters will aim to use structures that are characteristic of each language, and that they will try to sound natural and native in each language, so that their audience has the impression that a native speaker is using each language. This so-called 'translator invisibility' is considered a praiseworthy quality (but it also has been argued against; see Venuti, 1995, and further discussion below).

We expect interpreters to use the same structures in both languages when these constitute the majority pattern in both, but not when they are atypical or unusual in one of the two languages. In CASP for Bilingualism terms, we assume that professional interpreters have maximised their expressive power in both languages and are able to express meanings in each language just like native speakers. They are also expected to be maximally communicatively efficient in each language and to calibrate their output to the hearer's expectations. Maximise Common Ground is likely to be kept in check, however, more than in regular bilingual use, because if fully active, it may lead to less authentic outputs (or unusual- or awkward-sounding ones) in the target language. Translation training insists on authentic target text outputs, and translated text that reads or sounds like it has not been written or spoken in the target language is traditionally considered bad translation. Translations are praised if they do not reveal that they are translations (Venuti, 1995: 1):

A translated text, whether prose or poetry, fiction or nonfiction, is judged acceptable by most publishers, reviewers, and readers when it reads fluently, when the absence of any linguistic or stylistic peculiarities makes it seem transparent, giving the appearance that it reflects the foreign writer's personality or intention or the essential meaning of the foreign text – the appearance, in other words, that the translation is not in fact a translation, but the 'original'.

However, this insistence on not being able to tell it is a translation, which involves the translator's invisibility, has led to a reaction, namely the call to have more translator visibility. Venuti says that the prevalent insistence on fluency in English translation is apparent in different types of texts. The more fluent the translation, the more invisible the translator. This may sound at first like a good thing; that is, we are apparently getting what feels like direct access to the original author. In contrast, Venuti (1995: 20) argues that we can use translations of texts to become more aware of linguistic and cultural differences and let translation be the place where the other culture is manifested. For translations in the context of the law, the linguistic and cultural differences need to be brought to the fore, as we shall see, because if this is not done, important details about the case at hand may be missed or misunderstood.

An additional aspect that must be considered with reference to interpreting in particular, which is our key focus for testing the online competition amongst our processing principles, is the considerable amount of effort it requires (see Gile's 1997 'effort model' in interpreting). In addition to various cognitive and time pressures, this effort can also be attributed to the difficulty of finding equivalents for structures that require significant transformation in translation. Rojo, Ramos and Valenzuela (2014) measured the cognitive effort invested by participants using an eye-tracker to record their eye movements whilst they sight-translated a number of short stories containing the same sentence formulated as either a resultative construction (e.g. 'He hammered the handle straight') or as a predicative construction (e.g. 'He hammered the handle until it was straight'). A statistically significant difference was reported between the two types of constructions for all the parameters analysed (i.e. number of fixations, backtracks, total gaze time and changes in pupil size). The translation of the resultative version was found to demand greater cognitive effort than its non-resultative counterpart due to the lack of an equivalent resultative structure in Spanish with exactly the same form (see also Fernandez et al., 2017, on differences in bilinguals' reading times for acceptable vs. unacceptable constructions).

Let us now look at some language contrasts that represent a major source of difficulty and see how highly trained language professionals deal with them. We saw in Chapter 4 that bilinguals have more than one option available: keep the languages apart and sound authentic/natural in each, or add or omit details so as to maximise common ground and thus ease the cognitive pressure that comes from constantly making a complete switch from one pattern to another. What happens, then, when there are context-specific requirements whereby the translator must adhere to the original as much as possible whilst also producing a target output that sounds as if it were the original? How are language contrasts dealt with, online, under a high level of pressure and with such demanding contextual restrictions? Keeping the languages apart is easier when just one language is being spoken at a time (monolingual mode), but the context of interpreting is interesting because the ideal of sounding like a monolingual in each language needs to be pursued whilst both languages are highly active, in a bilingual mode.

6.5   Clash of Titans (Sorry, Patterns!) in Translation

Let us return to our two cognitive domains, motion and intentionality, which provided our case studies for bilingual memory (Chapter 5), and let us see how events in these two domains with their very different structure options are translated in legal contexts. The choice of these domains is again a principled one: how somebody moved and whether an act was committed on purpose or not is extremely important in judicial contexts, such as police investigations and court examinations. For instance, based on how somebody moved (e.g. running vs. limping) police officers can draw inferences about whether the person they are looking for is near or far from the scene of the crime or whether the person is hurt or not. We now know that speakers of typologically different languages differ with regard to how much and how often they talk about manner. Similarly, we are aware that some languages have distinct constructions for intentional vs. non-intentional events whilst others regularly use the same construction for both event types, which means that event descriptions can be unambiguous in one language but ambiguous in the other with respect to intentionality (Chapter 4).

Typological differences between languages make some meanings easier to express and some more difficult. As a result, some pieces of information about witnessed events may be more likely to be provided in some languages and not in others. By the same token, information may be present in the original and missing in translation and vice versa – not present in the original and added in translation – just because the habitual lexicalisation patterns in the target language (preferred ways of framing experience) make it easy vs. difficult to include certain information. A number of different translation strategies are resorted to in order to cope with the differences between two languages with respect to their lexical and grammatical patterns (see Ibarretxe-Antuñano & Filipović, 2013; Molés-Cases, 2016). It is the use of preferred patterns in the target language that creates the much-desired fluency in translation, and these are therefore generally prioritised at the cost of language-specific meanings expressed in the original. When we have a departure from a natural pattern of expression in the target language, we are faced with *translationese* – an output that resembles the original language. This was shown in a study of literary translations from German into Spanish (see Molés-Cases, 2016), whereby there was more information about manner of motion than would have been the case in Spanish original texts of comparable status because of the numerous instances of manner lexicalisations present in the German original texts (see also House, 2004 and Baumgarten & Özçetin, 2008 on how business communication translated into German is shaped by the style of the English original texts).

6.5.1   Motion in Translation

Let us look again at our contrasting patterns in English and Spanish, involving motion descriptions:

3a)   He ran out of the house, across the street and into the park.

3b)   Salió de la casa corriendo, cruzó la calle corriendo y entró en el parque corriendo.
'He exited the house running, crossed the street running and entered the park running.'

In (3a) only one verb is used in English, whilst Spanish speakers and translators have to use three verbs (underlined) in the same situation (3b). It is conspicuous that all three verbs in (3b) encode Path ('exited', 'crossed' and 'entered'), and that the Manner component rendered by the gerund ('corriendo' = 'running') has to be repeated after each path verb in the Spanish translation because we have to convey the message that the man ran all the time, which is the meaning expressed in the original sentence in English. Another translation alternative is to put the manner gerund at the beginning of the expression as in (3c):

3c)   Corriendo salió de la casa cruzó la calle y entró en el parque.
'Running he exited the house crossed the street and entered the park.'

A translator has to make choices in fitting one language to the other. By choosing (3b) as a translation for the English expression (3a), a translator would have emphasised Manner, which was not done in the original. Furthermore, the repetition of 'corriendo' ('running') with all three directional verbs in (3b) is stylistically awkward. The structure of (3c) is also problematic because it would mean, if applied generally to this language context, that a large number of sentences in English to Spanish translation would have to include a gerund at the beginning, which would be a very unusual pattern for Spanish. In addition, when multiple manners of motion are present in a motion event (see examples (1a)–(1c) in Chapter 5, Section 5.3), English speakers are more likely to express them, whilst Spanish speakers omit a great deal of manner information. Providing abundance of manner detail or highlighting manner is not part of the Spanish rhetorical style (Slobin, 1996). In fact, what Slobin (1996, 1997) showed is that habitually, when expressions such as the English in (3a) are translated, information on manner is most likely be omitted altogether. Finally, for some Spanish speakers, if 'corriendo' ('running') is added just once after the first verb as in (3d), this may elicit the interpretation that the running was happening all the time, for the remainder of the subject's trajectory, i.e. when crossing the street and entering the park:

3d)   Salió de la casa corriendo cruzó la calle y entró en el parque.
'He exited the house running crossed the street and entered the park.'

However, the meaning of running throughout in (3d) would be only an implicature in the Gricean sense (and therefore cancellable) rather than asserted, and thus easily deniable (as in 'I never said that he ran all the time, he only ran out of the house and then started walking!').

This typological difference between Spanish and English has resulted in different narrative styles in the two languages. Slobin (1996) analysed a number of novels in English and Spanish and their translations into Spanish and English respectively. He found that in literary contexts, information about manner is not rendered from the original into the translation in over 50 per cent of cases, since as we saw earlier, the Spanish pattern has numerous restrictions, lexical and syntactic, with regard to when and how manner can be expressed. This means that half of the time readers of the original text in English receive more dynamic event descriptions and have different mental imagery from readers of the Spanish translation. In English translations of Spanish original texts on the other hand, the situation is reversed: there are fewer instances of manner information in the original than in the translation. Translators make their motion expressions more in line with the English (target language) lexicalisation pattern by adding manner information, because otherwise it sounds awkward/unnatural/foreign. Constant use of path verbs, as in Spanish, is somewhat unusual in English (e.g. 'He ascended the stairs running' instead of 'He ran up the stairs'). These typological contrasts and their effects have now been documented in extensive research data and in a variety of contexts of use (literary texts, spoken discourse, metaphorical language; see Slobin, 2006) and at different stages of language acquisition (infants, children, adults; see Filipović & Ibarretxe-Antuñano, 2015 for detailed critical analysis).

In what is possibly the first attempt to apply linguistic typology to an analysis of forensic linguistic texts, Filipović (2007a, 2013b) accounts for differences between the original and the translation and considers their consequences for the understanding and interpretation of events. This research examined witness interviews in Spanish and their translations into English. Out of the total number of motion events in the Spanish original only about a fifth (21 per cent) of the descriptions contained manner verbs (in non-boundary-crossing events) with the rest of the descriptions (the majority, 79 per cent) containing path information only expressed with path verbs. This typologically conditioned preference for neutral or path verbs in Spanish is all the more striking because the events described were very dynamic, for example, muggings, robberies, domestic violence, manslaughter and so on, whereby we could reasonably expect many manners of motion. For instance, in a case of sexual harassment, an event that must have occurred with a highly salient (probably intense and aggressive) manner of motion, information on manner was conspicuously absent throughout the description of the event. The victim, who was a native speaker of Spanish, used hardly any manner verbs at all, e.g.:

4)   Me sali de la oficina y me fui. Y el se fue atras de mi, se fue, pero el se fue para
        alla y yo me vine para alla.
        Translation: 'I got out of the office and I left. And he went after me, he left, but
                    he went over there and I came over there.'

Similarly, in a description of a chase and knife attack (example 5) the Spanish descriptions contained very little information about the manner of motion in different segments of the violent activity described, which must have been very intense:

5)   ... y yo le cai atras, lo vi que traia la, la, la navaja y le cai atras y cuando le cai
        atras, muchos le caimos atras para agarrar al que agredio el muchacho.
        Translation: ' ... and I took off after him, I saw that he had the, the, the knife
                    and I took off after him and when I went after him a lot of us went
                    after him to grab the guy who had attacked the guy ...'

The original Spanish descriptions of the two situations in example (4) and (5) seem to lack dynamicity and intensity, which would undoubtedly have accompanied these events involving a sexual assault and a knife attack. However, the victim and the witness in the two respective cases were using the usual, typical and habitual Spanish pattern of expression, which does not give details about manner, even though such details could potentially be crucial in terms of creating an impression of the speed and flow of events, providing a better explanation of the situation and making clear, for example, why the victim (example 4) was unable to flee or escape her assailant. Such a lack of detail could have an impact on the victim's case, but the victim's language does not encourage the provision of such information habitually. Therefore, such information about the manner in which the events unfolded has to be sought explicitly.

Whilst these accounts sound natural in Spanish, the absence of manner verbs would make them sound very atypical in English. This is why, in the process of interpreting, information about the manner of motion can be, and often is, added spontaneously, because it is the most natural way to lexicalise motion events in English, as we can see from the following examples from police interview transcripts (see Filipović, 2007a and 2013b for further examples and discussion):

6)   ... entró   detras de mi ...
        'and enter-3SG.PST behind   me ...'
        Literal translation: 'and he entered behind me ... '
        Transcript translation: 'and he slipped in behind me ... '

7)   ... pero ... salió   por la seven.
              but ... exit-3SG.PST via the seven.
        Literal translation: 'but ... he went onto 7th Street.'
        Transcript translation: 'The suspect ran up 7th Street.'

8)   ... pero ... salió   por la   puerta detras.
           but ... exit-3SG.PST by   the   door back
           Literal translation: 'but ... he exited through the back door.'
           Transcript translation: 'but he ... ran out via the back door.'

Example (6) is taken from a sexual assault case. The interpreter appears to have already made up his mind about the suspect's guilt. There is no manner of motion in the victim's original statement cited in (6) and adding it in the translation suggests that the motion was sneaky and intentional and implicates the suspect's guilt. It may indeed have been the case that the suspect moved towards the victim in a sly manner and with the intention to assault her, but this was *inferred by the interpreter* rather than expressed by the victim, and the difference between the two is rather significant. The manner of motion in Spanish is also absent from the original descriptions in examples (7) and (8), but present in their English translations. During the interview from which these two examples are taken there was no information given in the original witness description in Spanish about how quickly the suspect or the witnesses that followed him were moving. However, information about the manner of motion was added by the interpreter on many occasions. As a consequence, the translation gives a picture of the suspects moving in a certain manner (e.g. running), whereas the original did not provide this information. Throughout that interview the English translation contains multiple uses of the verbs 'run' or 'chase' as equivalents for Spanish neutral or path verbs ('go', 'follow', etc.) that were used to describe the movements of both the suspect and the others involved at different points in the event. When these Spanish verbs were indeed translated with corresponding bare or path verbs in English, it was difficult to infer how quickly the suspect or the witnesses following him were moving, which, in turn, made it difficult to understand why the different witnesses were located at different places during the chase. In this specific case, it turned out in the end, after lengthy questioning about the location of the witnesses, that some were running, some were cycling, and some were walking fast; therefore, the manner of motion matters, but it has to be given in the original rather than be inferred and added in translation.

Since the interpreter knew that the situation being described in (7) and (8) involved the suspect being chased, and was therefore likely to be dynamic, this may have been the background motivation for the interpreter to add manner occasionally to the translation of motion events although the witness did not mention it explicitly in Spanish. It does not sound natural in English to describe a chase at length using neutral verbs such as 'follow' or 'go'. However, in general, adding manner of motion in the translation when it is not given in the original may have consequences when it comes to identifying a suspect or his whereabouts. The suspect could have run for a while and run into the restaurant, but then exited via the back door walking in order to avoid suspicion, in which case saying that the suspect ran out via the back door would have been an inaccurate translation and a false description.

It is clear that information about manner of motion is important for police investigation and judicial enquiry. It allows us to speculate about the suspect's physical state and location (e.g. if the suspect was running all the time, he could be tired and hiding in the search area; he could have gone further from the crime scene if was running than if he was limping; if he was running, it means he had not been wounded or hurt, etc.). The communicative consequence is that we could draw different conclusions about the event described from the Spanish original and from its English translation respectively. When there is a clash in patterns such as this between English and Spanish, it may be useful for interviewers to explicitly encourage speakers of languages like Spanish to provide details about the manner of motion during interrogation.

What we can conclude here in relation to manner of motion is that interpreters show us different strategies for resolving typological contrasts. Their attempt to sound natural in both languages (e.g. by using manner verbs in English even though no manner is mentioned in Spanish) is the result of enhanced emphasis on communicative efficiency in the target language (i.e. transmitting the message using the habitual language pattern of the hearer's language, English). We can assume that professional interpreters have already maximised their expressive power by mastering the means to express meanings in each language as native speakers do. We can also see elsewhere (Chapters 4 and 5) that bilinguals with equal proficiency in a bilingual mode tend to maximise common ground by using the Spanish motion lexicalisation pattern with the path expressed in the verb. The interpreters and translators in the discussed legal context could have adhered to this same pattern in their translations from Spanish into English, but they did not do so. Instead, they added manner information in English even though it was not present in the Spanish original, in both literary (Slobin, 1996, 1997) and non-literary contexts (Filipović, 2007a).

We also have to explain why interpreters do not seem to exhibit the same kind of linguistic behaviour as other fluent bilinguals. Interpreters seem to favour preferred language-specific patterns in each language rather than shared ones. That the principle Maximise Common Ground appears to be overpowered by Maximise Efficiency in Communication here is due to the *professional require-ment to sound natural in each language*, which is the established norm for professional translation, and which professional training insists on. When inter-preters use manner verbs in English translation instead of the path verbs as in the Spanish original they probably do not think of this as a big addition because they are not actually adding words or structures. They are still using a common syntactic category, a verb; the difference is only that it is a verb of manner, in line with the English (target language) preference for manner verbs instead of path verbs. Perhaps it is also the narrative context that leads them to believe that the described action was dynamic, especially if a manner verb was used once before in the original, for example at an earlier stage of the exchange.

Based on our discussion of these examples, it may be advisable to have interpreters sound a bit less natural in order to render all the meanings expressed in the original. There will be no prizes for translation here, but accuracy and equality in access to justice would be improved by a more faithful and exact rendering of what the speaker actually said.

6.5.2   Intentionality in Translation

As we saw in Chapter 4, some languages have more options for the explicit and unambiguous expression of intentionality (Spanish) than others (English). Furthermore, languages differ in terms of their usage conventions: it is not the case that intentional vs. non-intentional meanings cannot be differentiated in English, but we have seen that this is not done as regularly as it is in Spanish. The fact is that different languages have different patterns and restrictions (due to specific lexical and grammatical features) and the resulting usage habits crucially determine not only *how* information will be packaged but also *what kind* of information is likely to be given in an account of events and *how consistently*. Spanish has efficient packaging of different intentionality meanings and these meanings are signalled more regularly than in English. Consider the following examples:

9)   The man broke the glass.

10)   El hombre rompió el   vaso.
        'The man broke   the glass.'

11)   Se le rompió el vaso al hombre.
        'The man broke the glass (accidentally).'

In (9) we have the typical English expression for an event whereby a man broke a glass, but we cannot say whether it was done on purpose or not. On the other hand, in both examples (10) and (11), which are the possible translations into Spanish, we see that the man broke the glass, but the breaking was probably intentional in (10) and clearly non-intentional in (11). As we saw earlier, other languages have the same constructions as the one in (11) in Spanish, *the affective dative* (see Chapter 4, Section 4.3.3 for more details). For instance, we find the same distinction in Italian and Serbian (Italian: 'Mi si e roto il bichiere', and Serbian: 'Slomila mi se čaša' (both meaning 'To-me-the-glass-broke' = 'I broke the glass accidentally').

Sometimes when translating information about intentionality, it is not just a different construction that is required in translation but a different verb as well (underlined below):

12a)   John dropped the bottle.

12b)   Juan <u>tiró</u>   la   botella.
        'Juan threw the bottle.'

12c)   Se le <u>cayó</u> la botella a Juan.
        'Juan dropped the bottle (accidentally).'

Both (12b) and (12c) can be used in Spanish to translate the English example in (12a). The verb 'drop' in English is ambiguous with regard to intentionality, and the translator into Spanish must make a choice about which of the two meaning options (intentional or non-intentional) the speaker had in mind. This choice, however, should not fall upon the translator. Moreover, if the other way around was the case, i.e. that (12b) or (12c) are being translated into English, they could both have (12a) as the equivalent, which could lead to serious confusion and misinterpretation, possibly with severe real-life consequences (see discussion further below in this section). Lexically, grammatically and in actual usage there are no strict rules in English to force the interpretation one way or the other. This is why, if we want to be absolutely certain that we are understood in English we need to further specify intentionality, as was done in the following newspaper headline, for example, reporting on some refuse collectors who were behaving badly: 'Barnsley council has been forced to apologise after CCTV footage emerged of bin men *deliberately dropping bags of rubbish and throwing wheelie bins*' (www.telegraph.co.uk/news/2017/04/1 3/barnsley-council-apologise-bin-mens-totally-unacceptable-behaviour/).

Berk-Seligson (1983) notes that the way in which an event is framed in language may be a matter of choice. For example, in her study, when presented with the same illustrations showing a coin being dropped or a vase being broken some people chose to talk about the coin ('it fell', 'it was lost') and the vase ('it fell', 'it broke'), whereas others talked about the characters involved and what they did ('he dropped it', 'he lost it', 'she knocked it over', 'she broke it'). Berk-Seligson (ibid.) also notes that lexical choice in itself will greatly affect the interpretation of events. The decision to use one lexical item rather than another says something about how the participant wishes to present the characters in relation to the events they are involved in. Presumably, on these occasions, the speakers who are describing the events and the roles of the participants know exactly what they mean; that is, whether the involvement of the agent was voluntary or involuntary. It is people at the receiving end of the message that may interpret it differently. This can lead to miscommunication even in a monolingual situation, and a translation-mediated context adds another layer of complexity and further potential source of misunderstanding.

In the case of police interviews, an example can serve to illustrate the importance of drawing attention to this typological feature and the need for precision in translation (see Filipović, 2007a for details). 'Se me cayó en las escaleras' (meaning 'to-me-it-happened-that-she-fell on the stairs') was used extensively by a suspect who was describing what had happened to the victim. It was repeatedly translated into English as 'I dropped her on the stairs'. The English expression 'I dropped her' can refer to both intentional and non-intentional dropping; it is ambiguous and can therefore be used legitimately as a translation equivalent for the non-intentional expression in Spanish, so the interpreter was not, strictly speaking, at fault here. Throughout this particular interview the suspect was using the non-intentional expression in Spanish ('se me cayó' = 'It happened to me that she fell' or 'I dropped her accidentally') that clearly signals lack of intentionality on his part. In the English translation, however, this clearly non-intentional meaning was not conveyed. In addition, the police officer did not make the interviewing process any easier by asking 'Did she fall or did you drop her?' The police officer who was interviewing used the verb 'drop' in its intentional sense in order to draw a distinction between the accidental ('fall') and the intentional ('drop') action. The suspect responded 'no' to the question 'did she fall?' because technically, the victim did not fall – she herself was not in control of the motion because she was being carried. The suspect then said 'si, se me cayó' ('yes, to me it happened that she fell'), which was officially translated as 'Yes, I dropped her'. Thus, the suspect seemed to be confirming that the victim did not fall of her own accord and that he dropped her on purpose. However, what the suspect was actually stating was that he was involved in a dropping event, but that the dropping itself was non-intentional, an accident. The suspect's response was not marked as non-intentional in English, whilst it was undoubtedly non-intentional in Spanish. Consequently, the suspect was understood to be admitting guilt for an intentional act of throwing his victim down the stairs, which resulted in the victim's death. Particularly in those states or countries that still administer the death penalty, like the US state of California, where this interview took place, admitting to an intentional act of murder is not something that can be treated lightly and an imprecise translation that leads to the understanding that the suspect was doing precisely this would be not only be highly detrimental to the case, but could endanger the suspect's life. This is not to say that the interpreter was necessarily doing a bad job, since, as I explained, the English phrase 'I dropped her' can refer to both intentional and non-intentional acts of dropping.

So how can we deal with this problem of linguistic patterns clashing? We have a structure in English, the inchoative, for saying that something that happened was probably an accident, as in 'The glass broke', but this provides no specific information about any involvement on the part of an affected participant. In other words, the *English inchoatives cannot be used as equivalents to the Spanish affective dative* construction because they fail to express who the affected participant (i.e. the 'non-intentional agent') was. The English inchoative is closer to the Spanish *se*-construction *without the affective dative* ('se cayó' = 'X fell') because both express the outcome of an action without any information about an involuntary agent. But still, inchoative constructions in English are not the best translation equivalents even for the *se*-constructions without the affective dative in Spanish because they can be used in descriptions of both intentional and non-intentional events (see Filipović, 2013a, 2018), whilst when *se*-constructions are used, they refer to non-intentional events. Most importantly for us at present, it is the affective dative construction (such as 'se le cayó X' = 'to-him X fell') that is the most difficult one to render into English, and this is where our current focus lies.

In the case discussed here, using 'she fell' instead of 'I dropped her' as an equivalent for the Spanish affective dative construction 'se me cayó X' ('to-me X fell') would not work, as we explained above (the victim did not fall on her own). What about introducing an adverbial or a more extensive paraphrase, such as '*I dropped her accidentally*' or '*She fell from my arms*'? These solutions do not correspond perfectly to the Spanish affective dative construction either. In the former case we would be adding an additional element, the adverb, not present in the original and in the latter, a further specification is being added, also not present in the original, about how the victim was being carried (i.e. in the suspect's arms, but not over his shoulder, for example), which is not something that the speaker actually said. There no ideal solution here, it is vital to give at least some indication that a non-intentional meaning is intended by the speaker, even if this means interrupting the interview procedure when this is critically relevant.

Introducing additional words or phrases not explicitly mentioned in the original is something that trained interpreters eschew. In an experimental translation study, Hijazo-Gascón and Filipović (in preparation) found that, in contrast to Spanish-English bilinguals who did free encoding of video stimuli (Filipović, 2018; see Chapter 4), student trainee interpreters rarely added adverbs to make it clear whether something was done on purpose or not (e.g. 'He dropped the bag on purpose' vs. 'He dropped the bag by accident'). This is presumably because interpreters are trained not to add words that are not found in the original and they also aim to sound natural in the target language, which would not be achieved in English by constantly adding adverbials to indicate intentionality (or the lack thereof). Hijazo-Gascón and Filipović (in preparation) also have some initial findings indicating that student interpreters with English as the stronger language often use the ambiguous SVO structure to translate the Spanish affective dative construction into English (e.g. 'she dropped the vase'), whilst those with Spanish as their stronger language used passive or inchoative constructions more than SVO for this purpose ('the vase was/ got dropped' or 'the vase dropped down').

However, as noted above, using an inchoative (or passive) structure to translate the Spanish affective dative construction is not ideal since it tells us nothing about the involvement of the affected event participant, which is explicitly expressed in the Spanish affective dative construction. In order to fully maximise common ground, the non-intentional event participant would need to be clearly signalled as it is in Spanish, but doing so results in a marked/unusual/awkward structure (e.g. 'It happened to him that X broke', or something to this effect), which would not be a viable option for interpreters. We need to seek remedies for this dilemma, and adding an occasional adverb may not be such a bad solution.

It is interesting to point out here that previous research has noted that strategies used in simultaneous interpreting may differ between more experienced professionals and student interpreters. More experienced professional interpreters are believed to engage in more 'conceptually mediated translation', whilst student interpreters rely more on 'transcoding', that is, an automatic triggering of translation-equivalent structures (De Groot, 2011: 337; see also Tzou, Vaid & Chen, 2017). Conceptually mediated translation involves a full analysis of the input language in accordance with the grammar and semantics of this language and the emerging conceptual representations are then processed by the language system of the language into which the translation is made. This type of translation is also called 'natural translation' and is used by young children with no special training or knowledge of translation-equivalent structures. Transcoding on the other hand involves a direct replacement of source-language words and structures with the corresponding target ones. The more often the paired words or structures are used, the stronger the links between them and the more easily accessible each element becomes upon activation of its equivalent. Some have argued that professionals are the ones who could be expected to rely more on transcoding because they are likely to possess large stocks of readily accessible translation equivalents. For instance, Paradis (1994) sees the use of transcoding as a sign of professionalism. However, others argue the opposite: that transcoding indicates lack of expertise and that it negatively affects translation performance (Seleskovitch, 1976; see the detailed discussion in De Groot, 2011: 319–37).

Both views may actually be right. Fabbro, Gran and Gran (1991) suggest that experienced and trainee interpreters use both strategies, with the professionals engaging more in conceptually mediated interpreting, though when stressed or pressed for time their use of form-based strategies increases, and important conceptual distinctions from the original that are difficult to render in translation get lost. This is precisely what happened in the studies I have presented and discussed in this chapter.

We can see from these studies on motion and intentionality in translation that both experienced interpreters and student interpreters opt for translation equivalents that map onto shared semantic features in each language, but without rendering all the conceptual distinctions from the original. Interpreters may be drawing the relevant conceptual distinctions in their minds, but they are trained not to add explicit modification of speakers' statements that the speakers did not explicitly verbalise themselves, which is considered an unwarranted intervention (e.g. adverbs like 'on purpose' vs. 'accidentally'). Some interpreters may be more consistent than other in drawing the intentional vs. non-intentional meaning distinctions in English translations, for example by using the SVO construction only for intentional meanings, and the inchoative construction only for non-intentional ones as defaults (a study on individual interpreter consistency in translation choices is currently ongoing; Hijazo-Gascón and Filipović, in preparation). However, we would also need to check whether hearers as well as speakers actually detect these interpreter defaults or if they still interpret SVO structures sometimes as intentional and sometimes as non-intentional because they are indeed unspecified in English grammar with regard to intentionality (see Filipović, 2019b on some assumptions about verb meaning and lexical defaults in this context and on the need for future research).

What the study of intentionality in translation has shown is that it is important to determine in advance the exact points at which translation problems may occur between any two languages (see Filipović & Hijazo-Gascón, 2018, and also Hijazo-Gascón, 2019 for more examples). This can be achieved by studying both finely grained typological contrasts between languages and through analysis of real, authentic interactions amongst all the participants in a given social context (e.g. police interviewers, victims, witnesses or suspects and interpreters). We then need to implement these findings in the training of language professionals and legal practitioners, and in other fields involving high-risk contexts as well, such as air transportation, and the medical and pharmaceutical industries (see Trbojević, 2012), to ensure that potentially catastrophic consequences of miscommunication due to mistranslation are avoided.

As in the previous section on translation for motion expressions, we can draw the same conclusion here: *interpreters are not maximising common ground when translating intentionality as much as other bilinguals do because of their professional requirement to use typical structures of the target language* at the expense of rendering all the meaning details from the original. It would be worthwhile to test interpreters systematically under different conditions: for example when they are interpreting formally, at an official event, when they are interpreting in more relaxed circumstances (with fellow students or friends) or when they are not interpreting at all but talking to other bilinguals or monolinguals. This will be necessary in order to obtain a full picture of what happens with these trained language professionals when they are not working but just being bilinguals, and are under the influence of different external factors such as different interlocutors and different communication purposes.

6.6   Implications for Translation Theory and Practice

I have argued that proficient bilingual language use in situations that require simultaneous manipulation of both languages results in outcomes that our CASP for Bilingualism model can help us understand. The context of translating and interpreting creates a special environment in which we see bilingualism in action. Namely, it creates a situation characterised by competing motivations, whereby the principle of Maximise Common Ground competes head to head with Maximise Efficiency in Communication and with the requirements of this professional community to adhere to the grammar and usage preferences of the hearer's language. We can understand why this is so if we recall the definition of what being efficient in communication means. Communicative efficiency, as defined by Hawkins (2004, 2009, 2014) and adopted here, includes both speaker-oriented (production) and hearer-oriented (comprehension) goals. In the context of translating and interpreting, where the key goal is to produce outputs in the target language that sound as if they had been originally produced in that language, the hearer's expectations take priority.

This brings us to a concept which has been, and is still, at the heart of translation studies, namely the ideal of fluency in the target text (Venuti, 1995). Other considerations have also been identified as important in the study and performance of translation. The research has been prolific, especially within approaches guided by Skopos theory (Vermeer & Reiss, 2013 [1984]), which proposes that approaches to translation should be determined by the function of the product. In brief, the approach to be used in translation depends on who the target audience is. This essentially functionalist theory prioritises appropriateness of translation over pure linguistic equivalence, and this may indeed be the right way to go about translation in many contexts (e.g. in translations of novels, poems or in films). In legal contexts however, it is the linguistic equivalence of meaning that is the key criterion for adequate and successful translation, and crucially, the stakes are much higher if the translation does not achieve this crucial goal of preserving the exact same meaning as given in the original, as we have seen here.

There are different consequences for literary and legal texts if the same approach to translation (create a kind of 'natural feel' in the target language) is assumed in both. Meanings get lost in literary translation because of the typological differences between the original language and the language of the translation. As Slobin (1996, 1997) showed, a large proportion of manner verbs are not translated into Spanish in order to adhere to typological features of Spanish and the rhetorical style of the target language. When translation happens the other way around, from Spanish into English, information about manner is added even though it is not given in the original, for the same reasons. In literary contexts, this results in a more authentic narrative style, following the norms and preferences of the target language. However, in the translation of witness interviews it can create misunderstanding about what the witness said happened and it can lead investigations down the wrong path.

In the real-life legal cases that we discussed here (following Filipović, 2007a, 2013b) the analyses of translation samples clearly showed that interpreters were adhering more to the typical patterns of the target language. From the perspective of CASP for Bilingualism, we could have predicted, based on our discussions of bilinguals in non-professional contexts, that interpreters would maximise common ground when interpreting from one language to the other in order to minimise overall cognitive effort. However, we are also aware that maximising common ground may result in atypical/uncharacteristic/awkward target outputs. And as we saw in Chapter 3, it can lead occasionally to sounding unnatural, unauthentic and not in line with habitual rhetorical style or usage preferences (and in cases of unequal proficiency, it can result in ungrammaticality). In translation, this issue is of fundamental importance because, as emphasised before, the overarching key goal, in general, is to sound natural in the target language. Translations do not win awards for sounding like translations, as we have mentioned; they do so because they sound like the original. Thus, translators do not want to sound unnatural in the target language. This goal is deeply engrained in interpreting and translation training and it becomes a matter of automatic practice and routine. Now we can understand better why translators and interpreters from Spanish into English tend to add manner verbs in both literary and legal contexts, even though the original contains only path verbs, and why they do not systematically add adverbs to disambiguate intentionality. It is done for the purpose of adhering to the narrative style of the target text. Conversely, it sounds awkward to an interpreter's ear if he or she uses only path verbs in English or keeps adding adverbs to indicate presence vs. absence of intentionality with each verb that is used.

Another factor that needs mentioning is the fact that most bilingual interpreters have one stronger language even though some are truly born, raised and educated as bilinguals. The data from the studies presented in this chapter come from the United States, from cases where the interpreters' stronger language was English, so this could have influenced strict adherence to the English pattern. We know that when the stronger language of the bilingual is Spanish rather than English, the distinction between intentional and non-intentional events is regularly expressed in both languages (see Filipović, 2018; also see more details in Chapter 5). Therefore, a number of reasons specific to the context of interpreting and to the individual linguistic profiles of those involved need to be considered carefully (see also Hijazo-Gascón & Filipović, in preparation).

The theory and practice of translation needs to take a closer look at language typology and map out the cognitive and practical consequences of the typological conflicts in concrete situations. More empirical work is necessary, providing data and examples from different language combinations. There is also a need for more *explicit linguistic training of interpreters*, not just in the use of legal terminology and typical phrases, but also in the key differences in meaning between languages that can create significant difficulties in understanding. Similarly, legal (and other) professionals who work in bilingual contexts need to have their awareness raised about the relevant language contrasts that create difficulties in interpreter-assisted communication.

Where language professionals such as interpreters and translators have a responsibility is to ensure that, if speakers are using informal or ungrammatical constructions, slang vocabulary and hesitations whilst speaking, the same kinds of linguistic features should be rendered in the target text as well. This can have investigative importance (e.g. indicating level of education or social-group membership) and these features also relate to how listeners form opinions about their speakers, which is relevant for jury judgements (see, for example, Berg-Selikson, 2002 [1990]). Crucially, interpreters and translators must convey the meanings of words and constructions accurately and precisely from one language into another, and nothing must get in the way of this key goal in this context, not even the fear of sounding unnatural in translation.

6.7   Conclusion

The packaging of information in a language-specific way is so deeply rooted in our everyday experience and interactions with the world around us that we are often unaware that we are doing it, or that we absorb information from the world around us through the significant involvement of a system (or systems) of words and grammatical rules. When we have to learn and use two systems for organising experience at the same time, we have a special challenge – whether to use one system at a time or both together, and how. In this chapter we have considered bilinguals in action in a very particular context that involves constant use of two languages in the same communicative situation with two monolingual audiences. There is a special adjustability factor that is triggered by the specific requirements of this professional context: the ultimate goal of sounding authentic/natural in each language. This requirement, motivated by the principle of Maximise Efficiency in Communication, sometimes opposes the principle of Maximise Common Ground, which then results in outcomes with more detail in the original than in the translation, or vice versa. Our bilinguals-interpreters may be monitoring their outputs more stringently on such occasions than they would do if they were interpreting in informal contexts or if they were using their languages for ordinary communication with other bilinguals and monolinguals. This hypothesis, related to our adjustability (external) factors, is definitely worth testing in future research.

Studying the linguistic behaviour of the same participants under different situational conditions is the best way to test the CASP for Bilingualism predictions in relation to adjustability; that is, in relation to external factors. The role of the variability (internal) factors is more straightforward here: bilinguals with unequal proficiency in both languages should never carry out official interpreting, especially in highly sensitive contexts such as legal or medical ones. We illustrated this using an example of interpreting carried out by a heritage speaker, in which we saw that unbalanced proficiency impedes communication and could potentially lead to a negative perception of the interviewed suspect, leaving aside the ethical problems that pervade such communications (namley lack of access to impartial language assistance and, with reference to the context of US police interviews in particular, allowing the presentation of false evidence in order to elicit a confession; see Filipović & Abad Vergara, 2018 for further details).

Nevertheless, using professional interpreting is not exactly problem-free, as we saw in the case of translations of motion events and intentionality. Typological differences between languages make it difficult for interpreters to ensure that the original and the translation express exactly the same meanings and that the translation does not sound out of sync with target language norms and audience expectations.

So then, what is the solution then for legal translation and interpreting? In a nutshell, *maximise common ground within the limits of grammaticality* in each language and *do not worry about sounding unnatural in translation* – it is more important not to put lives at risk.

7 Conclusions and Future Directions

Life is all about connections. Rivers that run towards seas carry valuable nutrients that are then acquired, used and re-created as the same or similar nutrients, which then evaporate and fall down as rain into rivers that run towards seas. Language is all about connections too. In the flow of communication, we acquire, use and transform language and pass it on to the next generation of language-ready minds to start the process of acquisition, use and transformation of language all over again.

The more languages we speak the more minds we can connect with, which must be an advantage in itself. This has been the underlying tenet of this book, about to be concluded here. *Bilingualism is good for you*, regardless of whether and when there may be advantages or some (temporary, surmountable or compensated for) disadvantages in the process of becoming or being bilingual. Bilinguals (and multilinguals) can connect with more people through communication in different languages and they are also often bi-cultural (or multi-cultural), which enhances their adaptability to different environments and enriches their life experience. We have probed here for potential advantages and disadvantages in order to be able to understand how language and mind work together, and in order to make the most of the advantages of bilingualism whilst finding ways to contain any disadvantages. We have seen that memory for motion events in bilinguals may be impacted by the preference for the shared pattern of expression that is available in both languages (e.g. English and Spanish), which results in some aspects of the event (manner of motion) not being available as frequently or in as much detail as when just one of the two languages (English) is spoken (Chapter 5). But now that we are aware that this happens, we can make adjustments in situations where it matters, for example when interpreting, when teaching languages or when interviewing speakers of different languages who may be victims, suspects or witnesses.

Language typology tells us how similar or different two languages are in various respects and Applied Language Typology tells us *which* of these *similarities and differences matter in practice*. Some languages do not insist on certain pieces of information being regularly given, so the speakers may not be giving them, not because they do not want to, but because they *do not need to* or because it is *not easy or straightforward to do so*. Habitual lack of expression in a language may also result in less attention being paid to a particular aspect of the situation that does not need to be verbalised frequently or in great detail. If linguistic distinctions are obligatory in one language but only optional in another, as we saw with evidentiality (Chapter 4, Section 4.3.1), then their frequency may increase in that other language and become obligatory there too and potentially be grammaticalised during historical language change.

Many factors are responsible, often simultaneously, for a particular outcome in bilingual language use, and this is why having a multifactor model like CASP for Bilingualism is central to our study of bilingualism. As we saw in Chapter 3, and in subsequent chapters as well, only a multifactor model can capture the interplay of the many factors that are involved with their different strengths on different occasions.

The starting point in any discussion of bilingual outcomes must be the typological features of the respective languages in a specific cognitive or linguistic domain. As we saw in Chapter 4, our predictions will vary based on what languages share, partially or completely, as opposed to what they do not share. Different bilinguals will then maximise common ground, sometimes in similar ways to each other and sometimes differently. For instance, all bilinguals seem to adjust their lexical meanings so that the form-to-meaning mappings of both languages resemble each other closely. To this effect, they may use a more general term in one language to encompass meanings that are expressed by two or more different terms in another. They may also narrow down the meaning of a word so that it maps onto the same meaning as a related word in the other language. The cost to understanding and to overall communicative success in either language is usually not a major one in these cases, as explained in Chapter 4, Section 4.2.1. The cost to efficient communication is higher if common ground is maximised ungrammatically. All bilinguals also maximise common ground in grammar, with the result that they may use atypical structures in one of their languages because the common pattern is major in one language but minor in the other. Bilinguals with unequal proficiency often maximise common ground in ungrammatical ways, or in ways that balanced bilinguals would not, or at least not as frequently.

It is also important to highlight that not all typological contrasts are equal: we can follow George Orwell by saying that, some are more equal than others, as it were. Some contrasts matter more than others when it comes to their practical consequences for different professional fields (e.g., legal or medical), and these form the focus of our Applied Language Typology programme (Filipović, 2017a, 2017b). We need more research to be carried out on these contrasts in particular, and more documentation of their effects in different situations, as well as further confirmation of the assumption that teaching them explicitly is indeed helpful. By the same token, some clashes between typological patterns are more difficult to resolve in learning and processing than others. The higher the cost to efficient communication, the more incentivised bilinguals will be not to incur it. We saw that if basic word orders are too different, like the mirror-image contrasts between English (subject-verb-object, or SVO) and Japanese (subject-object-verb, or SOV), adult L2 learners acquire the correct head orderings early and do not maximise common ground by using use the same basic word order in both languages. On the other hand, when there is a partial overlap in word order, as in English and Spanish, bilinguals may try to make the overlap complete and use some word orders in English (such as verb-before-subject, or VS) that are ungrammatical in this language but grammatical in Spanish (recall e.g. *'Yesterday came my boyfriend'). The cost to efficient communication is still lower in these ungrammatical structures than in the case of using the Japanese word order in English because the verb still comes early, and the sentence can still be processed. Moreover, this VS pattern does actually exist in English as well, as a marginal option (recall 'I had my feet on the desk and in comes the boss!'). Thus, Spanish learners of L2 English use more ungrammatical word orders in their L2 than Japanese learners of L2 English, because they can get away with it and still communicate successfully. General typological proximity or distance is not a predictor on its own; rather, we need to consider what the possible common ground outputs are for each feature and how efficient, or not, one would be in communication. If an output impedes understanding to a considerable degree, as a Japanese word order in English would do, then this option is likely not be exercised. If, on the other hand, it does not prevent the message from getting through, as with VS word order in L2 English, then it may persist even until later stages of L2 acquisition (Filipović & Hawkins, 2013).

When there is a major typological contrast (between SVO and SOV basic word order), all bilinguals, even with beginner's proficiency in L2, use a different pattern for each language. However, we also noted that there is a possible way to maximise common ground even on occasions when two languages have mirror-image basic word orders (head-initial vs. head-final), but for this to happen, certain additional conditions need to be in place, namely geographical proximity and sociolinguistic circumstances conducive to language change (Gast, 2007; Heine & Kuteva, 2005; Ross, 1996, 2001).

Not all aspects of events would need to be described and expressed at all times, in any language. Intentionality may not matter on every occasion that an event is described, and it may not need to be explicitly specified every time. For example, some verbs refer to actions where substantial force was exerted and thus we do not need to say further whether something was done on purpose or not – it will be assumed if substantial force was involved (see Ibarretxe-Antuñano, 2012 for an excellent discussion of Spanish and Basque). However, there are occasions when a meaning, if not expressed explicitly and precisely, can lead to severe misunderstanding, with potentially serious consequences for the people involved, as we saw in the case of legal translation contexts (Chapter 6).

Early and balanced bilinguals are generally more efficient overall than late and unbalanced bilinguals, both in terms of processing efficiency and communication efficiency. When early and balanced bilinguals are using both their languages (within a single communicative situation, and also generally, in their lives), they are very incentivised to maximise common ground in both languages and they tend to use a common pattern in a variety of methodologically different tasks that either do or do not involve explicit use of language (e.g. categorisation tasks or similarity judgement tasks). When either pattern works for a specific task (e.g. gender-based categorisation of objects in Italian or German (Bassetti, 2007) or ambiguity resolution in syntactic attachment (Dussias, 2001), these bilinguals can and do 'choose' either of the two patterns in order to deal with the task at hand. These are prime examples of bilingual processing efficiency (see Filipović, 2014 for the original argument). On the other hand, they control their respective outputs better in each of their languages when they are in a monolingual mode and are communicatively efficient in each of their languages, coming close to monolingual norms in each, which is also the case for some late but highly proficient bilinguals. Late and unbalanced bilinguals, by contrast, will most likely use the pattern from their stronger language in both languages on such occasions (see Dussias & Sagarra, 2007; Fernandez, 2002). Late and unbalanced bilinguals may also switch between two patterns constantly and inefficiently in categorisation tasks, as was the case in the Lai, Rodriguez, and Narasimhan (2014) study, though it was not clear in that study if late bilinguals were also comparatively less balanced than the early ones. It can also be the case that, even if proficiency were balanced in both languages, the age of acquisition would still cause different processing strategies to be forged whereby early acquisition would foster maximising common ground and late acquisition the constant switching between the two systems. The two factors, age of acquisition and proficiency, can be disentangled in future research by including cross-comparisons of different groups: (a) the same age of acquisition-different proficiency levels (due to attrition or incomplete acquisition in one of the two groups), (b) different age of acquisition-same proficiency (early and very proficient late bilinguals) and (c) different age of acquisition and different proficiency (balanced early bilinguals and unbalanced L2 learners). Evidence discussed throughout this book seems to indicate that the ways in which late and unbalanced bilinguals maximise common ground differ in some respects from the ways in which early and balanced bilinguals do it. Unbalanced late bilinguals are more likely to maximise common ground even when they should not, or not do so when they could, as we saw in Chapter 4.

Even if a bilingual is balanced in both languages, some aspects of one language may 'pop up' when the other is spoken (e.g. atypical or ungrammatical patterns, or code-switches). This is why a bilingual is never a simple sum of two monolinguals. How often and what kind of 'pop-ups' occur will depend crucially on *multiple factors*, e.g. on how proficient the bilingual is in the language being spoken (which in the case of balanced bilingualism should be a high level), on who the interlocutors are (other bilinguals or two monolinguals, one in each language) and what the purpose of the communication is (formal vs. informal interaction). If the bilingual's interlocutor is a monolingual and the occasion is formal, then output control will be higher and production closer to the monolingual patterns of use than when the occasion is informal. The bilingual speaker may 'relax' the output monitor when communication is informal and 'allow' some *common ground* patterns to ease his processing load. The pressure on the output monitor must be even higher when conversing with two monolinguals at once, but the outputs are then much more difficult to control, even in an informal setting. A personal prime example for this is me trying to answer my mother's (Serbian) and my husband's (English) questions at once whilst at the same time conveying to each of them what the other one was saying! My use of structures acceptable (albeit not necessarily optimal) in both languages is then enhanced for efficient communication. When talking to a bilingual with the same two languages the output control is on higher alert in formal than informal situations but the overall pressure is less intense than with two different monolingual interlocutors simultaneously. Code-switching may or may not occur, and the readiness for it is there, but there is no pressure to completely switch between systems continuously.

I must point out here that it is not always clear that there is an overall stronger language and an overall weaker language. Bilinguals can have one language that is stronger in some respects (e.g. grammar) but weaker in another (e.g. lexicon, due to forgetting L1 words or not having learned L2 words). Therefore, an overall proficiency assessment is informative up to a certain point, but it is not an absolute predictor for outputs at each level of linguistic analysis. A multifactor model takes care of this by including finely grained typological differences (e.g. presence vs. absence of pattern overlap and frequency of the pattern in each language), as well as individual bilingual profiles (including acquisition histories and frequencies of use) and also details about the specific interaction environments the bilinguals find themselves in (interlocutor types and situation types).

From a long-term, historical perspective, we have seen arguments that late and unbalanced bilinguals may be more likely to cause their L2 to change in the direction of simplification, whilst early and balanced bilinguals are more likely to add form-to-meaning mappings that can complexify their languages due to the influence of one over the other (Trudgill, 2010, 2011). We also observed that bilingual influence can go in the opposite direction. Unbalanced late bilinguals can also apparently complexify their L2, and they can perhaps bring about long-term language change in their L2 if the social circumstances are right. In the studies we discussed, speakers of L1 Spanish/L2 English were adding expressions to specify intentionality in L2 English even though they are not obliged to do so in that language, just as speakers of L1 Turkish/L2 English were inclined to give information related to evidentiality (i.e. source of evidence) in their L2, which is not required. If the number of these L2 bilinguals were to surpass those of monolingual English speakers in a community, possibly with intermarriages and new generations of early bilinguals added to the mix, then the English spoken in such a community could change. This is a valid hypothetical possibility based on what we know about bilingual language contact and historical language change. The important point here is that L2 speakers can innovate by adding form–meaning mappings to their L2 from their L1; they do not simplify exclusively. For their additions to stick, and result in long-term change in the L2, they have to have strength in numbers. All bilinguals are incentivised to maximise common ground and they also want to be able to use as much material as possible from one language in the other. Frequency of specific form–meaning mappings in a language as well as frequency of use for each language by the bilinguals have a role to play in what is more likely to get introduced in one direction or the other. We may not have enough historical information to be able to say with certainty exactly what bilingualism looked like in Anglo-Saxon times, but we can be sure that there was a lot of it, and that both Celtic and Old Norse shaped the English we speak today – albeit to different degrees, probably due to sociolinguistic circumstances identified in the literature (Curzan, 2003; Trudgill, 2011).

Importantly, living in close proximity to or within another language community is not enough in itself as a basis for predictions about contact-induced language change. For instance, both Greek and Bulgarian speakers lived in the Turkish-speaking Ottoman Empire, but the former did not develop features under Turkish influence, such as evidentiality, whilst the latter did (see Chapter 4). We need to dig deeper into the historical record of what kind of social status was enjoyed by the different communities in order to understand why some changes occur whilst others do not. Lindstedt (2016) points out that Greek was a common language for all Orthodox peoples in the Ottoman Empire and as such enjoyed a special status. Greek also had the highest prestige in the Balkans and it was sometimes used as the language of diplomatic correspondence by the Ottoman central government as well (Horrocks, 1997). Lindstedt (2016: 65) points out further that the speakers of Turkish and Greek 'may not have been particularly motivated to learn other languages because others were expected to learn theirs'. Hence, Bulgarian would have been more likely to adopt features of Turkish than Greek would. Finally, we also discussed the fact that a socially subordinate language can influence a socially dominant one in locations where the socially inferior population is demographically dominant. For this we had the examples of Andean Spanish and Tariana Portuguese, which have acquired the feature of lexicalised evidentiality not present in mainland Spanish and Portuguese. Again, the innovation may have been started by L2 speakers who outnumbered the

Spanish- or Portuguese-speaking conquerors, and then got adopted and further reinforced in the use of early and balanced bilinguals.

What emerges clearly from this book is that we need to consider both psycholinguistic aspects of bilingualism, such as proficiency and dominance, and the sociolinguistic conditions under which languages are used (who is talking to whom and why), in addition to the other features of contact type that contribute to the long-term effects of bilingualism on the languages spoken (e.g. prestige status or demographic numbers of different bilingual types). Whilst ideas in this vein have been voiced before, as I acknowledge throughout these chapters, this book offers an integrated explanatory account of the general principles of bilingual language processing and of the ways in which multiple factors affect the outcomes of the interactions amongst these general principles. The various collaborations or competitions between principles, and the many factors outlined, constitute the complex adaptive system that is the bilingual linguistic system. The reason why we have often had seemingly contradictory reports and results in the literature about bilingual outputs can now be understood as the result of this push-pull relationship between the various factors involved, with different factors prevailing on different occasions. A multifactor model like CASP for Bilingualism is therefore necessary in any bilingual investigation and for any explanation related to bilingual language processing and language use. It provides us with a comprehensive picture of bilingualism in action and makes holistic predictions about the linguistic behaviours of different bilinguals in the same types of interactions (i.e. it captures bilingual variability) and of the same bilingual types in different types of interactions (i.e. it maps out bilingual adjustability).

Having multiple factors to consider does not make predictions easy, but it does not make them impossible. And in any case, there is no alternative. Bilingual linguistic behaviour is a complex adaptive system and any adequate account of it has to be a multifactor one. Making predictions using a multifactor model is necessary and inevitable. I outlined the ways in which this can be done in Chapter 3, and here I give just a brief summary. We start by delimiting the typological domain within which our multiple factors interact and then calibrate the predictions about outputs for this domain based on both the linguistic characteristics of the bilinguals and the different communicative situations in which they find themselves. So, for example, early bilinguals with equal proficiency in two languages (e.g. English and Spanish), who use them at an equal rate, will maximise common ground and draw the same distinctions in both languages (e.g. with respect to intentional vs. non-intentional causation), but possibly more so in a bilingual mode than in a monolingual. This prediction is potentially falsifiable, because they could still be maximising common ground to some extent and in certain domains more than others regardless of the mode, due to their habitual language use. We may also find that their witness memory may still be using resources from both languages even in a monolingual mode, something worth checking in future empirical investigations. If proficiency is higher in a language that makes more subtle distinctions in a lexical or grammatical domain (e.g. Spanish in the domain of intentionality again) and they use that language more frequently, they will draw the same distinctions in their other language that does not have them. If they are dominant in a language that does not make the relevant distinctions (e.g. English in the domain of intentionality), and the language that does make them is their weaker one, they will still maximise common ground, but in a different way – they will most likely not draw the relevant distinctions in both languages. Such 'avoidance-type' outputs by L2 learners (e.g. avoidance of the affective dative construction; see Chapter 4, Section 4.3.3), whilst atypical, may actually be grammatical, and then they can persist without being sanctioned. Explicit L2 instruction may be beneficial on this occasion. Unbalanced bilinguals are also less likely to adjust to different language modes and to control their weaker language outputs in comparison to balanced bilinguals, so we can hypothesise that language mode may have a weaker or no effect on their L2 outputs. On the other hand, the nature of the situation type (formal vs. informal) may prompt at least some unbalanced bilinguals to 'up the ante', as it were, and control their outputs better when the occasion is formal (Dewaele, 2001). Some of these predictions have been confirmed in previous chapters, whilst some await further exploration and confirmation or refutation (e.g. on whether and when some long-term habits and parallel activation would still produce the same outcomes in a monolingual mode as they do in a bilingual mode, or whether the outcomes would be more in line with monolingual norms).

Future research is needed in many areas of bilingualism; for instance, in child language development amongst bilinguals. The issue of increasing vs. decreasing 'convergence' (i.e. maximising common ground in lexical labelling and representation) is still unresolved. Do bilinguals start with separate lexical systems for the two languages that come closer together or do they start with one that diverges into two? The literature is still divided on this. Storms, Ameel and Malt (2015) showed that bilingual children may start with two systems which then gradually merge into one until at least the age of 14. Other studies seem to show that a common system is shared from early on, with a common grammatical pattern being used in both languages by a bilingual child, in spite of its being ungrammatical in one of the two languages (e.g. Yip & Matthews, 2007). Storms et al. (2015) allow for the possibility that the conflicting results in the literature may be due to the fact that their own methodology permits them to study only children from 5 years of age and above, whilst other studies that report early convergence may have looked at younger children (e.g. Nicoladis, 2002; Yip & Matthews, 2007). Again, multiple factors are likely to be relevant, such as relative proficiency and frequency of use in each language, nature of immersion (balanced bilingualism at home vs. classroom learning) as well as the specific typological domain in question (i.e. depending on the nature of the overlap between the two languages; see Chapter 4) and the context of specific interactions (monolingual vs. bilingual). It may be the case that both camps (the increasing and the decreasing convergence theories) are actually right: the complete convergence/overlap assumed very early on (e.g. before age of 5, or to be determined) can then be replaced by separate representations, which are kept apart even when they do not need to be, and which begin to merge again slowly, maybe between the age of 5 and 14, as Storms et al. (2015) documented, when, in our terms, bilinguals 'realise' the advantages of maximising common ground. They then settle into having a system in which common ground is maximised in an optimal way, that works in both languages, and whereby the initial ungrammatical maximising of common ground has been replaced with the appropriate way of doing it, with semantically and grammatically matching patterns in both lexicon and grammar.

Another avenue of research that may be fruitful is that of explicit instruction in language learning and teaching. We saw in Chapter 4 that explicit instruction about the relevant typological contrast can have benefits for memory in an L2 that lead to better performance by that group than by L1 speakers, who seem not to be aware of the relevant conceptual distinctions in their native language (Koster & Cadierno, 2018). Raising awareness about typological similarities and differences between languages should have a place in the language learning and teaching curriculum. It is unrealistic to expect of L2 learners that they should be able to infer some, possibly very important, nuances in meaning and use, because classroom exposure and occasional immersion is rarely sufficient for that. Explicit instruction may also be needed in order to prevent incorrect inferences about meaning and usage in an L2. *Language Awareness* is an ongoing movement initiated by Eric Hawkins (1984), who proposed raising language awareness in the classroom by various means including incorporating simple contrastive analysis to serve as an interface between mother-tongue and foreign-language study. Experimental teaching that raises foreign-language learners' awareness of contrasts between the mother tongue and the foreign language has been shown to facilitate the learning of difficult foreign-language structures (Kupferberg & Olshtain, 1996).

What we also currently need is a detailed and critical overview of methodologies in the field, focusing on the reliability and validity of the different measures used in the literature as well as assessment of what works and what does not work as a method in testing a specific feature of bilingual language use. As we saw in Chapter 4, the variety of methodologies used in this context is vast, and different methodologies seem to lead to diverging conclusions, which should not be the case. We must tread carefully when we generalise our claims, and in any case, much more finessed, finely grained, domain-specific investigations need to be carried out before any sweeping generalisations can be attempted about bilingual processing. Using CASP for Bilingualism may help us reach research generalisations faster whilst also enabling us to develop a holistic rather than partial view of the complex adaptive system that bilingual language is.

We also need more empirical data, from more language pairs in diverse linguistic and cognitive domains, and more information about the linguistic behaviour of different bilingual types under different interactional conditions. Further study of language and memory as well as bilingual language use in diverse professional contexts under different circumstances, as exemplified here, will lead to further discoveries about the bilingual mind and how it works. Interaction itself emerges as the key to understanding bilingualism, both within and across minds. Languages interact within a bilingual mind, and these interactions are reinforced through further interactions in contact both with other bilinguals and with monolinguals. Depending on which types of interactions are more frequent for a particular bilingual speaker, she or he will have certain patterns of linguistic behaviour and certain outputs more firmly entrenched than others. Repetitive success in communication strengthens the patterns that lead to success. If one pattern is successful in both languages, it will be favoured in both if they are both used equally frequently, and the memories of success will be reinforced (as in balanced bilingualism). If one of the two languages is used more often, then the patterns from that language that can lead to successful communication in both will be favoured since they will be represented and remembered as successful more often than the patterns from the other, less frequently used language. This is when we see more of the majority patterns from the stronger language being used in the weaker language, where they either constitute the minority pattern or, if common ground is stretched too much, result in an ungrammatical pattern.

All these products of bilingual language use can develop from being atypical or ungrammatical to typical and grammatical. This is because performance is the source of what becomes grammaticalised in languages (Hawkins, 1994, 2004, 2014) and if enough speakers are using a particular language pattern within the community (i.e. if the level of bilingualism is high and permeates many different facets of social interactions), bilingual linguistic performance can result in significant changes to the language as a whole, for monolingual populations as well.

Bilingualism has contributed in fundamental ways to both the lexicons and the grammars of languages as we know them today, and it is likely to continue doing so in the future. This is why the future of *language research must place bilingualism at the very core of its concerns*. The different factors and their interactions need to be considered by any model or approach to bilingualism that wants to do justice to the richness and complexity of the facts. The CASP for Bilingualism principles have been formulated in a way that is intended to make them compatible with, and neutral to, different theoretical approaches, in the interests of achieving greater interdisciplinarity in studies of the bilingual mind and bilingual behaviour.

It is my hope that this book will inspire further research that leads to new discoveries about bilingualism within and across minds, and about language and mind more generally.

References

Abutalebi, J., Cappa, S. F. & Perani, D. (2009). What can functional neuroimaging tell us about the bilingual brain? In J. F. Kroll & A. M. B. De Groot, eds., *Handbook of Bilingualism*. Oxford: Oxford University Press, pp. 497–515.

Aikhenvald, A. (2002). *Language Contact in Amazonia*. Oxford: Oxford University Press.

Aksu-Koç, A. & Slobin, D. I. (1986). A psychological account of the development and use of evidentials in Turkish. In C. Wallace & J. Nicholas, eds., *Evidentiality: The Linguistic Coding of Epistemology*. New York, NY: Ablex, pp. 159–67.

Altarriba, J. (2002). Bilingualism: Language, memory and applied issues. *Online Readings in Psychology and Culture* 4(2). https://dx.doi.org/10.9707/2307-0919 .1034.

Altarriba, J. & Basnight-Brown, D. M. (2007). Methodological considerations in performing semantic- and translation-priming experiments across languages. *Behavior Research Methods* 39, 1–18.

Altarriba, J. & Isurin, L., eds. (2013). *Memory, Language, and Bilingualism: Theoretical and Applied Approaches*. Cambridge, UK: Cambridge University Press.

Ameel, E., Malt, B., Storms, G. & Van Assche, F. (2009). Semantic convergence in the bilingual lexicon. *Journal of Memory and Language*, 60, 270–90.

Ameel, E., Storms, G., Malt, B. C. & Sloman, S. A. (2005). How bilinguals solve the naming problem. *Journal of Memory and Language*, 53, 60–80.

Antoniou, K., Grohmann, K. K., Kambanaros, M. & Katsos, N. (2016). The effect of childhood bilectalism and multilingualism on executive control. *Cognition* 149, 18–30.

Arslan, S., Bastiaanse, R. & Felser, C. (2015). Looking at the evidence in visual world: Eye-movements reveal how bilingual and monolingual Turkish speakers process grammatical evidentiality. *Frontiers in Psychology*. doi:http://dx.doi.org/10.3389/fp syg.2015.01387.

Aske, J. (1989). Path predicates in English and Spanish: A closer look. In *Proceedings of the Fifteenth Annual Meeting of the Berkeley Linguistics Society*. Berkeley, CA: Berkeley Linguistics Society, pp. 1–14.

Athanasopoulos, P. (2009). Cognitive representation of colour in bilinguals: The case of Greek blues. *Bilingualism: Language and Cognition* 12, 83–95.

Athanasopoulos, P. (2011). Cognitive restructuring in bilingualism. In A. Pavlenko, ed., *Thinking and Speaking in Two Languages*. Bristol: Multilingual Matters, pp. 29–65.

Athanasopoulos, P., Bylund, E., Montero-Melis, G., et al. (2015). Two languages, two minds: Flexible cognitive processing driven by language of operation. *Psychological Science* 26(4), 518–26.

Athanasopoulos, P., Damjanovic, L., Krajciova, A. & Sasaki, M. (2011). Representation of colour concepts in bilingual cognition: The case of Japanese blues. *Bilingualism: Language and Cognition* 14(1), 9–17.

Athanasopoulos, P., Derring, B., Wiggett, A. Kuipers, J. -R. & Thierry, G. (2010). Perceptual shift in bilingualism: Brain potentials reveal plasticity in pre-attentive colour perception. *Cognition* 116, 437–43.

Atkinson, R. C., & Shiffrin, R. M. (1968). Human memory: A proposed system and its control processes. In K. W. Spence & J. T. Spence, eds., *The Psychology of Learning and Motivation* (vol.2). Orlando, FL: Academic Press, pp. 89–195.

Baker, C. (2011). *Foundations of Bilingual Education and Bilingualism (*5th ed.) Clevedon, UK: Multilingual Matters.

Bartolotti, J. & Marian, V. (2013). Bilingual memory: Structure, access and processing. In J. Altarriba & L. Isurin, eds., *Memory, Language, and Bilingualism: Theoretical and Applied Approaches*. Cambridge, UK: Cambridge University Press, pp. 7–47.

Basnight-Brown, D. M. (2014). Models of lexical access and bilingualism. In R. R. Heredia & J. Altarriba, eds., *Foundations of Bilingual Memory*. New York, NY: Springer, pp. 85–107.

Basnight-Brown, D. M. & Altarriba, J. (2007). Differences in semantic and translation priming across languages: The role of language direction and language dominance. *Journal of Memory and Cognition* 35, 953–65.

Bassetti, B. (2007). Grammatical gender and concepts of objects in bilingual children. *International Journal of Bilingualism* 11, 251–73.

Bassetti, B. & Cook, V., eds. (2011). *Language and Bilingual Cognition*. New York, NY: Psychology Press.

Baumgarten, N. & Özçetin, D. (2008). Linguistic variation through language contact in translation. In P. Siemund & N. Kintana, eds., *Language Contact and Contact Languages*. Amsterdam/Philadelphia: John Benjamins, pp. 293–316.

Benmamoun, E., Montrul, S. & Polinsky, M. (2013a). Defining an 'ideal' heritage speaker: Theoretical and methodological challenges. Reply to peer commentaries. *Theoretical Linguistics*, 39(3–4), 259–94.

Benmamoun, E., Montrul, S. & Polinsky, M. (2013b). Heritage languages and their speakers: Opportunities and challenges for linguistics. *Theoretical Linguistics*, 39(3–4), 129–81.

Ben Zeev, S. (1977). Mechanisms by which childhood bilingualism affects understanding of language and cognitive structures. In P. A. Hornby, ed., *Bilingualism: Psychological, Social and Educational Implications*. New York, NY: Academic Press, pp. 29–55.

Berk-Seligson, S. (1983). Sources of variation in Spanish verb construction usage: The active, dative, and the reflective passive. *Journal of Pragmatics*, 7, 145–168.

Berk-Seligson, S. (2002 [1990]). *The Bilingual Courtroom: Court Interpreters in the Judicial Process*. Chicago, IL: The University of Chicago Press.

Berk-Seligson, S. (2009). *Coerced Confessions: The Discourse of Bilingual Police Interrogations*. Berlin: Mouton de Gruyter.

Berk-Seligson, S. (2011). Negotiation and communicative accommodation in bilingual police interrogations: A critical interactional sociolinguistic perspective. *International Journal of Sociology of Language* 207, 29–58.

Bernolet, S., Hartsuiker, R. & Pickering, M. (2013). From language-specific to shared syntactic representations: The influence of second language proficiency on syntactic sharing in bilinguals. *Cognition* 127, 287–306.

Berthele, R. (2012). On the use of PUT verbs by multilingual speakers of Romansh. In A. Kopecka & B. Narasimhan, eds., *The Events of Putting and Taking: A Crosslinguistic Perspective*. Amsterdam: John Benjamins, pp. 145–66.

Bialystok, E. (1999). Cognitive complexity and attentional control in the bilingual mind. *Child Development* 70, 636–44.

Bialystok, E. (2007). Cognitive effects of bilingualism: How linguistic experience leads to cognitive change. *International Journal of Bilingual Education and Bilingualism* 10(3), 210–23.

Bialystok, E., Craik, F. I. M. & Freedman, M. (2007). Bilingualism as protection against the onset of symptoms of dementia. *Neuropsychologia* 45, 459–64.

Bialystok, E., Craik, F. I. M., Grady, C., et al. (2005). Effect of bilingualism on cognitive control in the Simon task: Evidence from MEG. *Neuroimage* 24, 40.

Bialystok, E, Craik, F. I.M. & Ruocco, A. C. (2006). Dual-modality monitoring in a classification task: The effects of bilingualism and ageing. *Quarterly Journal of Experimental Psychology* 59(11), 1968–83.

Bialystok, E., Craik, F. I. M. & Ryan, J. (2006). Executive control in a modified antisaccade task: Effects of aging and bilingualism. *Journal of Experimental Psychology: Learning, Memory, and Cognition* 32, 1341–54.

Bialystok, E. & Martin, M. M. (2004). Attention and inhibition in bilingual children: Evidence from the dimensional change card sort task. *Developmental Science* 7, 325–39.

Birdsong, D. (2005). Interpreting age effects in second language acquisition. In J. F. Kroll & A. M. B. De Groot, eds., *Handbook of Bilingualism: Psycholinguistic Approaches*. New York, NY: Oxford University Press, pp. 109–27.

Birdsong, D. (2006). Age and second language acquisition and processing: A selective overview. *Language Learning*, 56, 9–48.

Birdsong, D. & Molis, M. (2001). On the evidence for maturational constraints in second-language acquisition. *Journal of Memory and Language* 44, 235–49.

Bloom, P., Peterson, M. A., Nadel, L. & Garrett, M. F., eds. (1999). *Language and Space*. Cambridge, MA: MIT Press.

Bloomfield, L. (1935). Linguistic aspects of science. *Philosophy of Science* 2(4), 499–507.

Borg, A. (1985). *Cypriot Arabic: A Historical and Comparative Investigation into the Phonology and Morphology of the Arabic Vernacular Spoken by the Maronites of Kormakiti Village in the Kyrenia District of North-Western Cyprus*. Stuttgart: Deutsche Morgenländische Gesellschaft.

Boroditsky, L., Schmidt, L. A. & Phillips, W. (2003). Sex, syntax and semantics. In D. Gentner & S. Goldin-Meadow, eds., *Language and Mind: Advances in the Study of Language and Thought*. Cambridge, MA: MIT Press, pp. 61–79.

Bricker, V. (1999). Color and texture in the Maya language of Yukatan. *Anthropological Linguistics* 41(3), 283–307.

Broadbent, D. E. (1958). *Perception and Communication*. New York, NY: Oxford University Press.

Brown, A. & Gullberg, M. (2011). Bidirectional cross-linguistic influence in event conceptualisation? Expressions of Path among Japanese learners of English. *Bilingualism: Language and Cognition* 14(1), 79–94.

Brysbaert, M. & Duyck, W. (2010). Is it time to leave behind the revised hierarchical model of bilingual language processing after fifteen years of service? *Bilingualism: Language and Cognition* 13, 359–71.

Bylund, E. (2011). Language-specific patterns in event conceptualisation: Insights from bilingualism. In A. Pavlenko, ed., *Thinking and Speaking in Two Languages*. Bristol: Multilingual Matters, pp. 108–42.

Bylund, E. & Athanasopoulos, P. (2014). Linguistic relativity in SLA: Towards a new research programme. *Language Learning* 64(4), 952–85.

Bylund, E. & Jarvis, S. (2011). L2 effects on L1 event conceptualisation. *Bilingualism: Language and Cognition* 14(1), 47–59.

Cadierno, T. (2008). Motion events in Danish and Spanish: A focus on form pedagogical approach. In S. De Knop & T. De Rycker, eds., *Cognitive Approaches to Pedagogical Grammar*. Berlin: Mouton de Gruyter, pp. 259–94.

Cadierno, T. (2010). Motion in Danish as a second language: Does the learner's L1 make a difference? In Z.-H. Han &T. Cadierno, eds., *Linguistic Relativity in SLA*. Clevedon, UK: Multilingual Matters, pp. 1–33.

Cadierno, T. (2017). Thinking for speaking about motion in a second language. Looking back and forward. In I. Ibarretxe-Antuñano, ed., *Motion and Space across Languages: Theory and Applications*. Amsterdam: John Benjamins, pp. 279–300.

Cadierno, T., Ibarretxe-Antuñano, I. & Hijazo-Gascón, A. (2016). Semantic categorisation of placement verbs in L1 and L2 Danish and Spanish. *Language Learning*, 66(1), 191–223.

Caldwell-Harris, C. L. & Ayçiçeği-Dinn, A. (2009). Emotion and lying in a non-native language. *International Journal of Psychophysiology* 71, 193–204.

Campbell, L. (2013). *Historical Linguistics: An Introduction*. Cambridge, MA: MIT Press.

Caskey-Simons, L. A. & Hickerson, N. P. (1977). Semantic shift and bilingualism: Strategist vs. evaluative functions of the anterior cingulate cortex. *Proceedings of the National Academy of Sciences* 97, 1944–8.

Chamoreau, C. & Léglise, I. (2012). *Dynamics of Contact-Induced Language Change*. Berlin: Mouton De Gruyter.

Chiswick, B. R. & Miller, P. W. (2008). Why is the payoff to schooling smaller for immigrants? *Labour Economics* 6, 1317–40.

Cifuentes-Férez, P. & Rojo, A. (2015). Thinking for translating: A think-aloud protocol on the translation of manner-of-motion verbs. *Target* 27, 273–300.

Clark, H. H. (1996). *Using Language*. Cambridge, UK: Cambridge University Press.

Comrie, B. (2008). Inflectional morphology and language contact, with special reference to mixed languages. In P. Siemund & N. Kintana, eds., *Language Contact and Contact Languages*. Amsterdam: John Benjamins, pp. 15–32.

Cook, V. (1991). The poverty of the stimulus argument and multicompetence. *Second Language Research* 7(2), 103–17.

Cook, V. (1992). Evidence for multicompetence. *Language Learning* 42(4), 557–91.

Cook, V. (1995). Multi-competence and the learning of many languages. *Language, Culture and Curriculum* 8(2), 93–8.

Cook, V. & Bassetti, B. (2011). *Language and Bilingual Cognition*. New York, NY: Psychology Press.

Costa, A., Foucart, A., Hayakawa, S., Aparici, M. & Apesteguia, J. (2014). Your morals depend on language. *PLoS ONE* 9(4). https://doi.org/10.1371/journal.pone.0094842.

Costa, A., Hernández, M. & Sebastián-Gallés, N. (2008). Bilingualism aids conflict resolution: evidence from the ANT task. *Cognition* 106(1), 59–86.

Costa, A., Miozzo, M. & Caramazza, A. (1999). Lexical selection in bilinguals: Do words in the bilingual's two lexicons compete for selection? *Journal of Memory and Language* 41, 365–97.

Coventry, K., Valdés, B. & Guijarro-Fuentes, P. (2010). Thinking for speaking and immediate memory for spatial relations. In Z.-H. Han & T. Cadierno, eds., *Linguistic Relativity in SLA*. Clevedon, UK: Multilingual Matters, pp. 84–101.

Craik, F. I. M. (2002). Levels of processing: Past, present . . . and future? *Memory* 10 (5–6), 305–18.

Craik, F. I. M. & Lockhart, R. S. (1972). Levels of processing: A framework for memory research. *Journal of Verbal Learning and Verbal Behavior* 11, 671–84.

Curzan, A. (2003). *Gender Shifts in the History of English*. Cambridge, UK: Cambridge University Press.

Dahl, O. (2004). *The Growth and Maintenance of Linguistic Complexity*. Amsterdam: John Benjamins.

Danker, J. D. & Anderson, J. R. (2010). The ghosts of brain states past: Remembering reactivates the brain regions engaged during encoding. *Psychological Bulletin* 136, 87–102.

Davidoff, J., Davies, I. & Roberson, D. (1999). Colour categories in a stone-age tribe. *Nature* 398, 203–4.

De Bot, K. (1992). A bilingual production model: Levelt's 'speaking' model adapted. *Applied Linguistics* 13, 1–24.

De Groot, A. M. B. (1992). Bilingual lexical representation: A closer look at conceptual representations. In R. Frost & L. Katz, eds., Orthography, Phonology, Morphology, and Meaning. Amsterdam: Elsevier, pp. 389–412.

De Groot, A. M. B. (1993). Word-type effects in bilingual processing task: Support for a mixed representational system. In R. Schreuder & B. Weltens, eds., *The Bilingual Lexicon*. Amsterdam: John Benjamins, pp. 27–51.

De Groot, A. M. B. (1997). The cognitive study of translation and interpretation: Three approaches. In J. H. Danks et al., eds., *Cognitive Processes in Translation and Interpreting*. London: Sage, pp. 25–56.

De Groot, A. M. B. (2011). *Language and Cognition in Bilinguals and Multilinguals: An Introduction*. New York, NY: Psychology Press.

De Groot, A. M. B. (2014). About phonological, grammatical and semantic accents in bilinguals' language use and their cause. In L. Filipović & M. Pütz, eds., *Multilingual Cognition and Language Use* [Human Cognitive Processing Series 44]. Amsterdam: John Benjamins, pp. 229–62.

De Groot, A. M. B., Dannenburg, L. & Van Hell, J. G. (1994). Forward and backward word translation in bilinguals. *Journal of Memory and Language* 33, 600–29.

De Houwer, A. (1995). Bilingual language acquisition. In P. Fletcher & B. MacWhinney, eds., *The Handbook of Child Language*. Oxford, UK: Blackwell, pp. 219–50.

DeKeyser, R. M. (2000). The robustness of critical period effects in second language acquisition. *Studies in Second Language Acquisition* 22, 499–533.

Dewaele, J.-M. (2001). Activation or inhibition? The interaction of L1, L2 and L3 on the language mode continuum. In J. Cenoz, B. Hufeisen & U. Jessner, eds., *Cross-*

Linguistic Influence in Third Language Acquisition: Psycholinguistic Perspectives. Clevedon, UK: Multilingual Matters, pp. 69–89.

Dewaele, J-M. (2004). Blistering barnacles! What language do multilinguals swear in?! *Estudios de Sociolinguistica* 5(1), 83–105.

Dijkstra, T. and Van Heuven, W. (2002). The architecture of the bilingual word recognition system: From identification to decision. *Bilingualism: Language and Cognition* 5, 175–97.

Dimitropoulou, M., Duñabeitia, J. A. & Carreiras, M. (2011). Masked translation priming effects with low proficient bilinguals. *Memory and Cognition* 39, 260–75.

Dingemanse, M. & Enfield, N. J. (2014). Let's talk: Special report. Scientific American Mind, September, pp. 64–9.

Döpke, S. (1998). Competing language structures: The acquisition of verb placement by bilingual German–English children. *Journal of Child Language* 25, 555–84.

Dörnyei, Z. (2009). *The Psychology of Second Language Acquisition.* Oxford: Oxford University Press.

Dussias, P. E. (2001). Sentence parsing in fluent Spanish-English bilinguals. In J. Nicol, ed., *One Mind, Two Languages: Bilingual Language Processing.* London, UK: Blackwell Publishing, pp. 159–76.

Dussias, P. E. (2003). Syntactic ambiguity resolution in second language learners: Some effects of bilinguality on L1 and L2 processing strategies. *Studies in Second Language Acquisition* 25, 529–57.

Dussias, P. & Sagarra, N. (2007). The effect of exposure on syntactic parsing in Spanish- English bilinguals. *Bilingualism: Language and Cognition* 10(1), 101–16.

Ellis, A. W. & Lambon Ralph, M. A. (2000). Age of acquisition effects in adult lexical processing reflect loss of plasticity in maturing systems: Insights from connectionist networks. *Journal of Experimental Psychology: Learning, Memory and Cognition* 26, 1103–23.

Ellis, N. C. (1998). Emergentism, connectionism and language learning. *Language Learning* 48(4), 631–664.

Ellis, N. C. (2008). Usage-based and form-focused language acquisition: The associative learning of constructions, learned-attention, and the limited L2 state. In P. Robinson & N. C. Ellis, eds., *Handbook of Cognitive Linguistics and Second Language Acquisition.* London, UK: Routledge, pp. 372–405.

Ellis, N. & Cadierno, T. (2009). Constructing a second language. *Annual Review of Cognitive Linguistics* 7, 111–39.

Ellis, N. C. & Hennelly, R. A. (1980). A bilingual word-length effect: Implications for intelligence testing and relative ease of mental calculation in Welsh and English. *British Journal of Psychology* 71, 43–51.

Ellis, N. C. & Larsen-Freeman, D. (2009). Constructing a second language: Analyses and computational simulations of the emergence of linguistic constructions from usage. In N. C. Ellis &D. Larsen-Freeman, eds., *Language as a Complex Adaptive System.* Chichester, UK: Wiley-Blackwell, pp. 90–125.

Ellis, R. (1994). *The Study of Second Language Acquisition.* Oxford, UK: Oxford University Press.

Emonds, J. E. & Faarlund, J. T. (2014). *English: The Language of the Vikings.* Olomouc, Czech Republic: Palacký University.

Engemann, H., Harr, A.-K. & Hickmann, M. (2012). Caused motion events across languages and learner types: A comparison of bilingual first and adult second language acquisition. In L. Filipovic & M. Pütz, eds., *Multilingual Cognition and Language Use* [Human Cognitive Processing Series 44]. Amsterdam: Benjamins, pp. 263–88.

Ervin, S. M. (1961). Semantic shift in bilingualism. *American Journal of Psychology* 74, 361–72.

Fabbro, F. (1999). *The Neurolinguistics of Bilingualism: An Introduction.* Hove, UK: Psychology Press.

Fabbro, F., Gran, B., & Gran, L. (1991). Hemispheric specialization for semantic and syntactic components of language in simultaneous interpreters. *Brain and Language* 41, 1–42.

Færch, C. & Kasper, G. (1987). Perspectives on language transfer. *Applied Linguistics* 8, 111–36.

Fausey, C. & Boroditsky, L. (2010). Subtle linguistic cues influence perceived blame and financial liability. *Psychonomic Bulletin and Review* 17, 644–50.

Fausey, C. & Boroditsky, L. (2011). Who dunnit? Cross-linguistic differences in eye-witness memory. *Psychonomic Bulletin and Review* 18, 150–57.

Fenyvesi, A. (1994). Language contact and language death: The case of Hungarian. MA dissertation, University of Pittsburgh.

Fernandez, E. M. (1995). *Processing Strategies in Second Language Acquisition: Some Preliminary Results.* Paper presented at GASLA (Generative Approaches to Second Language Acquisition) '95, CUNY Graduate School and University Center, New York, NY.

Fernandez, E. M. (2002). Relative clause attachment in bilinguals and monolinguals. In R. R. Heredia & J. Altarriba, eds., *Bilingual Sentence Processing.* Amsterdam: Elsevier, pp. 187–215.

Fernandez, E. M., de Souza, R. A. & Carando, A. (2017). Bilingual innovations: Experimental evidence offers clues regarding the psycholinguistics of language change. *Bilingualism: Language and Cognition* 20(2), 251–68.

Field, F. W. (2002). *Linguistic Borrowing in Bilingual Context.* Amsterdam: John Benjamins.

Filipović, L. (1999). Language-specific expression of motion and its use in narrative texts. MPhil dissertation, University of Cambridge.

Filipović, L. (2007a). Language as a witness: Insights from cognitive linguistics. *Speech, Language and the Law* 14(2), 245–67.

Filipović, L. (2007b). *Talking about Motion: A Crosslinguistic Investigation of Lexicalisation Patterns.* Amsterdam: John Benjamins.

Filipović, L. (2008). Typology in action: Applying insights from typological contrasts. *International Journal of Applied Linguistics* 18(1), 42–61.

Filipović, L. (2009). Motion events in semantic typology and eyewitness interviews. *Language and Linguistics Compass* 3(1), 300–13.

Filipović, L. (2010a). Typology meets witness narratives and memory: Theory and practice entwined in cognitive linguistics. In E. Tabakowska et al., eds., *Cognitive Linguistics in Action: Theory to Application and Back.* Berlin: Mouton de Gruyter, 269–91.

Filipović, L. (2010b). Thinking and speaking about motion: Universal vs. language-specific effects. In G. Marotta et al., eds., *Space in Language.* Pisa: University of Pisa Press, 235–48.

Filipović, L. (2010c). Aspectual meanings in two cognitive domains: A constructional approach to aspect in Serbian. *Constructions and Frames* 2(1), 74–89.

Filipović, L. (2011). Speaking and remembering in one or two languages: Bilingual vs. monolingual lexicalisation and memory for motion events. *International Journal of Bilingualism* 15, 466–85.

Filipović, L. (2013a). The role of language in legal contexts: A forensic cross-linguistic viewpoint. In M. Freeman & F. Smith, eds., *Law and Language: Current Legal Issues* 15. Oxford, UK: Oxford University Press, pp. 328–43.

Filipović, L. (2013b). Constructing causation in language and memory: Implications for access to justice in multilingual interactions. *International Journal of Speech, Language and the Law* 20, 1–19.

Filipović, L. (2014). Efficiency of the bilingual mind: Clues from processing, memory and second language acquisition studies. In L. Filipović & M. Pütz, eds., *Multilingual Cognition and Language Use: Processing and Typological Perspectives* [Human Cognitive Processing Series 44]. Amsterdam: John Benjamins, pp. 205–27.

Filipović, L (2016). *May* vs. *might* in the judgement on certainty: The difference between L1 and L2 English speakers. *Applied Linguistic Review* 7(2), 181–201.

Filipović, L. (2017a). Applied Language Typology: Applying typological insights in practice. *Languages in Contrast* 17(2), 255–78.

Filipović, L. (2017b). Applying language typology: Practical applications of research on typological contrasts between languages. In I. Ibarretxe-Antuñano, ed., *Motion and Space across Languages and Applications* [Human Cognitive Processing Series 59]. Amsterdam. John Benjamins, pp. 399–418.

Filipović, L. (2018). Speaking in L2 but thinking in L1: Language-specific effects on memory for causation events in English and Spanish. *International Journal of Bilingualism* 22, 180–98.

Filipović, L. (2019a). Police interviews with suspects: Communication problems in evidence-gathering and possible solutions. *Pragmatics and Society* [Special issue] 10 (1), 9–31.

Filipović, L. (2019b). Bilingual memory advantage: Bilinguals use a common linguistic pattern as an aid to recall memory. *International Journal of Bilingualism* https://doi.org/10.1177/1367006918814381.

Filipović, L. & Abad Vergara, S. (2018). Juggling investigation and interpretation: The problematic dual role of police officer-interpreter. *Law and Language* 5(1), 62–79.

Filipović, L. & Geva, S. (2012). Language-specific effects on lexicalisation and memory of motion events. In L. Filipović & K. Jaszczolt, eds., *Space and Time across Languages and Cultures Vol. 2: Language Culture and Cognition*. Amsterdam: John Benjamins, pp. 269–82.

Filipović, L. & Hawkins, J. A. (2013). Multiple factors in second language acquisition: The CASP model. *Linguistics* 51, 145–76.

Filipović, L. & Hawkins, J. (2018). The Complex Adaptive System Principles model for bilingualism: Language interactions within and across bilingual minds. *International Journal of Bilingualism*. Pre-print at: https://doi.org/10.1177/1367006918781076.

Filipović, L. & Hijazo-Gascón, A. (2018). Interpreting meaning in police interviews: Applied Language Typology in a forensic linguistics context. *Vigo International Journal of Applied Linguistics VIAL* 15, 67–104.

Filipović, L. & Ibarretxe-Antuñano, I. (2015). Motion. In E. Dąbrowska & D. Dagmar, eds., *Handbook of Cognitive Linguistics* [Handbooks of Linguistics and Communication Science 39]. Berlin: Mouton de Gruyter, 536–45.

Filipović, L., Slobin, D. I. & Ibarretxe-Antuñano, I. (2013). *Language Language(s) and memory: Rules of engagement in monolinguals vs. bilinguals.* Paper at Association for Psychological Science 25th Anniversary Conference, Washington, USA.

Filipović, L. & Vidaković, I. (2010). Typology in the L2 classroom: Second language acquisition from a typological perspective. In M. Pütz & L. Sicola, eds., *Inside the Learner's Mind: Cognitive Processing in Second Language Acquisition.* Amsterdam: John Benjamins, pp. 269–91.

Flecken, M. (2010). *Event Conceptualisation In Language Production of Early Bilinguals.* Utrecht: LOT Dissertation publications.

Forbes, J. N., Poulin-Dubois, D., Rivero, M. R. & Sera, M. D. (2008). Grammatical gender affects bilinguals' conceptual gender: Implications for linguistic relativity and decision making. *Open Applied Linguistic Journal* 1, 68–76.

Francis, W. (1999). Cognitive integration of language and memory in bilinguals: Semantic representation. *Psychological Bulletin* 125, 193–222.

Frazier, L. & Clifton, C. (2000). On bound variable interpretations: The LF-only hypothesis. *Journal of Psycholinguistic Research* 29, 125–39.

Frenck-Mestre, C. (2002). An on-line look at sentence processing in the second language. In R. R. Heredia and J. Altarriba, eds., *Bilingual Sentence Processing.* Amsterdam: Elsevier, pp. 217–36.

Friedman, V. A. (2003). *Turkish in Macedonia and Beyond: Studies in Contact, Typology and Other Phenomena in the Balkans and the Caucasus* [Turcologica, 52]. Wiesbaden: Otto Harrassowitz.

Gast, V. (2007). From phylogenetic diversity to structural homogeneity: On right-branching constituent order in Mesoamerica. *Sky Journal of Linguistics* 20, 171–202.

Gathercole, V. C. M. (2015). Are we at a socio-political and scientific crisis? *Cortex* 73, 345–46.

Gathercole, V. M. (2016). Factors moderating proficiency in bilingual speakers. In E. Nicolaidis & S. Montanari, eds., *Bilingualism across the Lifespan: Factors Moderating Language Proficiency.* Washington, DC: Mouton de Gruyter/ American Psychological Association, pp. 123–40.

Gathercole, V. C. M., & Moawad, R. A. (2010). Semantic interaction in early and late bilinguals: All words are not created equal. *Bilingualism: Language and Cognition* 13, 385–408.

Gathercole, V.C. & Thomas, E.M. (2009). Bilingual first language development: Dominant language takeover, threatened minority language take-up. *Bilingualism: Language and Cognition* 12(1), 213–37.

Gell-Mann, M. (1992). Complexity and complex adaptive systems. In J. A. Hawkins & M. Gell-Mann, eds., *The Evolution of Human Languages.* Redwood City, CA: Addison-Wesley, pp. 3–18.

Genesee, F., Paradis, J. & Cargo, M. B., eds. (2004). *Dual Language Development and Disorder: A Handbook of Bilingualism and Second Language Learning.* Baltimore, MD: Paul H. Brookes.

Gentner, D. & Goldin-Meadow, S., eds. (2003). *Language in Mind: Advances in the Study of Language and Thought.* Cambridge, MA: MIT Press.

Gibbons, J. (2003). *Forensic Linguistics*. Oxford, UK: Blackwell.

Gile, D. (1997). Conference interpreting as a cognitive management problem. In J. H. Danks, G. M. Shreve, S. B. Fountain & M. McBeath, eds., *Cognitive Processes in Translation and Interpreting*. London, UK: Sage, pp. 96–214.

Giles, H., Coupland, J., & Coupland, N. (1991). *Contexts of Accommodation: Developments in Applied Sociolinguistics*. Cambridge, UK: Cambridge University Press.

Giles, H., & Smith, P. M. (1979). Accommodation theory: Optimal levels of convergence. In H. Giles & R. N. St. Clair, eds., *Language and Social Psychology*. Oxford, UK: Blackwell, pp. 45–65.

Gollan, T. H., Montoya, R. I. & Werner, G. (2002). Semantic and letter fluency in Spanish-English bilinguals. *Neuropsychology* 16, 562–76.

Green, D. W. & Abutalebi, J. (2013). Language control in bilinguals: The adaptive control hypothesis. *Journal of Cognitive Psychology* 25(5), 515–30.

Grice, P. H. (1957). Meaning. *The Philosophical Review* 66, 377–88.

Grosjean, F. (1992). Another view of bilingualism. In R. Harris, ed., *Cognitive Processing in Bilinguals*. Amsterdam/New York: North Holland, pp. 51–62.

Grosjean, F. (1998). Studying bilinguals: Methodological and conceptual issues. *Bilingualism: Language and Cognition* 1(2), 131–49.

Grosjean, F. (2001). The bilingual's language modes. In J. Nicol, ed., *One Mind, Two Languages: Bilingual Language Processing*. Oxford, UK: Blackwell, pp. 1–22.

Grosjean, F. (2010). *Bilingual: Life and Reality*. Cambridge, MA: Harvard University Press.

Gullberg, M. (2009). Reconstructing verb meaning in a second language: How English speakers of L2 Dutch talk and gesture about placement. *Annual Review of Cognitive Linguistics* 7, 222–45.

Hakuta, K., Bialystok, E. & Wiley, E. (2003). Critical evidence: A test of the Critical-Period Hypothesis for second-language acquisition. *Psychological Science* 14, 31–8.

Hale, S. (2004). *The Discourse of Court Interpreting: Discourse Practices of the Law, the Witness, and the Interpreter*. Amsterdam: John Benjamins.

Hale, S. (2007). *Community Interpreting*. Palgrave Macmillan: Basingstoke.

Hale, S. (2014). Interpreting culture. Dealing with cross-cultural issues in court interpreting. *Perspectives: Studies in Translatology* 22, 321.

Han, Z.-H. (2010). Grammatical morpheme inadequacy as a function of linguistic relativity: A longitudinal case study. In Z.-H. Han & T. Cadierno, eds., *Linguistic Relativity in SLA*. Clevedon, UK: Multilingual Matters, pp. 154–82.

Harrington, M. (1992). Working memory capacity as a constraint on L2 development. In R. J. Harris, ed., *Cognitive Processes in Bilinguals*. Amsterdam: Elsevier, pp. 123–35.

Harris, C. (2010). Bilingual speakers in the lab: Psychophysiological measures of emotional reactivity. *Journal of Multilingual and Multicultural Development* 25 (2–3), 223–47.

Hartsuiker, R. J., Beerts, S., Loncke, M., Desmet, T. & Bernolet, S. (2016). Cross-linguistic structural priming in multilinguals: Further evidence for shared syntax. *Journal of Memory and Language* 90, 14–30.

Hartsuiker, R. J. & Pickering, M. (2008). Language integration in bilingual sentence production. *Acta Psychologica* 128(3), 479–89.

Hartsuiker, R. J., Pickering, M. J., & Veltkamp, E. (2004). Is syntax separate or shared between languages? Cross-linguistic syntactic priming in Spanish-English bilinguals. *Psychological Science* 15(6), 409–14.

Hasko, V. (2010). The role of thinking for speaking in adult L2 speech: The case of (non) unidirectionality encoding by American learners of Russian. In Z.-H. Han & T. Cadierno, eds., *Linguistic Relativity in SLA*. Clevedon, UK: Multilingual Matters, pp. 34–58.

Hatzidaki, A., Branigan, H. P. & Pickering, M. J. (2011). Co-activation of syntax in bilingual language production. *Cognitive Psychology* 62, 123–50.

Hawkins, E. (1984). *Awareness of Language: An Introduction*. Cambridge, UK: Cambridge University Press.

Hawkins, J. A. (1978). *Definiteness and Indefiniteness: A Study in Reference and Grammaticality Prediction*. London, UK: Croom Helm.

Hawkins, J. A. (1986). *A Comparative Typology of English and German: Unifying the Contrasts*. London, UK: Routledge.

Hawkins, J. A. (1994). *A Performance Theory of Order and Constituency*. Cambridge, UK: Cambridge University Press.

Hawkins, J. A. (2004). *Efficiency and Complexity in Grammars*. Oxford, UK: Oxford University Press.

Hawkins, J. A. (2009). An efficiency theory of complexity and related phenomena. In G. Sampson, D. Gil & P. Trudgill, eds., *Language Complexity as an Evolving Variable*. Oxford, UK: Oxford University Press, pp. 252–68.

Hawkins, J. A. (2014). *Cross-Linguistic Variation and Efficiency*. Oxford, UK: Oxford University Press.

Hawkins, J. A. & Filipović, L. (2012). *Criterial Features in L2 English: Specifying the Reference Levels of the Common European Framework*. Cambridge, UK: Cambridge University Press.

Hawkins, J. A. & Gell-Mann, M., eds. (1992). *The Evolution of Human Languages Santa Fe Institute Studies in the Sciences of Complexity: Proceedings Volume XI*. Reading, MA: Addison-Wesley.

Hayes, A. & Hale, S. (2010). Appeals on incompetent interpreting. *Journal of Judicial Administration* 20(2), 119–30.

Heine, B. (2008). Contact-induced word order change without word order change. In P. Siemund & N. Kintana, eds., Language Contact and Contact Languages. Amsterdam/Philadephia: John Benjamins, pp. 31–60.

Heine, B. & Kuteva, T. (2005). *Language Contact and Grammatical change*. Cambridge, UK: Cambridge University Press.

Hendriks, H., Hickmann, M. & Demagny, A. C. (2008). How English native speakers learn to express caused motion in English and French. *Acquisition et Interaction en Langue Étrangère* 27, 15–41.

Heredia, R. R. & Altarriba, J., eds. (2014). *Foundations of Bilingual Memory*. New York, NY: Springer.

Heredia, R. R. & Cieslicka, A. B. (2014). Bilingual memory storage: Compound-coordinate and derivatives. In R. R. Heredia & J. Altarriba, eds., *Foundations of Bilingual Memory*. New York, NY: Springer, pp. 11–39.

Hernandez, A. E., Martinez, A. & Kohnert, K. (2000). In search of the language switch: An fMRI study of picture naming in Spanish-English bilinguals. *Brain and Language* 73, 421–31.

Hijazo-Gascón, A. (2018). Acquisition of motion events in L2 Spanish by German, French and Italian speakers. *Language Learning Journal* 46(3), 241–62.

Hijazo-Gascón, A. (2019). Translating accurately or sounding natural? The interpreters' challenges due to semantic typology and the interpreting process. *Pragmatics and Society* [special issue] 10(1), 73–96.

Hijazo-Gascón, A. & Filipović, L. (in preparation). Interpreting caused motion and resultative constructions: A bidirectional English-Spanish study. University of East Anglia, ms.

Hoff, E., Core, C., Place, S., Rumiche, R., Señor, M. & Parra, M. (2012). Dual language exposure and early bilingual development. *Journal of Child Language* 39, 1–27.

Hohenstein, J., Eisenberg, A. & L. Naigles (2006). Is he floating across or crossing afloat? Cross-linguistic influences of L1 and L2 in Spanish–English bilingual adults. *Bilingualism; Language and Cognition* 9(3), 249–61.

Hopper, P. J. and Thompson, S. A. (1980). Transitivity in grammar and discourse. *Language* 56, 251–95.

Horrocks, G. (1997). *Greek: A History of the Language and Its Speakers*. London/ New York: Longman.

House, J. (2004). English as a lingua franca and its influence on texts in other European languages. In G. Garzone & A. Cardinaletti, eds., *Mediazione Linguistica e Interferenza*. Milano: FrancoAgneli, pp. 21–48.

Hsin, L., Legendre, G. & Omaki, A. (2013). Priming cross-linguistic interference in Spanish–English bilingual children. In *Proceedings of the 37th Annual Boston University Conference on Language Development*. Somerville, MA: Cascadilla Press, pp. 165–77.

Huddleston, R. & Pullum, G. K. (2002). *The Cambridge Grammar of the English Language*. Cambridge, UK: Cambridge University Press.

Hulk, A. (1997). The acquisition of French object pronoun by a Dutch/French bilingual child. In A. Sorace, C. Heycock & R. Shillcock, eds., *Language Acquisition: Knowledge, Representation and Processing*. Edinburgh, UK: Edinburgh University Press, pp. 521–6.

Hulstijn, J. (2018). An individual-differences framework for comparing nonnative with native speakers: Perspectives from BLC theory. Language Learning. doi:https://doi .org/10.1111/lang.12317.

Ibarretxe-Antuñano, I. (2012). Placement and removal events in Basque and Spanish. In A. Kopecka & B. Narasimhan, eds., *The Events of Putting and Taking: A Crosslinguistic Perspective*. Amsterdam: John Benjamins, pp. 123–43.

Ibarretxe-Antuñano, I. & Filipović, L. (2013). Lexicalisation patterns and translation. In A. Rojo & I. Ibarretxe-Antuñano, eds., *Cognitive Linguistics and Translation*. Berlin: Mouton de Gruyter, pp. 253–84.

Ingham, B. (1994). The effect of language contact on the Arabic dialect of Afghanistan. In J. Aguade, F. Corriente & M. Marugán, eds., *Actas de Congreso Internacional sobre Interferencias Lingüísticas Arabo-Romances y Paralelos*. Zaragoza: Navarro, pp. 287–308.

Jared, D., Poh, R. P. Y. & Paivio, A. (2013). L1 and L2 picture naming in Mandarin-English bilinguals. A test of bilingual dual coding theory. *Bilingualism: Language and Cognition* 16, 383–96.

Jarvis, S., O'Malley, M., Jing, L. et al. (2013). Cognitive foundations of crosslinguistic influence. In J. W. Schwieter, ed., *Innovative Research and Practices in Second Language Acquisition and Bilingualism*. Amsterdam: John Benjamins, pp. 287–308.

Jarvis, S. & Pavlenko, A., eds. (2010 [2007]). *Crosslinguistic Influence in Language and Cognition*. London, UK: Routledge.

Johanson, L. (2003). Evidentiality in Turkic. In A. Y. Aikhenvald & R. M. W. Dixon, eds., *Studies in Evidentiality*. Amsterdam: John Benjamins, pp. 273–90.

Johnson, J. S. & Newport, E. L. (1989). Critical period effects in second language learning: The influence of maturational state on the acquisition of English as a second language. *Cognitive Psychology* 21, 60–99.

Kellerman, E. (1983). Now you see it, now you don't. In S. Gass & L. Selinker, eds., *Language Transfer in Language Learning*. Rowley, MA: Newbury House, pp. 112–34.

Kersten, A., Meissner, C., Lechuga, J., et al. (2010). English speakers attend more strongly than Spanish speakers to manner of motion when classifying novel objects and events. *Journal of Experimental Psychology: General*, 139, 638–53.

Keysar, B., Hayakawa, S.L. & An, S. G. (2012). The foreign-language effect: Thinking in a foreign tongue reduces decision biases. *Psychological Science* 23, 661–8.

Koornneef, A. (2008). *Eye-Catching Anaphora*. Utrecht: LOT International Dissertation Series.

Koster, D. & Cadierno, T. (2018). The effect of language on recognition memory in first language and second language speakers: The case of placement events. *International Journal of Bilingualism*. https://doi.org/10.1177/1367006918763140.

Kousta, S.-T., Vinson, D. P. & Vigliocco, G. (2008). Investigating linguistic relativity through bilingualism: The case of grammatical gender. *Journal of Experimental Psychology: Learning, Memory and Cognition* 34, 843–58.

Kredens, K. & Morris, R. (2010). Interpreting outside the courtroom: 'A shattered mirror?' Interpreting in legal contexts outside the courtroom. In M. Coulthard & A. Johnson, eds., *The Routledge Handbook of Forensic Linguistics*. Abingdon, UK: Routledge, pp. 455–72.

Kroll, J. F. & Bialystok, E. (2013). Understanding the consequences of bilingualism for language processing and cognition. *Journal of Cognitive Psychology (Hove)* 25(5). doi:https://doi.org/10.1080/20445911.2013.799170.

Kroll, J. F. & De Groot, A. M. B. (1997). Lexical and conceptual memory in the bilingual: Mapping form to meaning in two languages. In A. M. B. De Groot & J. F. Kroll, eds., *Tutorials in Bilingualism: Psycholinguistic Perspectives*. Mahwah, NJ: Lawrence Erlbaum, pp. 169–99.

Kroll, J. F., Dussias, P. E., Bogulski, C. A. & Valdes Kroff, J. R. (2008). Juggling two languages in one mind: What bilinguals tell us about language processing and its consequences for cognition. In B. Ross, ed., *Psychology of Learning and Motivation*, vol. 56. San Diego: Academic Press, pp. 229–62.

Kroll, J. F. & Stewart, E. (1994). Category interference in translation and picture naming: Evidence for asymmetric connections between bilingual memory representations. *Journal of Memory and Language* 33, 149–74.

Kroll, J. F., Van Hell, J. G., Tokowicz, N. & Green, D. W. (2010). The revised hierarchical model: A critical review and assessment. *Bilingualism: Language and Cognition*, 13, 373–81.

Kupferberg, I. and Olshtain, E. (1996). Explicit contrastive instruction facilitates the acquisition of difficult l2 forms. Special issue on cross-linguistic approaches to language awareness. *Language Awareness* 5, 149–65.

Kupisch, T., Lein, T., Barton, D. et al. (2013). Acquisition outcomes across domains in adult simultaneous bilinguals with French as weaker and stronger language. *Journal of French Language Studies*. doi:https://doi.org/10.1017/ S0959269513000197.

Lai, V. T., Rodriguez, G. G. & Narasimhan, B. (2014). Thinking-for-speaking in early and late bilinguals. *Bilingualism: Language and Cognition* 17, 139–52.

Larrañaga, P., Treffers-Daller, J., Tidball, F. & Gil Ortega, M.-C. (2012). L1 transfer in the acquisition of manner and path in Spanish by native speakers of English. *International Journal of Bilingualism* 16(1), 117–38.

Lee, P. (1996). *Whorf Theory Complex: A Critical Reconstruction* [Studies in the History of Language Sciences 81]. Amsterdam: John Benjamins.

Leisiö, L. (2001). Morphosyntactic convergence and integration in Finland Russian. Academic dissertation. University of Tampere, Finland.

Lemmens, M. (2002). The semantic network of Dutch posture verbs. In J. Newman, ed., *The Linguistics of Sitting, Standing, and Lying*. Amsterdam: John Benjamins, pp. 103–39.

Lemmens, M. (2006). Caused posture: Experiential patterns emerging from corpus research. In A. Stefanowitsch & S. Gries, eds., *Corpora in Cognitive Linguistics* (vol. 2). Berlin: Mouton de Gruyter, pp. 261–96.

Lenneberg, E. H. (1967). *The Biological Foundations of Language*. New York, NY: Wiley & Sons.

Levelt, W. J. M. (1989). *Speaking: From Intention to Articulation*. Cambridge, MA: MIT Press.

Levinson, S. (2000). *Presumptive Meanings*. Cambridge, MA: MIT Press.

Levinson, S. C. (2003). *Space in Language and Cognition*. Cambridge, UK: Cambridge University Press.

Levinson S. & Wilkins, G., eds. (2006). *Grammars of Space*. Cambridge, UK: Cambridge University Press.

Li, W. (2000). *The Bilingualism Reader*. London, UK: Routledge.

Lindstedt, J. (2016). Multilingualism in the Central Balkans in late Ottoman times. In M. Makartsev & M. Wahlström, eds., *In Search of the Center and Periphery: Linguistic Attitudes, Minorities, and Landscapes in the Central Balkans* [Slavica Helsingiensia, vol. 49]. Helsinki: University of Helsinki, Department of Modern Languages, pp. 51–67.

Loebell, H. & Bock, K. (2003). Structural priming across languages. *Linguistics* 41(5), 791–824.

Loftus, E. F. & Palmer, J. C. (1974). Reconstruction of auto-mobile destruction: An example of the interaction between language and memory. *Journal of Verbal Learning and Verbal Behavior* 13, 585–9.

Lohndal, T. & Westergaard, M. (2016). Grammatical gender in American Norwegian heritage language: Stability or attrition. *Frontiers in Psychology* 7: doi:https://doi.org/10.3389/fpsyg.2016.00344.

Lopez, B. & Vaid, J. (2018). Divergence and overlap in bilingual conceptual representation: does prior language brokering experience matter? *Bilingualism: Language and Cognition* 21(1), 150–61.

Lucy, J. A. (1992). *Language Diversity and Thought*. Cambridge, UK: Cambridge University Press.

Lucy, J. A. (2014). Methodological approaches in the study of linguistic relativity. In L. Filipović & M. Pütz, eds., *Multilingual Cognition and Language Use: Processing and Typological* Perspectives. Amsterdam: John Benjamins, pp. 17–44.

Lucy, J. & Gaskins, S. (2003). Interactions of language type and referent type in the development of nonverbal classification preferences. In D. Gentner & S. Goldin-Meadow, eds., *Language in Mind: Advances in the Study of Language and Thought.* Cambridge, MA: MIT Press, pp. 465–92.

Luk, G., De Sa, E. & Bialystok, E. (2011). Is there a relation between onset age of bilingualism and enhancement of cognitive control? *Bilingualism: Language and Cognition,* 14, 588–95.

Macizo, P. & Bajo, M. T. (2006). Reading for repetition and reading for translation: Do they involve the same processes? *Cognition* 99, 1–34.

Mack, M. (1986). A study of semantic and syntactic processing in monolinguals and fluent early bilinguals. *Journal of Psycholinguistic Research* 15, 463–88.

MacLaury, R. (1997). *Color and Cognition in Mesoamerica: Constructing Categories as Vantages.* Austin, TX: University of Texas Press.

MacWhinney, B. (2005). A unified model of language acquisition. In J. F. Kroll & A. M. B. De Groot, eds., *Handbook of Bilingualism: Psycholinguistic Approaches.* New York: Oxford University Press, pp. 49–67.

MacWhinney, B., Malchukov, A. & Moravcsik, E., eds. (2014). *Competing Motivations in Grammar and Usage.* Oxford, UK: Oxford University Press.

Mägiste, E. (1982). Automaticity and interference in bilinguals. *Psychological Research,* 44, 29–43.

Mägiste, E. (1985). Development of intra- and interlingual interference in bilinguals. *Journal of Psycholinguistic Research* 14, 137–54.

Malt, B. C., Sloman, S. A. & Gennari, S. P. (2003). Speaking versus thinking about objects and actions. In D. Gentner & S. Goldin-Meadow, eds., *Language in Mind: Advances in the Study of Language and Thought.* Cambridge, MA: MIT Press, pp. 81–111.

Manterola, J. (2012). The Basque articles -a and bat and recent contact theories. In C. Chamoreau & I. Léglise, eds., *Dynamics of Contact-Induced Language Change.* Berlin: Mouton de Gruyter, pp. 231–63.

Marian, V. & Neisser, U. (2000). Language-dependent recall of autobiographical memories. *Journal of Experimental Psychology – General* 129(3), 361–8.

Marinova-Todd, S. H., Marshall, D. B. & Snow, C. E. (2000). Three misconceptions about age and L2 learning. *TESOL Quarterly* 34(1), 9–34.

Matsumoto, A. & Stanny, C. J. (2006). Language-dependent access to autobiographical memory in Japanese-English bilinguals and US monolinguals. *Memory* 14(3), 378–90.

McDonald, J. L. (2000). Grammaticality judgment in a second language: Influence of age of acquisition and native language. *Applied Psycholinguistics* 21, 395–423.

McDonald, J. L. (2006). Beyond the critical period: Processing-based explanations for poor grammaticality judgment performance by late second language learners. *Journal of Memory and Language* 55, 381–401.

McLaughlin, B. (1978). *Second Language Acquisition in Childhood.* Hillsdale, NJ: Lawrence Erlbaum.

McWhorter, J. H. (2009). What else happened to English? A brief for the Celtic Hypothesis. *English Language and Linguistics* 13 Special Issue 02/July 2009, 163–91.

Meillet, A. (1982) [1906]. Comment le mots changent les sens. *Linguistique historique et linguistique Générale* (1982 [1906]), 230–71.

Mellow, J. D. (2008). The emergence of complex syntax: A longitudinal case study of the ESL development of dependency resolution. *Lingua* 118, 499–521.

Michael, E. & Gollan, T. H. (2005). Being and becoming bilingual: Individual differences and consequences for language production. In J. F. Kroll & A. M. B. De Groot, eds., *Handbook of Bilingualism: Psycholinguistic Approaches*. New York, NY: Oxford University Press, pp. 389–407.

Miyake, A. & Friedman, N. P. (1998). Individual differences in second language proficiency: Working memory as language aptitude. In A. F. Healy and L. E. Bourne, eds., *Foreign Language Learning: Psychological Studies on Training and Retention*. Mahwah, NJ: Erlbaum, pp. 339–64.

Molés-Cases, T. (2016). *La traducción de los eventos de movimiento en un corpus paralelo alemán español de literatura infantil y juvenil*. Frankfurt am Main: Peter Lang.

Montrul, S. (2004). *The Acquisition of Spanish: Morphosyntactic Development in Monolingual and Bilingual L1 Acquisition and in Adult L2 Acquisition*. Amsterdam: John Benjamins.

Montrul, S. (2008). *Incomplete Acquisition in Bilingualism. Re-Examining the Age Factor*. Amsterdam: John Benjamins.

Montrul, S. (2015). Dominance and proficiency in early and late bilingualism. In C. Silva-Corvalán & J. Treffers-Daller, eds., *Language Dominance in Bilinguals: Issues of Measurement and Operationalisation*. Cambridge, UK: Cambridge University Press, pp. 15–35.

Montrul, S. & Ionin, T. (2010). Transfer effects in the interpretation of definite articles by Spanish heritage speakers. *Bilingualism: Language and Cognition* 13, 449–73.

Montrul, S. & Ionin, T. (2012). Dominant language transfer in Spanish heritage speakers and L2 learners in the interpretation of definite articles. *The Modern Language Journal* 96(1), 70–94.

Mulayim, S., Lai, M. & Norma, C. (2015). *Police Investigative Interviews and Interpreting: Context, Challenges, and Strategies*. Boca Raton, FL: CRC Press.

Müller, N. (1998). Transfer in bilingual first language acquisition. *Bilingualism: Language and Cognition* 1(3), 151–71.

Müller, N. & Hulk, A. (2001). Cross-linguistic influence in bilingual language acquisition: Italian and French as recipient languages. *Bilingualism: Language and Cognition* 4, 1–53.

Muysken, P. (2000). *Bilingual Speech: A Typology of Codemixing*. Cambridge, UK: Cambridge University Press.

Muysken, P. (2005). Psycholinguistic modelling in language contact. *International Journal of Bilingualism* 9(3–4), 511–18.

Muysken, P. (2013). Language contact outcomes as the result of bilingual optimisation strategies. *Bilingualism: Language and Cognition* 16(4), 709–30.

Myers-Scotton, C. (2006). *Multiple Voices: An Introduction to Bilingualism*. Oxford, UK: Blackwell.

Nicol, J., Teller, M. & Greth, D. (2001). Production of verb agreement in monolingual, bilingual and second-language speakers. In J. Nicol, ed., *One Mind, Two Languages: Bilingual Language Processing*. Oxford, UK: Blackwell, pp. 117–58.

Nicoladis, E. (2002). What's the difference between 'toilet paper' and 'paper toilet'? French–English bilingual children's crosslinguistic transfer in compound nouns. *Journal of Child Language* 29(4), 843–63.

Nicoladis, E. (2006). Cross-linguistic transfer in adjective-noun strings by preschool bilingual children. *Bilingualism: Language and Cognition* 9, 15–32.

Nicoladis, E. & Montanari, S., eds. (2016). *Bilingualism across the Lifespan: Factors Moderating Language Proficiency*. Washington, DC: Mouton de Gruyter/ American Psychological Association.

Nida, E. (1964). *Toward a Science of Translating: With Special Reference to Principles and Procedures Involved in Bible Translating*. Leiden: Brill.

O'Grady, W. (2005). *Syntactic Carpentry: An Emergentist Approach to Syntax*. Mahwah, NJ: Lawrence Erlbaum.

O'Grady, W. (2008). The emergentist program. *Lingua* 118, 447–64.

Odlin, T. (1989). *Language Transfer: Cross-Linguistic Influence in Language Learning*. Cambridge, UK: Cambridge University Press.

Opitz, B. & Degner, J. (2012). Emotionality in a second language: It's a matter of time. *Neuropsychologia* 50(8), 1961–7.

Paivio, A. (1986). *Mental Representations: A Dual Coding Approach*. New York, NY: Oxford University Press.

Papp, K., Johnson, H. A. & Sawi, O. (2015). Bilingual advantages in executive functioning either do not exist or are restricted to very specific and undetermined circumstances. *Cortex* 69, 265–78.

Papp, K., Johnson, H. A. & Sawi, O. (2016). Should the search for bilingual advantages in executive functioning continue? *Cortex* 74, 305–314.

Paradis, M. (1994). Toward a neurolinguistics theory of simultaneous translation: The framework. *International Journal of Psycholinguistics* 10, 319–35.

Paradis, M. (1997). The cognitive neuropsychology of bilingualism. In A. M. B. De Groot & J. F. Kroll, eds., *Tutorials in Bilingualism: Psycholinguistic Perspectives*. Mahwah, NJ: Erlbaum, pp. 331–54.

Paradis, M. (2000). Generalizable outcomes of bilingual aphasia research. *Folia Phoniatrica and Logopaedia* 52, 54–64.

Paradis, M. (2004). *A Neurolinguistic Theory of Bilingualism*. Amsterdam: John Benjamins.

Paradis, J. & Genesee, F. (1996). Syntactic acquisition in bilingual children: Autonomous or independent. *Studies in Second Language Acquisition* 18, 1–25.

Pavlenko, A. (2005). Bilingualism and thought. In A. De Groot & J. F. Kroll, eds., *Handbook of Bilingualism: Psycholinguistic Approaches*. Oxford, UK: Oxford University Press, pp. 433–53.

Pavlenko, A., ed. (2011). *Thinking and Speaking in Two Languages*. Clevedon, UK: Multilingual Matters.

Pavlenko, A. (2014). *The Bilingual Mind and What It Tells Us about Language and Thought*. Cambridge, UK: Cambridge University Press.

Pavlenko, A. & Jarvis, S. (2002). Bidirectional transfer. *Applied Linguistics* 23(2), 190–214.

Pavlenko, A. & Malt, B. (2011). Kitchen Russian: Cross-linguistic differences and first-language object naming by Russian–English bilinguals. *Bilingualism: Language and Cognition* 14(1), 19–45.

Peal, E. & Lambert, M. (1962). The relation of bilingualism to intelligence. *Psychological Monographs* 72, 1–23.

Penfield, W. & Roberts, L. (1959). *Speech and Brain Mechanisms*. Princeton, NJ: Princeton University Press.

Pienemann, M. (1998). *Language Processing and Second Language Development: Processability Theory.* Amsterdam & Philadelphia: John Benjamins.

Polinsky, M. (1995). Cross-linguistic parallels in language loss. *Southwest Journal of Linguistics* 14(1–2), 87–123.

Polinsky, M. (2008). Without aspect. In G. G. Corbett & M. Noonan, eds., *Case and Grammatical Relations*. Amsterdam: John Benjamins, pp. 263–82.

Polinsky, M. (2016). Bilingual children and adult heritage speakers: The range of comparison. *International Journal of Bilingualism*. doi:https://doi.org/10.1177/1367006916656048.

Poplack, S. (1980). Sometimes I'll start a sentence in Spanish y termino en español: Toward a typology of code-switching. *Linguistics* 18(7–8), 581–618.

Potter, M., So, K.-F., Von Eckardt, B. & Feldman, L. (1984). Lexical and conceptual representation in beginning and more proficient bilinguals. *Journal of Verbal Learning and Verbal Behavior* 23, 23–38.

Pountain, C. (2003). *Exploring the Spanish Language*. London, UK: Hodder Arnold.

Prince, A. & Smolensky, P. (1993). *Optimality Theory: Constraint Interaction in Generative Grammar*. Cambridge, MA: MIT Press.

Pulvermuler, F., Hauk, O., Nikulin, V. & Ilmoniemi, R. (2005). Functional links between motor and language systems. *European Journal of Neuroscience* 21, 793–7.

Quirk, R, Greenbaum, S., Leech, G. & Svartvik, J. (1985). *A Comprehensive Grammar of the English Language*. London, UK: Longman.

Ramscar, M., Sun, C. C., Hendrix, P., & Baayen, H. (2017). The mismeasurement of mind: Life-span changes in paired-associate-learning scores reflect the 'cost' of learning, not cognitive decline. *Psychological Science*. doi:https://doi.org/10.1177/0956797617706393.

Rappaport, G. (1990). Sytuacja językowa Amerykanów polskiego pochodzenia w Teksasie. In M. Władysław, ed., *Język polski w świecie. Zbiór studiów*, Warsaw/Cracow: Państwowe Wydawnictwo Naukowe, pp. 159–78.

Rizzolatti, G. & Arbib, M. A. (1998). Language within our grasp. *Trends in Neuroscience* 21(5), 188–94.

Roberson, D., Davidoff, J., Davies, I. R., & Shapiro, L. R. (2005). Colour categories: Evidence for cultural relativity hypothesis. *Cognitive Psychology* 50, 378–411.

Roberts, F., Margutti, P. & Takano, S. (2011). Judgments concerning the valence of inter-turn silence across speakers of American English, Italian, and Japanese. *Discourse Processes* 8(5), 331–54.

Rogers, C. L. (2006). Effects of bilingualism, noise and reverberation on speech perception by listeners with normal hearing. *Applied Psycholinguistics* 27, 465–85.

Rohde, D. L. T. & Plaut, D. C. (2003). Less is less in language acquisition. In P. Quinlan, ed., *Connectionist Models of Development*. Hove, UK: Psychology Press, pp. 189–231.

Rojo, A. (2015). Translation meets cognitive science: The imprint of translation on cognitive processing. *Multilingua* 34(6), 721–46.

Rojo, A., Ramos, M. & Valenzuela, J. (2014). The emotional impact of translation: A heart rate study. *Journal of Pragmatics*, 71, 31–44.

Rosenberg, P. (2005). Dialect convergence in the German language dialects. In P. Auer, F. Hinskens & P. Kerswill, eds., *Dialect Change: Convergence and Divergence in European Languages*. Cambridge, UK: Cambridge University Press, pp. 221–35.

Ross, M. D. (1996). Contact-induced change and the comparative method: Cases from Papua New Guinea. In M. Durie & M. D. Ross, eds., *The Comparative Method reviewed: Regularity and Irregularity in Language Change*. Oxford, UK: Oxford University Press, 180–217.

Ross, M. D. (2001). Contact-induced change in Oceanic languages in North-West Melanesia. In A. Y. Aikhenvald & R. M. Dixon, eds., *Areal Diffusion and Genetic Inheritance: Problems in Comparative Linguistics*. Oxford, UK: Oxford University Press, 134–66.

Ruiz, C., Paredes, N., Macizo, P. & Bajo M. T. (2008). Activation of lexical and syntactic target language properties in translation. *Acta Psychologica* 128(3), 490–500.

Runnqvist, E., Gollan, T. H., Costa, A. & Ferreira, V. C. (2013). A disadvantage in bilingual sentence production modulated by syntactic frequency and similarity across languages. *Cognition* 129, 256–63.

Saunders, B. & van Brakel, J. (1997). Are there non-trivial constraints on color categorisation? *Brain and Behavioural Sciences* 20, 167–228.

Savić, J. (1995). Structural convergence and language change: Evidence from Serbian/English code-switching. *Language in Society* 24, 475–92.

Schmidt, R. (1990). The role of consciousness in second language learning. *Applied Linguistics* 11, 129–58.

Schmidt, R. (1993). Awareness and second language acquisition. *Annual Review of Applied Linguistics* 13, 206–26.

Schmiedtová, B. von Stutterheim, C. & Caroll, M. (2011). Language-specific patterns in event construal of advanced second language speakers. In A. Pavlenko, ed., *Thinking and Speaking in Two Languages*. Bristol, UK: Multilingual Matters, pp. 66–107.

Schmitt, E. (2000). Overt and covert codeswitching in immigrant children from Russia. *International Journal of Bilingualism* 4, 9–28.

Schmitz, K., Di Venanzio, L. & Scherger, A.-L. (2016). Null and overt subjects in Italian and Spanish heritage speakers in Germany. *Lingua* 180, 101–23.

Schooler, J. W. & Engstler-Schooler, T. Y. (1990). Verbal overshadowing of visual memories: Some things are better left unsaid. *Cognitive Psychology* 22, 36–71.

Schrauf, R. W., Pavlenko, A. & Dewaele, J.-M. (2003). Bilingual episodic memory: An introduction. *International Journal of Bilingualism* 7, 221–33.

Schrauf, R. W., & Rubin, D.C. (1998). Bilingual autobiographical memory in older adult immigrants: A test of cognitive explanations of the reminiscence bump and the linguistic encoding of memories. *Journal of Memory and Language* 39(3), 437–57.

Schwartz, A. & Kroll, J. F. (2006). Bilingual lexical activation in sentence context. *Journal of Memory and Language*, 55, 197–212.

Scontras, G., Fuchs, Z. & Polinsky, M. (2015). Heritage language and linguistic theory. *Frontiers in Psychology*. doi:https://doi.org/10.3389/fpsyg.2015.01545.

Seleskovitch, D. (1976). Interpretation: A psychological approach to translating. In R. Brislin, ed., *Translation: Applications and Research*. New York, NY: Gardner Press, pp. 92–116.

Serratrice, L., Sorace, A., Filiaci, F. & Baldo, M. (2009). Bilingual children's sensitivity to specificity and genericity: Evidence from metalinguistic awareness. *Bilingualism: Language and Cognition* 12(2), 239–57.

Serratrice, L., Sorace, A. & Paoli, A. (2004). Crosslinguistic influence at the syntax–pragmatics interface: Subjects and objects in English–Italian bilingual and monolingual acquisition. *Bilingualism: Language and Cognition* 7(3), 183–205.

Shapiro, L., Hestvik, A., Lesan L. & Garcia, A. R. (2003). Charting the time-course of VP-ellipsis sentence comprehension: Evidence for an initial and independent structural analysis. *Journal of Memory and Language* 49, 1–19.

Shin, J.- A. & Christianson, K. (2009). Syntactic processing in Korean–English bilingual production: Evidence from cross-linguistic structural priming. *Cognition* 112, 175–80.

Siegel, J. (2012). Two types of functional transfer in language contact. *Journal of Language Contact*, 5, 187–215.

Silva-Corvalán, C. (1994). *Language Contact and Change: Spanish in Los Angeles*. Oxford, UK: Clarendon Press.

Silva-Corvalán, C. (2014). *Bilingual Language Acquisition: Spanish and English in the First Six Years*. Cambridge, UK: Cambridge University Press.

Silva-Corvalán, C. & Treffers-Daller, J. (eds.) (2015). *Language Dominance in Bilinguals: Issues of Measurement and Operationalisation*. Cambridge, UK: Cambridge University Press.

Singleton, D. (2005). The critical period hypothesis: A coat of many colours. *International Review of Applied Linguistics in Language Teaching* 43, 269–85.

Slobin, D. I. & Aksu, A. A. (1982). Tense, aspect and modality in the use of the Turkish evidential. In P. J. Hopper, ed., *Tense-Aspect: Between Semantics and Pragmatics*. Amsterdam: John Benjamins, pp. 185–200.

Slobin, D. I. (1987). Thinking for speaking. *Proceedings of the Thirteenth Annual Meeting of the Berkeley Linguistic Society*. Berkeley, CA: Berkeley Linguistic Society, pp. 435–44.

Slobin, D. I. (1996). Two ways to travel: Verbs of motion in English and Spanish. In M. Shibatani & S. A. Thompson, eds., *Grammatical Constructions – Their Form and Meaning*. Oxford, UK: Clarendon Press, pp. 195–219.

Slobin, D. I. (1997). Mind, code, and text. In J. Bybee, J. Haiman & S. Thompson, eds., *Essays on Language Function and Language Type*. Amsterdam: John Benjamins, pp. 437–67.

Slobin, D. I. (2000). Verbalised events: A dynamic approach to linguistic relativity and determinism. In S. Niemeier & R. Dirven, eds., *Evidence for Linguistic Relativity*. Amsterdam: John Benjamins, pp. 107–38.

Slobin, D. I. (2003). Language and thought online: Cognitive consequences of linguistic relativity. In D. Gentner & S. Goldin-Meadow, eds., *Language in Mind: Advances in the Study of Language and Thought*. Cambridge, MA: MIT Press, pp. 157–91.

Slobin, D. I. (2006). What makes manner of motion salient? Explorations in linguistic typology, discourse, and cognition. In M. Hickmann & S. Robert, eds., *Space in Languages: Linguistic Systems and Cognitive Categories*. Amsterdam: John Benjamins, pp. 59–81.

Slobin, D. I. (2016). Thinking for speaking and the construction of evidentiality in language contact. In M. Güven, D. Akar, B. Öztürk & M. Kelepir, eds., *Exploring the*

Turkish Linguistic Landscape: Essays in Honor of Eser Erguvanlı-Taylan [Studies in Language Companion Series 175]. Amsterdam: John Benjamins, pp. 105–20.

Soares, C., & Grosjean, F. (1984). Bilinguals in a monolingual and a bilingual speech mode: The effect on lexical access. *Memory and Cognition* 12, 380–6.

Sperber, D. & Wilson, D. (1986). *Relevance: Communication and Cognition*. Oxford, UK: Blackwell.

Stam, G. (2010). Can a L2 speaker's patterns of thinking for speaking change? In Z.-H. Han & T. Cadierno, eds., *Linguistic Relativity in SLA*. Clevedon: Multilingual Matters, pp. 59–83.

Storms, G. Ameel, E. & Malt, B. C. (2015). Development of cross-language lexical influence. *International Journal of Bilingual Education and Bilingualism* 18(5), 529–47.

Talmy, L. (1985). Lexicalisation patterns: Semantic structure in lexical forms. In T. Shopen, ed., *Language Typology and Syntactic Description*. Cambridge, UK: Cambridge University Press, pp. 57–149.

Talmy, L. (1991). Path to realisation: A typology of event conflations. *Proceedings of the Berkeley Linguistic Society* 17, 480–519.

Talmy, L. (2000). *Toward a Cognitive Semantics* (vols. 1 & 2). Cambridge, MA: MIT Press.

Taylor I. & Taylor, M. M. (1990). *Psycholinguistics – Learning and Using Language*. Englewood Cliffs, NJ: Prentice Hall.

Thelin, N. (1990). Verbal aspect in discourse: On the state of the art. In N. Thelin, ed., *Verbal Aspect in Discourse*. Amsterdam: John Benjamins, pp. 3–88.

Thierry, G. & Wu, Y. J. (2007). Brain potentials reveal unconscious translation during foreign language comprehension. *Proceedings of the National Academy of Sciences* 104, 12530–5.

Tokowicz, N., Michael, E. B. & Kroll, J. F. (2004). The roles of study-abroad experience and working-memory capacity in the types of errors made during translation. *Bilingualism: Language and Cognition* 7(3), 255–72.

Tooley, K. M., Traxler, M. J. & Swaab, T. Y. (2009). Electrophysiological and behavioural evidence of syntactic priming in sentence comprehension. *Journal of Experimental Psychology: Learning, Memory, and Cognition* 35, 19–45.

Torbio, A. J. (2004). Convergence as an optimisation strategy in bilingual speech: Evidence from codeswitching. *Bilingualism: Language and Cognition* 7, 165–73.

Tosun, S., Vaid, J. & Geraci, L. (2013). Does obligatory linguistic marking of source of evidence affect source memory? A Turkish/English investigation. *Journal of Memory and Language* 69(2), 121–34.

Traxler, M. J. (2008). Structural priming among prepositional phrases: Evidence from eye-movement. *Memory and Cognition* 36, 659–74.

Traxler, M. J. (2012). *Introduction to Psycholinguistics: Understanding Language Science*. Chichester, UK: Wiley-Blackwell.

Trbojević, I. (2012). Modal hedges in para-pharmaceutical product instructions: Some examples from English and Serbian. *LFE: Revista de lenguas para fines específicos* 18, 71–92.

Tristram, H. (2004). Diglossia in Anglo-Saxon England, or what was spoken Old English like? *Studia Anglica Posnaniensia* 40, 87–100.

Tristram, H. (2006). Why don't the English speak Welsh? In N. J. Higham, ed., *Britons in Anglo-Saxon England*. Woodbridge, UK: Boydell, pp. 192–214.

Trudgill, P. (2010). *Investigations in Sociohistorical Linguistics: Stories of Colonisation and Contact*. Cambridge, UK: Cambridge University Press.

Trudgill, P. (2011). *Sociolinguistic Typology: Social Determinants of Linguistic Complexity*. Oxford, UK: Oxford University Press.

Trueswell, J. C. & Papafragou, A. (2010). Perceiving and remembering events crosslinguistically. *Journal of Memory and Language* 63, 64–82.

Trujillo, J. (2003). The difference in resulting judgments when descriptions use high-manner versus neutral-manner verbs. Senior Dissertation, University of California Berkeley.

Tversky, B. (2011). Tools for thought. In B. Benedetti & V. Cook, eds., *Language and Bilingual Cognition*. New York, NY: Psychology Press, pp. 131–9.

Tzou, Y.-Z., Eslami, Z. R., Chen, H.-C. & Vaid, J. (2012). Effect of language proficiency and degree of formal training in simultaneous interpreting on working memory and interpreting performance: Evidence from Mandarin–English speakers. *International Journal of Bilingualism* 16(2), 213–27.

Tzou, Y.-Z., Vaid, J. & Chen, H.-C. (2017). Does formal training in translation/ interpreting affect translation strategy? Evidence from idiom translation. *Bilingualism: Language and Cognition* 20(3), 632–41.

Vaid, J. & Meuter, R. (2017). Languages without borders: Reframing the study of the bilingual mental lexicon. In M. Libben, M. Goral & G. Libben, eds., *Bilingualism: A Framework for Understanding the Mental Lexicon*. Amsterdam: John Benjamins, pp. 7–26.

Valdés, G. & Figueroa, R. (1996). *Bilingualism and Testing: A Special Case of Bias*. New York, NY: Ablex.

Van Heuven, W. J. B., Dijkstra, T. & Grainger, J. (1998). Orthographic neighborhood effects in bilingual word recognition. *Journal of Memory and Language* 39, 458–83.

Van Hell, J. G., Abdollahi, F., Adams, K. D. & Li, P. (2017). Electrophysiological and behavioral signatures of mapping novel word forms to meaning in beginning child and adult second language learners. Paper at the 11th International Symposium on Bilingualism, Limerick, Ireland, June 2017. Colloquium: *Semantic Representation and Processing in Bilingual Speakers*.

Van Hell, J. G., & De Groot, A. M. B. (2008). Sentence context modulates visual word recognition and translation in bilinguals. *Acta Psychologica* 128, 431–51.

Van Hell, J. G. & Dijkstra, T. (2002). Foreign language knowledge can influence native language performance in exclusively native contexts. *Psychonomic Bulletin & Review* 9(4), 780–9.

Van Hell, J. G. & Kroll, J. F. (2013). Using electrophysiological measures to track the mapping of words to concepts in the bilingual brain: A focus on translation. In J. Altarriba & L. Isurin, eds., *Memory, Language, and Bilingualism: Theoretical and Applied Approaches*. New York, NY: Cambridge University Press, pp. 126–60.

Vasić, N. (2006). *Pronoun comprehension in agrammatic aphasia: The structure and use of linguistic knowledge*. Utrecht: LOT International Dissertation Series.

Venuti, L. (1995). *The Translator's Invisibility: A History of Translation*. London/ New York: Routledge.

Vermeer, H. J. &Reiss, K. (2013 [1984]). *Towards a General Theory of Translational Action: Skopos Theory Explained*. London, UK: Routledge.

Vigliocco, G. & Filipović Kleiner, L. (2004). From mind in the mouth to language in the mind. *Trends in Cognitive Sciences* 8, 5–7.

Vigliocco, G. & Hartsuiker, R. J. (2002). The interplay of meaning, sound, and syntax in sentence production. *Psychological Bulletin* 128(3), 442–72.

Wardlow-Lane, L. & Ferreira, V. S. (2008). Speaker-internal vs. speaker-external forces on utterance form: Do cognitive demands override threats to referential success? *Journal of Experimental Psychology: Leaning, Memory and Cognition* 34, 1466–81.

Weber, K., and Indefrey, P. (2009). Syntactic priming in German-English bilinguals during sentence comprehension. *Neuroimage* 46(4), 1164–72.

Webster, N. (1961). *Webster's Third New International Dictionary of the English Language Unabridged*. Springfield, MA: Merriam-Webster.

Weinreich, U. (1966[1953]) *Languages in Contact: Findings and Problems*. London/ Paris: Mouton.

Wenzell, V. (1989). Transfer of aspect in the English oral narratives of native Russian speakers. In H. Dechert & M. Raupach, eds., *Transfer in Language Production*. Norwood, NJ: Ablex, pp. 71–97.

Whitacker, S. F. (1987). Might may be right? *English Today* 11, 35–6.

Wolff, P., & Ventura, T. (2003). When Russians learn English: How the meaning of causal verbs may change. In B. Beachley, A. Brown & F. Conlin, eds, *Proceedings of the Twenty-Seventh Annual Boston University Conference on Language Development* Boston, MA: Cascadilla Press, pp. 822–33.

Wolleb, A. (2015). Syntactic representations in the bilingual mind: The role of executive function and pragmatics in cross-language priming. PhD dissertation. The Arctic University of Norway, Center for Advanced Studies in Theoretical Linguistics (CASTL).

Yip, V. & Matthews, S. (2007). *The Bilingual Child: Early Development and Language Contact*. Cambridge, UK: Cambridge University Press.

Yow, W. Q. & Li, X. (2015). Balanced bilingualism and early age of second language acquisition as the underlying mechanism of a bilingual executive control advantage: Why variations in bilingual experiences matter. *Frontiers in Psychology*. doi:https:// doi.org/10.3389/fpsyg.2015.00164.

Yu, Z. & Schwieter, J. W. (2015). Recognizing the effects of language mode on the cognitive advantages of bilingualism. *Frontiers in Psychology*. doi:https://doi.org/10 .3389/fpsyg.2018.00366.

Zuengler, J. (1991). Accommodating in native-nonnative interactions: Going beyond the 'what' to the 'why' in second-language research. In H. Giles, J. Coupland & N. Coupland, eds., *Contexts of Accommodation*. New York, NY: Cambridge University Press, pp. 223–44.

Language Index

Name Index

Subject Index

accent, 36
  bilingual accent, 36
accents
  semantic accent, 36–7
access to justice, 149, 151, 162
acquisition, 5, 7, 9, 11–15, 17, 19, 21, 23, 28–9,
  31, 35–6, 39, 43, 48–9, 52–3, 56–7, 61,
  63–4, 66, 71, 89, 93, 97, 103–4, 110–11,
  114–15, 118–20, 145, 158, 172, 174–6
  bilingual acquisition, 5, 12, 23, 28, 35, 43,
    56, 65, 93, 104, 115, 120
  L2 acquisition, 15, 17, 36, 48–9, 63–4, 89,
    104, 111, 174
  second language acquisition, 29, 35, 52–3,
    56, 71
activation, 31–4, 36–42, 48, 66, 68, 91, 113,
  122, 148, 166, 179
  parallel activation, 36–7, 39–41,
    68, 179
adjustability, 56, 66, 178
  adjustability factors, 5–6, 67, 70, 118, 148,
    170–1. *See also* external factors
age of acquisition, 5, 11, 13, 15–16, 28–9, 49,
  67, 112, 135, 137, 175
agent, 101, 128, 131–2, 140, 163–5
agreement, 44, 108, 111
ambiguity, 18, 20–1, 45, 59, 76, 108, 134,
  141, 175
aspect, 5, 22, 24, 86–9, 105–6
aspectuality, 74, 86–90
attrition, 13, 28–9, 52–3, 66, 82, 100, 175

balanced bilingualism, 14, 23, 108, 111, 176,
  180–1
balanced bilinguals, 4, 13, 19, 26, 31, 44, 89,
  102–3, 108, 111, 113, 126, 132, 134–5,
  173, 175–6, 178–9

CASP, 5–6, 10, 51–6, 66–77, 79–83, 86, 90–1,
  94–5, 98, 109, 115, 118, 120, 122, 126,
  132–3, 135–6, 138, 144, 150, 154, 168–9,
  171, 173, 178, 181–2

categorisation, 8, 14, 20, 36, 39, 45, 47, 49, 74,
  76, 99, 109, 111, 115, 123, 175
causation, 101, 127–8, 130, 132, 178
classroom, 1, 19, 36, 77, 80, 145, 180
cognates, 34–5, 37–8, 100
cognition, 8, 23, 29, 46–8, 91, 116, 122–3, 127,
  144, 145
cognitive effort, 155, 169
cognitive load, 61
collaboration, 51, 75, 148, 178
colour, 5, 36, 47, 74, 77–8, 109–10,
  138
common ground, 18, 43, 60, 63, 69, 74, 80,
  89–90, 94–5, 98, 100, 104, 110, 113,
  143, 174, 176, 181, *See also* maximize
  common ground
communication, 2–3, 5–6, 10–11, 14, 20, 25–7,
  30–1, 34, 40–1, 54, 57–9, 61, 63–5, 68–9,
  79, 82, 99–100, 102–4, 109–10, 112, 114,
  116–17, 144, 146–7, 151, 153, 168,
  170–6, 181, *See also* maximize
  efficiency
communicative situation, 1–3, 5–6, 11, 23,
  28, 30–3, 51–2, 55–6, 66–70, 75, 80,
  90, 95, 98, 113–14, 126, 135, 146, 170,
  175, 178
competing motivations, 71, 150, 168
competition, 37–9, 51, 56, 60, 69–71,
  75, 90, 114, 118, 136, 146, 148,
  155, 178
complex adaptive system, 6, 56, 178, 181
complexity, 58, 60, 87, 89, 95, 163
comprehension, 4, 36–7, 42, 58, 66, 98, 168
conceptualisation, 35, 37, 46–8
convergence, 30–1, 36, 52–3, 76, 93,
  179–80
cross-linguistic influence, 5, 52–3, 66, 85

discourse, 7, 30, 53, 74, 81, 91, 96, 103, 105–8,
  146, 158
dominance, 4–5, 13–14, 28–30, 49, 67, 83, 90,
  144, 178

210